Bouncing Back

Bouncing Back

How to Stay in the Game When Your Career Is on the Line

Andrew J. DuBrin

McGraw-Hill, Inc.

New York St. Louis San Francisco Auckland Bogotá
Caracas Lisbon London Madrid Mexico Milan
Montreal New Delhi Paris San Juan São Paulo
Singapore Sydney Tokyo Toronto

Library of Congress Cataloging-in-Publication Data

DuBrin, Andrew J.
   Bouncing back : how to stay in the game when your career is on the
line / Andrew J. DuBrin.
        p.   cm.
   Includes index.
   ISBN 0-07-017901-8 :   — ISBN 0-07-017900-X (pbk.) :
   1. Career changes.   2. Unemployment—Psychological aspects.
3. Execuives—Employment.   4. Executives—Life skills guides.
I. Title.
HF5384.D83   1992
650.14′024658—dc20   91-27944
                                                              CIP

1 2 3 4 5 6 7 8 9 0   DOC/DOC   9 7 6 5 4 3 2 1

ISBN   0-07-017901-8   {HC}
ISBN   0-07-017900-X   {PBK}

*The sponsoring editor for this book was James H. Bessent, Jr., the editing
supervisor was Fred Dahl, and the production supervisor was Donald Schmidt.
It was set in Baskerville by McGraw-Hill's Professional Book Group composition
unit.*

Printed and bound by R. R. Donnelley & Sons Company.

To Drew R. DuBrin, who has helped so many people overcome severe adversity

Contents

Preface

The adversity facing managers and staff professionals in corporate America and Canada has reached epidemic proportions. Much of this adversity has been created by mergers and acquisitions, hostile takeovers, and leveraged buyouts. Approximately 4000 to 8000 mergers and acquisitions take place annually in the United States and Canada. Organizations combining with each other usually result in downsizings or restructurings accompanied by confusion, intense conflict, and heavy politicking. Furthermore, more than one million middle managers and professionals have lost their jobs during the last decade.

Adding to the turmoil, many of the companies that acquired other businesses in the 1980s are now divesting most of their acquisitions. They have decided that it is more productive to concentrate on their core businesses. When a subsidiary is sold, another merger or acquisition takes place, reigniting the flames of adversity.

Shortly after beginning my investigation of how managers and professionals overcome adversity, one consistent finding surfaced. Virtually all successful people have experienced major adversity in their careers. Furthermore, if given an opportunity, most of these people who have made successful comebacks enjoy talking about their experiences. Resilient people are proud of their ability to engage in face-to-face combat with adversity and emerge victorious.

Coping with adversity is necessary for achieving a successful career. Learning how to prepare for career downturns and how to manage them is part of climbing the corporate ladder. In the words of columnist Mitch Broder, "This nation has been built by men and women who were strengthened by adversity and learned from their mistakes."[1]

Adversity is very subjective: It doesn't exist until you perceive it to exist. One person whose holdings are devalued by 75 percent in the wake of a stock market plunge might say, "I'm virtually wiped out. My life savings have gone down the drain in one afternoon." Another person holding a comparable portfolio of stocks might say, "On paper my portfolio has lost 75 percent of its value. However, since I don't intend to sell any stocks now, I haven't lost anything." The first person would experience adversity, while the second would be facing only a minor annoyance.

Despite the subjectivity of adversity, there are certain overwhelming, uncomfortable, and catastrophic circumstances that create career adversity for most people. Among these setbacks and crises are:

Being fired

Losing your job because of a takeover

Falling out of power

Being demoted

Being bypassed for promotion

Entering into severe conflict with your boss

Having your budget cut drastically

Being investigated for charges of sexual harassment despite your innocence

The self-employed can add to this list losing a big chunk of business to a competitor, a business partner absconding with funds, or the business burning down during a busy season. In this book we emphasize the adversity created by corporate mergers and takeovers, but the other types of adversity just mentioned are also included.

Our book is based on people who have experienced these adversities and then made a comeback instead of crumbling. Most of these people are not public figures, executive superstars, or prominent athletes. Instead they represent the backbone of managers and professionals in a variety of businesses of all sizes, government agencies, research laboratories, and educational institutions. In many places throughout this book, however, we supplement the original observations of myself and my researchers with accounts of well-known people. I agree with the courses of action taken by most, but not all, of the people in the stories presented. However, I think it is important to present a wide range of solutions to handling adversity.

Aside from having studied and written about adversity in the past, this author has weathered enough of it to take a personal interest in the subject. I've twice experienced major television and magazine appearances being canceled at the last moment, been deposed from a job I enjoyed, had two of my properties burn down, and felt the adversity of an athletic injury. All the circumstances just mentioned created tough emotional sledding for me.

The purpose of this book is to help you do a better job of bouncing back, of recovering from present or future adversity. Our primary focus is career adversity, but many of the techniques and insights will apply equally well to making a comeback in your personal life. Pondering the ideas presented here can also help you work through the emotional baggage of old adversities, thus freeing up more energy to face the challenges of today and tomorrow.

As you read this book, watch carefully for certain recurring themes of how people successfully handle adversity. Do not be concerned that some of these themes overlap and may be variations of each other. The important point is to grab any idea that can help you bounce back from adversity. Ten recurring themes in overcoming adversity are:

1. Adversity should propel you into a problem-solving mode in which you explore many different alternative solutions to your problem.

2. Resilient people reach out to others for emotional support when faced with adversity. Rather than going it alone, they turn to their family and friends for support and encouragement.

3. Resilient people face adversity with a high level of confidence that they will regain their equilibrium. They believe strongly in their own capacity to get the job done.

4. If you want to overcome adversity you need to be overwhelmingly persistent. The resilient person keeps trying until something takes him or her over a career hurdle.

5. An optimistic and positive spirit is crucial for getting through hard times.

6. If you want to work your way out of a mess, take the same well-planned, professionally detached approach you use to solve any other vexing business problem.

7. Adversity is a wonderful learning experience, and heightens your problem-solving ability.

8. Rather than suffer from a "post-traumatic stress disorder" (or shell shock) after a setback, the resilient person jumps back into the fray.

9. Resilient people are willing to take prudent risks. If you want to overcome a major setback you will often have to gamble with your time, money, or other resources.

10. To overcome adversity it is necessary to avoid self-defeating, coun-

terproductive behavior such as wallowing in self-pity or fleeing into substance abuse.

Acknowledgments

My primary thanks on this project go to my past research assistants and students who have given their mental and physical energy to this project. Thanks also to my editor at McGraw-Hill, Jim Bessent, for seeing merit in my manuscript. I thank also all those who created circumstances whereby bouncing back was a personal necessity for me. Without these people and the circumstances they created, my writing on this topic might have been sterile and detached. The writing of this book has converted all my past antagonists and detractors into collaborators.

Carol Bowman, the woman in my life, receives my gratitude for enhancing the quality of my life. Thanks are due my offspring, Drew, Douglas, and Melanie, for their continuing interest in my work. Thank you also, Kristine Bowman, for your interest. Finally, I pay tribute to the comebacks of Tom Bowman and Andrew Drake.

Andrew J. DuBrin

Bouncing Back

1

The Inner Core of the Resilient Manager

A comment by a psychiatric nurse gives you insight into how resilient people differ from those who cannot handle pressure. I asked her what kind of problems business and professional people experienced that brought them into her hospital for care. She told me, "Almost anything can unglue our patients. Sometimes they have had a fight with their boss, their spouse, or their child. Or they can't cope with asking for a raise, finding a new job, or entertaining relatives over the holidays. They are very brittle inside."

Unlike these patients, resilient managers and professionals are internally flexible rather than brittle. They have a tough inner core that can withstand severe and multiple pressures. Resilient people have an inner strength of character that colors their perception of adverse circumstances. They do not accept the idea that they have experienced defeat or failure. Successful executives reveal that they don't even think about failure and don't even use the word. Instead, they rely on synonyms such as "mistake," "glitch," "bungle," and "setback."[1]

Understanding the inner core or personality of resilient managers and professionals can help you become more resilient. Although some aspects of personality are determined before birth, other aspects can be developed and honed. A case in point is that fear of public speaking is quite universal. Yet with practice and useful suggestions, most managers and professionals can learn to control their anxiety enough to make a company presentation. People can also learn to change their attitudes toward handling adversity. For example, instead of blaming others for all your setbacks, you can learn to assume some responsibility for your adverse circumstances. A good starting point in becoming more resilient is to examine your tendencies toward having a survivor personality.

Do You Have a Survivor Personality? Resilient managers are survivors—they may get wounded in corporate mergers and other battles, but they land on their feet without too much permanent damage. Psychologist Salvatore Didato has researched the personality of people who survive in the face of extreme adversity, both in their careers and personal lives. His analysis shows that survival in a crisis depends on a number of personal factors. A hardiness of spirit, resilience to stress, and a positive attitude are all necessary to get through adversity. The following quiz gives you some preliminary insight into your survival tendencies.[2]

Answer the following statements by assigning numbers 1, 2, or 3: 1 = not true, 2 = somewhat true, and 3 = very true. Then read on for explanations.

_____ 1. I feel a sense of dedication to some aspects of my life (i.e., to my family, school, church, community, etc.)

_____ 2. I am satisfied with the rate of progress toward the goals I have set for myself.

_____ 3. It's better to be smart than lucky.

_____ 4. When good things happen they come about because of hard work.

_____ 5. People can get their own way if they just keep trying.

Answer statements 6 through 8 true (T) or false (F):

_____ 6. It's best to adapt as well as possible to changes in life because there's not much one can do to alter fate.

_____ 7. It has always been hard for me to adjust to life changes (e.g., to a new job, school, neighborhood, etc.).

_____ 8. I usually find it hard to trust others and to build friendships.

Explanations. As a group, survivors have these personality traits in common and the quiz reflects them:

1. A sense of involvement in something they are doing in life. A commitment to something (a person, cause, a group). There is a dedication and a purpose to their lives (Items 1 and 2).

2. A feeling of control over their life. A certitude that the outcomes in living are the direct result of their abilities and efforts (Items 3, 4, 5, and 6).

3. The courage to be open to change. The self-confidence to face the unexpected and to make new adjustments (Items 7 and 8).

In contrast to these favorable survivor qualities, persons most vulnerable to breakdown under heavy stress often have a high power drive (a need to be dominant over others) and a high degree of inhibition about expressing it. Such types may curb their power drive (assertiveness, aggressiveness, competitiveness, etc.) in a socially approved way. All too often, however, they become ineffectual or immobilized when adversity strikes.

Interpreting Your Score. Total your points for Items 1 through 5. Give yourself one point for each false answer to Items 6, 7, and 8. Add up all your points (maximum points possible is 18).

15–18 points: You are an above-average survivor with the resilience to carry on and be supportive of others if a crisis hits.

11–14 points: You are average in times of high stress and, though it may take somewhat longer than it would for a high scorer, you can cope with most setbacks.

8–10 points: You're vulnerable to adversity. Try to become more involved in a worthy life goal. Work at developing a more positive, self-confident attitude.

In the rest of the chapter we examine some of the characteristics just described in more depth, and present the stories of several people who have demonstrated these characteristics and related actions. And the case histories presented throughout this book are about people with survivor personalities.

Bouncing Back Characteristic 1: Taking Charge of Your Own Life

Comeback Scenario 1: Peter Stam, Creative Director

Besides being a creative director for a New York advertising agency, Peter Stam was actively involved in raising his two sons, restoring a Manhattan brownstone, engaging in various civic activities, and writing a novel. And whenever he could squeeze it in he would take exotic vacations such as a trip to Sri Lanka.

Stam's pace prompted a close friend to remark: "I got tired just thinking about all the things he does. I just know that someday it's all going to catch up with him. It *has* to!"

One would have thought that "someday" had arrived when Mr. Stam's widowed mother had a fatal heart attack. She died at age 78 while operating a retirement home for approximately 20 women. Suddenly Stam had inherited a business to run. It was a business about which he knew very little because he and his mother had not discussed her business affairs.

"I remember wondering, what was I going to do? Who was going to serve the meal that very night for the residents in the home?" he later recounted. "Of course, my mother had some help, so that was a naive question. But the suddenness with which I had to deal with both my own grief, and a radically altered personal situation—I now owned a business!—had my head free falling for a while. I quickly landed on solid ground thanks to the support of my wife, my kids, and the agency. Then I began to do what I thought had to be done."

Stam initially established priorities, formulated a master plan based on his thoughts and discussion with his family, then mustered all of his energies and skills in juggling his life and a business 1,200 miles away.

"Every Monday through Thursday I dealt with eccentrically creative people, demanding clients, life in New York, and teaching my eldest son how to use our home computer," he recalled. "Then from Friday through Sunday I dealt with ordinary, small town people, food purchasing and inventory, and arranging outings for elderly ladies. They were two very different worlds."

Stam's plan was to sell the retirement home within a year and use the proceeds to open his own advertising agency. He accomplished that within eight months. Before operating his agency he took a short vacation to visit his mother's older sister who still lived in a small city in upstate New York. His mother grew up there, and it was in her home town that he fully experienced his grief for the first time over her loss.

Psychologically hardy individuals, like Peter Stam, take charge of their own lives instead of blaming problems on external circumstances. If a hardy executive makes a costly mistake, he or she is likely to accept responsibility for the blooper and then attempt to clean up the chaos. The hardy manager has three general characteristics:

Bouncing Back Characteristic 2:
Belief in Your Control

Hardy managers believe that they can control, or at least influence, the events they experience. Peter Stam demonstrated this characteristic in managing his time to meet a hectic schedule. After the initial shock of learning about his mother's death, he seized control of these stressful events and consequences by establishing priorities. Stam temporarily shelved his civic activities and working on his novel. A less direct way of seizing control was to plan for something he had wanted to do for a long time—open his own agency.

Bouncing Back Characteristic 3:
Commitment to the Task

Initially Stam had no interest in operating a retirement home. Yet at the same time he was uncomfortable with the idea of a group of elderly ladies becoming victims of neglect or absentee management. Carrying out the role of a hardy (or resilient) manager, he accepted the added responsibility and committed himself to the welfare of the retirement home residents.

Bouncing Back Characteristic 4:
Responding to Challenge

When change is thrust upon them, hardy managers do not wallow in a self-pity or "Why me?" attitude. Instead they accept reality and try to squeeze out whatever advantages can be found in the situation. The hardy manager responds to challenge by sizing up what needs to be done to create order out of chaos. Peter Stam clearly accomplished this feat.[3]

Hardiness also hinges on two other factors—a good physical constitution and social support. Being in good physical health and being able to rely on friends for emotional support helps people withstand the ravages of adversity.

Bouncing Back Characteristic 5:
Ownership of the Problem

Studies of the reaction of crisis victims provide useful clues to the nature of resilient managers. The crises studied included robbery, rape, and radiation poisoning. People who accepted some responsibility for crises they have experienced, coped better than those people who blamed all their misfortune on others. Self-blame when carried to extremes can be harmful. However, victims who accept some responsibility for a crisis may also have a feeling of control. Self-blame helped victims cope by giving them the opportunity to modify their behavior in such a way that would help them avoid becoming a victim in the future.

Accepting some responsibility for adverse circumstances thus reduces a sense of vulnerability: if you can exert control over what happens to you, it is possible to ward off some adversity. Because you feel you own the problem, you are more likely to do something about it.

Comeback Scenario 2: John Dentworth, Marketing Manager

Harry Rogers, a manager of executive resources in a large company, has observed how accepting some blame for an adversity helps a manager make a comeback. According to Harry, no "derailed" manager ever climbed back on the tracks to advancement until that person took ownership of the problems that led to derailment. Derailment occurs when a manager was expected to rise in the organization, and who wants to advance, is fired, demoted, or stalled because of problems he or she creates. Derailment can also occur when you resist policies of the new owners. Harry's successful attempts at salvaging John Dentworth, a manager in his company, illustrate the importance of accepting some blame for career adversity:

> Harry was called in by the company president to see if he could straighten out John, a manager who was described in his performance appraisals as abrupt, arrogant, and a poor listener. Because of these behaviors, he was passed over for the general managership of West Coast operations.
>
> When Harry first met with John, he reviewed the record, and summarized the criticism made of John by top executives. John denied all the criticisms, and blamed other people for his problems. "I'm the one who did the work," said John. "I'm the one who found the answers." Harry then suggested that John send a questionnaire to others who had worked with him, asking them about his personal style.
>
> John agreed and selected 13 people to complete the questionnaires. All 13 agreed that John was an outstanding decision maker and a marketing genius; but he was heavy-handed with subordinates. He attempted to control people rather than work with them.
>
> John calmed down a bit but was still not convinced. Harry then sent him to an interpersonal workshop to learn how he was per-

ceived by others. John listened as the members of the group depicted him in exactly the same terms as the people back in the office: bright and talented, but arrogant and intolerant of people less capable than himself.

Although the feedback from others and the coaching by Harry was painful, John slowly took an active role in his derailment. John agreed to an assessment by an outside psychologist, and attended a listening workshop. The evaluation of the psychologist fit the other feedback John had been receiving.

John soon began to see that he needed to change his ways of dealing with people. Several months later, John was among five people formulating a marketing plan for a new product. John worked out an analysis at his personal computer, and came back to the meeting prepared to ram through his ideas. Suddenly he realized, however, that other people in the room had different opinions. Before laying out his plan, John gave everyone time to talk. During the next hour, the group reached a consensus decision that was close to John's formulation. He was slowly learning that problem solving involved more than brilliant analysis. "You know," he said to Harry the next day, "being brilliant is never enough."

The organization was pleased enough with John's progress to give him a lateral transfer to a new division as a vice president with a staff of six people. He was back on track toward becoming a general manager.[4]

The message is that until you accept the fact you may have been a contributor to adversity you face, you will not be able to bounce back. In rare circumstances, such as a fire, your contribution to the adversity may have been very minor. Yet even here you must ask yourself, "What steps did I take to prevent the fire?"

Bouncing Back Characteristic 6: Indomitable Spirit

The single most important core trait of resilient people is their persistence, combative spirit, or indomitable spirit. They inch their way forward rather than surrendering in the midst of adversity.

Adversity at the Highest Levels. A well-known example, like him or not, is President Richard M. Nixon. After resigning from office rather than face the prospects of impeachment, Nixon went into temporary exile. Four years later, however, a Gallup Poll indicated that Nixon was included in the list of the ten most admired men in the United States. Against all the predictions of his complete collapse, Richard Nixon has survived and is still in demand. The former president prides himself in his indomitable spirit. Managers and professionals of lesser renown than Nixon can also help us understand the workings of an indomitable spirit.

Comeback Scenario 3: George Pagano, Small Business Owner

At age 33, George Pagano was already a successful home repair subcontractor. "I did lots of roofing and framing," he said. "The money was good and I was young. You really have to be agile to climb around on those roof rafters. And you have to be quick. Time is money when you are self-employed. I figured I'd always be able to do it."

One split second of carelessness changed his plans abruptly. Deep in thought as he returned home one night from a movie, he ran a stop sign. The next morning he regained consciousness in the hospital to find he had a badly shattered right leg. After two surgeries and four months of physical therapy, the doctors gave George the bad news—he would have to find a different line of work.

"I was stunned," said George. "At age 33, I was out of business. I had my life savings invested in my business and I had no marketable talents except carpentry. It took me two months to get over my self-pity and start looking for a way out of my problem. I still had my van and my carpenter's tools, but what good were they when I walked with a cane and couldn't even climb a ladder?"

The answer came to George the next week when he read a newspaper article about the current widespread interest in restoration of older homes. He had excelled in cabinet making and woodworking during his trade school and apprenticeship. "It suddenly dawned on me that I could combine the interest in restored buildings and my talent for woodworking and make a decent living for myself, bad leg or no bad leg."

George then methodically capitalized upon his network:

- He obtained letters of reference about his woodworking skills from his trade school.
- He contacted previous customers who would vouch for his dependability and meticulous work.
- He had business cards printed indicating that his trade was "restorations," and handed the cards to lumber dealers and other carpenters.
- He telephoned the local historical society and let them know he was available for restorative work.

Next, George placed a classified ad. Nothing happened, so he reran the ad. "This time I got one inquiry. I quickly estimated the job and to my surprise, landed the job. You have no idea how excited I was. I was on my way back."

Pagano Restorations has since established a solid reputation for superior restorative work done promptly and reasonably. He has hired a helper to do the more strenuous work. At last report George has more work than he can handle. With the continuing interest in older homes, George sees no end to the available job opportunities for him. "It's a satisfying job that requires time and patience. But I love it. I made a good living as a carpenter before. I knew I could make good again."

George Pagano teaches an important lesson: An indomitable spirit can propel you toward redirecting your career if that is what it takes to enable you to bounce back.

Bouncing Back Characteristic 7:
High Self-Esteem and
Self-Confidence

People with high self-esteem tend to perform better on many tasks than their counterparts with less self-esteem. High self-esteem therefore helps you make a comeback. If you have a positive image of your own worth, it gives you the boost in self-confidence that you need to recover from adversity. The process is cyclical. If you have enough self-esteem to get through adversity, others admire you. As a result, your self-esteem receives another boost. An important underlying reason is that self-esteem is determined largely by how others perceive you.

Comeback Scenario 4: Laura Baker,
Computer sales Representative

The words of Laura Baker illustrate how self-esteem and self-confidence can fuel a comeback:

> Three years ago I hit a low point in my life. The company I worked for was involved in scandal about paying kickbacks to a few school and city administrators in exchange for a few major contracts. I wasn't directly involved in offering the kickbacks, but I was the sales representative on one of the unethically handled accounts. As you can imagine, I got tarred with the same brush.
>
> About the same time, my boyfriend was arrested for selling cocaine to stockbrokers in his office. In a two-week period I faced unemployment and the necessity to either help my boyfriend through his turmoil or leave him. At first I thought the world was caving in

on me, but then I realized I was still a good person. I admit I should have been more perceptive about the wrongdoings of my firm and my boyfriend. Yet I had done nothing wrong.

I had the self-confidence to face the world in a positive way. I told prospective employers that they could check out my story. I didn't offer kickbacks to anyone. My only error on the job was having too much trust in my employer. Based on my good sales record, I did find a comparable job. I also decided to help my boyfriend through his rough times. So what if a few people thought I was too forgiving. I have enough confidence in myself to stick with my own inclinations.

Laura's confident view of herself enabled her to look past the criticism surrounding her firm, and present a positive view to the world. The same technique can work for you. Being caught in adverse circumstances does not mean that your self-confidence should be lowered. It is time instead to look upon the good deeds that you have done.

Bouncing Back Characteristic 8: Avoidance of Self-Pity

Another core attitude of resilient career people is that they avoid feeling sorry for themselves. Self-pity is a negative thought that blocks constructive action. The person who wallows in self-pity runs the risk of spending too much time in introspection and not enough time plotting a comeback. A case in point is the attitudes expressed by an economist in her handling of job adversity.

Comeback Scenario 5: Linda Tsao Yang, Economist

In 1980, Yang was appointed by Governor Jerry Brown as the savings and loan commissioner for California. Two and one half years after her term began, Yang opposed Citicorp's attempt to take over the ailing Fidelity Savings and Loan of California. She believed that the pending takeover was in violation of state law. Yang's position placed her in conflict with federal regulators and certain members of the Brown administration.

Yang then expressed her views in the op-ed section of *The New York Times*. Charges of insubordination faced her the next day. Yang was suspended with pay from her job and denied access to her office and files by Brown's chief of staff. "First I felt shame," Yang recalls. "After that, anger and frustration. But the worst kind of enemy in that kind of difficult situation is self-pity. When you find yourself in a crisis, the less you focus on yourself, the more you're able to deal with it. I became concerned with the honor of the office, of women and of the Asian-American community. I stepped outside myself."[5]

After a week, Yang was reinstated to her position, and remained until the end of the Brown administration a few months later. Next, she returned to head her consulting firm, Linda Tsao Yang and Associates. Instead of feeling sorry for herself, Yang swung into constructive action. If you are placed in a very adverse situation, I recommend you do the same thing.

Comeback Scenario 6: Ken Stone, Tool Repair Shop Owner

Stone, the owner of Mr. Pneumatic Tool in New York State, shares a similar attitude to Yang's about coping with adversity. Although his business experience is limited, Stone's marketing edge is that he makes tool repairs quickly and reliably. He expected his business to gross $250,000 in its third year of operation. Stone said he will not let his blindness get in his way of success. "I used to go to a school for the blind, and all they taught me was to rely on the sighted world. You can't feel sorry for yourself. You've got to put one foot in front of the other and keep moving."[6]

Stone's lesson is a dramatic one because it takes tremendous determination to repair tools without the benefit of sight. You can profit from his experiences by not feeling sorry for yourself when you have a challenge to overcome.

Bouncing Back Characteristic 9: Able to Handle Disappointment

To make a comeback you have to be able to cope with the disappointment that made the comeback necessary. Being able to handle disappointment is also necessary because of the inevitability of disappointment when your work involves influencing others. Ultimately some people are going to resist your influence attempts over an important issue such as spearheading a new program, approving your candidate for a promotion, or seeking approval for a new budget. You are also liable to face disappointment when you are demoted after a takeover because the predator firm wants their person in power.

Abraham Zaleznik and Manfred F. R. Ket de Vries examined the psychology of corporate people. They observed that people who want power and responsibility, or who are creative, are especially vulnerable when reality deviates from their wishes or intentions. Instead of being an omen of continued failure, these periods of disappointment often stimulate growth and outstanding performance.[7]

Dealing with Loss and Bewilderment.   Much of the progress depends on the quality of the psychological work the individual accomplishes under the feelings of loss and bewilderment that often accompany disappointment. The outcome is determined by the quality of the person and the courage he or she can mobilize. Also important is the richness of his or her talents, and the ability to take a careful look at ourselves.

One of the biggest challenges is that current disappointments are linked to those experienced earlier in life. In the process of thinking through a disappointment, the person recognizes that it is not possible to reach certain goals, and therefore may be willing to drop certain goals. By so doing, these often unrealistic goals no longer place a demand on the person's behavior. Simultaneously the person discovers new possibilities for work and pleasure. These possibilities are blocked as long as the person is intent on obtaining rewards to make up for felt losses of the past.

There is irony in the solutions to the problems of disappointment. The deepest irony is in discovering that we have been mourning losses that were never sustained and yearning for a past that never existed. At the same time the person ignores the real capabilities for shaping the present.

Putting Theory to Use.   How might the theorizing just presented relate to making your own comeback? One example is that some people are seeking the approval from their bosses that they never received from their parents.

Self-Defeating Scenario 1: Jacques Chartrand, Clothing Designer

A clothing designer had worked for three months on a reversible sports jacket. His boss, the merchandising vice president, rejected the idea stating that, "Not only is your idea tacky, it's been tried and failed many times in the past." The designer had a difficult time coping with this rejection and disappointment because his father had rejected so many of his attempts at creativity. Until the designer can separate boss rejection from parental rejection, he will continue to suffer major disappointments when his product ideas are rejected.

You too may arrive at a point in your career where you will have to disassociate an authority figure in the present from one in the past. Your boss might act like a parent, but don't confuse him or her with being one of your parents.

Bouncing Back Characteristic 10: Getting Up One More Time Than You Have Been Knocked Down

Courage is a big contributor to resiliency. You need it both in the midst of adversity, and to stage a comeback once the adversity has run its course. When a company is facing a crisis, the key people involved in survival need moral courage. A crisis survival plan may lead to the company getting sued. Your largest creditors will sue your company for as much as possible. Courageous members of the survival team will understand that winning means getting up one more time than they have been knocked down.[8]

Courage Helps Deal with Rejection.   Courage is also important to the resilient person because it helps one deal with rejection. Successful sales people learn to courageously handle rejection by denying its existence. Victor Kiam believes that successful sellers flip the situation around by rejecting rejection. (As you probably know Kiam is the man who liked Remington Shavers so much, he bought the company.) In Kiam's words: "For successful sellers every slammed door becomes a source of energy and excitement, something that starts the adrenaline pumping for the impending challenge: to pry that door back open."[9] Kiam recounts an early experience of his that illustrates how courage can help a person cope with rejection:

Comeback Scenario 7: Victor Kiam, Undergarment Seller

Several decades ago I was making my rounds in Tupelo, Mississippi, selling bras, girdles, and other undergarments for the Playtex Corp. When I arrived at one small shop, I found the owner busy sweeping the floor. Extending my hand, I introduced myself, told him I was a Playtex representative, and paused.

Silence.

Undeterred, I opened my sample case and began my pitch. As I did, I could almost see rage swelling up inside the man. Before I could pull out a single item, he began sweeping me out of the store with forceful strokes of the broom. Shocked, I asked what I had done to offend him. He continued pushing me toward the door. As I opened my mouth to protest, he gathered all his strength for one final shove that sent me barreling into the street. When the dust cleared, I found myself flat on my behind in the middle of the side-walk.

This was no subtle rejection. I would have been well within my rights to harbor a bitter grudge against the shopkeeper. But rather than indulge my emotions, I cast off the rejection and grew deter-mined to uncover the cause of the man's hostility.

After chatting with some other sales representatives and store owners in the area, I found that the shopkeeper had a legitimate complaint. Thanks to my predecessor, the man had so overstocked his store that much of his capital was tied up in excess merchandise.

To right a bad situation, I arranged a deal. One of my larger ac-counts would purchase the shopkeeper's inventory at cost. Needless to say, I made a friend. The next time I called on the shopkeeper, the broom was tucked safely away in the closet and I received the warmest of greetings. The man said he would become a loyal Playtex customer. And though he never became one of my largest accounts, I could always depend on his orders.

If I had sunk into depression following that early, violent rejec-tion, I would have certainly lost the account. At that point, I doubt if any sales representative would have been able to reclaim it. Thank-fully, I didn't, and for the rest of my time with Playtex I had one less slamming door to contend with.[10]

Kiam displayed courage in his willingness to deal further with the irate shopkeeper after the physical punishment he received. Neverthe-less, one might question the level of Kiam's self-esteem at that point in his career. If his self-esteem had been higher he might not have ac-cepted physical abuse from a customer without retaliating verbally or physically. Yet I see an important message here for you. If you are re-jected by a key person in your work environment, have the courage to not let the rejection overwhelm you. It is part of trying to assert yourself and become or remain successful.

Bouncing Back Characteristic 11: Willingness to Take Risks

Risk taking is necessary to make a comeback that places you at or be-yond the level you were struck with before adversity. Almost all the people described in this book are sensible risk takers. When George Pagano decided to become a home restorer, he took the risk of going bankrupt while waiting for customers. A safer alternative for George would have been to take a retail or factory job. Such a course of action, however, would not have constituted a comeback. George would not have recaptured the job satisfaction he experienced as a subcontractor before his automobile accident.

Risk taking is necessary because the chances may be a small part of a particular comeback route to being successful. Many corporate executives who are laid off because of a merger or acquisition, hostile takeover, or leveraged buyout pursue the risky comeback path of self-employment. The chances of becoming a successful entrepreneur are at best 50-50 even for a well-designed business. Failed self-employment represents a multiple loss. The failed entrepreneur loses personal assets, borrowed money, and a good credit rating. Opportunity costs, the money the person could have earned by taking a relatively secure job, must also be added to the loss.

Comebacks within Large Organizations.   Comebacks, of course, can also be made within the context of a large organization. Here too, a risk-taking attitude is necessary to make the dramatic moves required to turn around adverse circumstances. Even if the adverse circumstances do not represent a personal catastrophe such as being involved in a scandal, they can create personal adversity. For example, if an executive cannot guide the company out of trouble, his or her reputation may become permanently tarnished.

Comeback Scenario 8: Don Lennox, Former Navistar CEO

Don Lennox's struggle at International Harvester (now Navistar), illustrates how risk-taking can turn around a crisis and ward off personal adversity at the same time. He looks back upon his experiences:

> The biggest crisis I faced in my career was an organizational problem. The problem occurred around the time I joined International Harvester. Top management, with the assistance of outside consultants, decided that the company's poor performance was due to their five business units being run as a centralized organization. We reorganized the five new businesses. However, the end result was five bureaucratic businesses instead of one. We therefore attempted to identify those who had the potential to be innovative. It was found that many of the employees couldn't or wouldn't change. We eliminated these employees.

Lennox also launched a far-reaching move to reduce IH's operating expenses. "Without risking some substantial debt there was no way out of our hole. The important thing was to get rid of nonperforming assets."

The construction equipment unit was sold to Dresser Industries, Inc. Lennox also took IH out of the manufacture of truck axles and transmission, airliner tow truck, and off-highway haulers. Divestments were also made of the life insurance business and numerous joint ventures such as mining. "We had to take the chance of giving up some businesses with future potential in order to survive at the moment."

During this period of divestments, Lennox closed the Fort Wayne truck plant that had been a company fixture since 1923. Two thousand workers were laid off, all that remained of the 10,000 who had worked there in 1979. To some old-timers, Lennox recalls, "Fort Wayne *was* International Harvester, but in the end I concluded that we had to get rid of the plant. I doubted the plant could be turned to profitability because it had not turned a profit in 20 years."

> I was able to convince the organization that our drastic efforts were in the employees' best interests because bankruptcy was impending. Most employees came to believe that action was necessary. I certainly had self-doubts about what I was doing, and a deep concern for the havoc that was created. Making those brutal cutbacks was the most unpleasant task in my life. It was such a depressing way to operate. Employees were getting laid off and orders to vendors were eliminated when a product was discontinued.
>
> I finally experienced elation when the agricultural business was sold off in 1984. At that point I felt we were home free. We gambled that employee morale could be held at an acceptable level after we eliminated the business on which the company was founded.

Few career people are placed in a Lennox's position of risking selling off a company's core business. Yet there is an important lesson here. To overcome lingering adversity, drastic surgery may be required. If, for example, your career satisfaction is so low that it is a continuous source of stress, switching careers would represent a prudent risk.

Bouncing Back Characteristic 12: Decisiveness in the Midst of Turmoil

Decisiveness is an important attribute of a resilient manager. The inner core of the resilient person includes a capacity and desire to move swiftly and decisively in the midst of turmoil. Without such decisiveness, the adverse situation is likely to get further out of hand. Decisiveness, similar to the other characteristics discussed so far, is closely linked to other traits and behaviors. For example, the decisive person is usually courageous and willing to take risks. One such person is Bal Dixit, the president of Newtex, a manufacturer of heat repellent cloth used to replace asbestos.

Comeback Scenario 9: Bal Dixit, President of Newtex

A native of India, Dixit emigrated to the United States in 1964, and founded his company in 1978. After two years of painstaking effort to establish a market for his product and build a factory, Newtex suffered a fire two days before the annual stockholder's meeting. Bal vividly recalls seeing smoke billowing from the roof of his factory. When the doors were opened, oxygen fed the flames, creating an extremely dangerous situation. Although the company had fire insurance, thoughts raced through Bal's mind about the loss of customer confidence, employee morale, and a cancelled stockholder's meeting.

Bal Dixit's immediate action was to get everyone out of the building. While his office called the fire department, Bal sprayed the fire with an extinguisher, but the fire raged out of control. The television news teams were at the scene of the fire along with the fire department. Bal wanted to get control of information communicated to the press, and he wanted to divert a panic by employees and business associates.

Damage Control.   As soon as the fire was under control, Bal called all the employees into the office to discuss the major setback. His goal was to provide leadership and an optimistic attitude for his employees to follow. Bal told them if they pitched in to help, he would guarantee their job security. Every employee present was given an emergency assignment and told not to discuss the fire with anyone. Bal would field all questions from customers and the media. The employees worked day and night to clean up the soot and the damaged equipment.

Every bit of damage was carefully documented with the total cost accounted for in detail. Bal made the quick decision to go ahead with repairs before the insurance claims were covered so that the company would not lose valuable time. Contractors were called in immediately to repair the roof and the treatment tower in which the fire started. The roof was repaired that weekend and within two weeks the tower was back in operation.

When the stockholders walked into the factory two days later, they were aware of the fire but the true extent of damage was not apparent.

Dixit and his employees moved so swiftly that only one major customer was aware of the fire. Although Dixit thinks that his attention to the fire diverted some of his marketing efforts, Newtex met its sales forecast for the quarter. Since that time the company has continued to grow, and Bal Dixit has received a New York State award for excellence in small business.

It would be hard to deny that much of the future of his company was insured by Dixit's decisive action. Employees still refer to that night as the "Dixit Fixit." Bal Dixit's decisiveness in taking immediate action to reverse the fire damage vastly contributed to his leadership excellence. If you are faced with potential catastrophe, or even a lesser adversity, be decisive. It will give forward thrust to your comeback.

Bouncing Back Characteristic 13: Moderate Indulgence in Pleasure

Fun lovers in the office may not be the most effective at rebounding from adversity. Resilient managers and professionals tend to be more work- than pleasure-oriented. Many powerful people are pleasure-oriented, but many of these people have not had to cope with much adversity. A study of 88 corporate executives showed that some of the people who get the biggest bang out of life were having career problems. It was showed that people who indulge moderately in pleasure can deal with setbacks and focus on the qualities that help them get ahead.[11]

Although somewhat disheartening, this moderate indulgence in pleasure of resilient people is explainable. Such an attitude helps them focus more on their comeback rather than finding a temporary escape from pain by indulging in pleasure. We are not recommending that you give up on pleasure. Better yet is to work hard and play hard. This way when adversity strikes, you will have a strong enough work orientation to help you over the rough spots.

Bouncing Back Characteristic 14: Realistic Perspective

Managers with a good capacity to overcome adversity have a realistic perspective of their world. They accept the fact that some frustration and disappointment are inevitable in corporate America. A middle manager employed by Manufacturers Hanover Trust Co. during one of its belt-tightening phases, reveals the type of realistic perception that fosters resiliency:

> Some days it's difficult to get up and go to work. But I still have things I want to accomplish. If not for the company, then for myself. The most important thing for me is supporting my family. So if nothing else, I sit down and hate this, but I know it's important for my family. The majority of people I know who are sitting here, toughing it out, are doing it for their families. And maybe you say to yourself, "Hey, it's no better anywhere else."

Action Tips

If you want to become a resilient person, attempt to develop the characteristics and traits in the following checklist. If you already possess them, hone them further. Such development or honing will help you bounce back from adversity.

1. Take charge of your own life.
2. Believe that you can control the events you experience.
3. Be committed to the key task of your comeback.
4. Assume some ownership of the problem that led to your adversity.
5. Develop an indomitable spirit.
6. Maintain high self-esteem and self-confidence.
7. Avoid self-pity.
8. Accept disappointment in stride.
9. Remember that winning means getting up one more time than you have been knocked down.
10. Be willing to take prudent risks.
11. Be decisive in the midst of turmoil.
12. Enjoy pleasure but not to the exclusion of enjoying hard work.
13. Maintain a realistic perspective.

2

Handling Yourself After the Merger or Takeover

One day you face a new reality at work. Your company is now part of another corporate entity. The new entity could have come about in several ways. Your company may have taken over another firm, your company might have been acquired by another, or your company has been bought by your own management or an outside agent.

Adversity may be facing you under all these circumstances. Your job might be in jeopardy to reduce duplication of effort or costs. Or you might be demoted and reporting to someone who appears less qualified than you. At a minimum, you may be required to manage in a maze of confusion, low morale, low productivity, and political infighting as workers become preoccupied with saving their hides. Here we look at ways to survive this ordeal. More so than in other chapters, we urge you to follow these suggestions in step-by-step fashion as each one applies to you:

> Read the handwriting on the wall. → Maintain a high profile. → Sell yourself to the retention interviewer and major customers. → Develop a lean and mean operating style. → Avoid a "them-versus-us" mentality. → Avoid displaying bitterness. → Deal positively with the merger consultant. → Show that you can adapt to the changes. → React positively to your new boss. → Obtain your share of resources during downsizing. → Remember that there is life after termination.

Bouncing Back Characteristic 15:
Read the Handwriting on
the Wall

Many postmerger managers deny the reality that their job is in jeopardy. Instead of taking action to find a new position or to preserve their present one, they choose to believe that somebody else will get axed. Denial in this sense is distorting the objective facts of a situation because they are so anxiety provoking. The denial process leads postmerger managers to ignore the handwriting on the wall about job loss, or to think it spells out a co-worker's name.[1]

There are certainly good reasons for wanting to deny the prospects of having to search for a new position outside the company. Most pension benefits are still not portable, and finding a new job could mean enduring the agony of relocation. The agony might include not being able to sell one's house at a fair price because the market is already glutted with other victims of a merger or purge.

Conduct a Job Search While Still Employed. Despite the inconvenience and disruption of finding a new position, it is better to conduct your search while still employed. An axiom of the recruiting business is that employed managers are easier to place than the unemployed. Although you may have been asked to leave for circumstances beyond your control, potential employers might be suspect. Many believe that only the poor performers are invited out of the organization during a downsizing. Many prospective employers think to themselves, "If you're so hot, why didn't the company keep you around to help increase productivity?" The stereotype that unemployed managers and professionals are inferior persists despite all the productive people who have been forced out of jobs in recent years.

How can one overcome denial if the process is automatic, and almost unconscious? Encourage feedback from a knowledgeable third party. Run your circumstances by that person, and have him or her restate what you said. An example, "What I've heard you say is that you haven't been invited to an important meeting ever since the merger took place. Furthermore, your boss hasn't asked your opinion in weeks."

Signals of Problems Ahead. Following is a description of many subtle, and not so subtle messages that all convey the same information—you are about to be terminated or demoted. Being alert to these signals can trigger you into finding a more secure position for yourself.

You find yourself out of the loop. Mysteriously, you are no longer included in a variety of important communication events such as meetings, receiving important memos, and informal meetings at the home of the general manager. Being out of the loop is the most general piece of ominous handwriting on the wall. Many of the other signs described below are a subset of no longer being part of the in-group.

Project, task force, or committee assignments no longer come your way. Be especially wary if another person performing comparable work has been given such assignments. It could mean the organization only intends to keep one of you, and the other person is being favored.

Several months have passed since you have received a luncheon invitation from an important person. It could mean that in order to increase productivity, the company is cutting down on the time and expense involved in business luncheons. Because top-level managers will rarely forgo this sacred expense account luxury, not being invited may mean that your power has diminished.

You are moved to a smaller office, without a plausible explanation offered. The move is even more significant when your request for refurbishing the office is denied. Most likely the company has no intention of making you extra comfortable during the balance of your stay.

A manager from another department suddenly becomes interested in knowing all he or she can about your operation, and your opinion about many company matters. This person might be earmarked to add your job to his or her responsibilities. Your brain is being picked now because it is obvious you would be less cooperative after being given your notice.

You are not invited to a major meeting about reorganization. The meeting probably included a discussion of how your function could be eliminated or consolidated. Not even mobsters would invite a person to a meeting about his or her own funeral.

You ask a team member to help you on a project, and the person refuses. The explanation is that your boss has pulled him or her away from your unit temporarily. The implication of this refusal is that your boss no longer thinks you are important enough to ask before bypassing your authority. Because you are on the hit list, you stop receiving normal courtesies. Besides, the organization no longer thinks what you are doing is valuable.

You do not receive a "stay bonus." If you are regarded as a key person in the new corporate entity, you might be offered a special payment to remain after the reorganization takes place. Often the bonus entails a week's pay for each month you stay on for the next six months. Not every postmerger company offers such a bonus, so not receiving one is not a surefire sign of being on the hit list. Yet if several other managers at your level received a stay bonus, and you did not, your days could be numbered.

Being as objective as you can, it is obvious that you are no longer doing relevant work. In fact, you are often creating work for yourself by asking for appointments to see important people. Your purpose is to let them know that you are available for an assignment. An early sign that your work is losing its relevance, is when your workday begins to pass more slowly. The slowness comes about because performing trivial work is boring and anxiety provoking for a person with self-respect.

Only routine messages appear in your electronic-mail. Almost all of the information sent to you also appears on the screens of everybody else. For example, the only two messages you received last week were (1) an announcement that the company was having a sale of surplus office furniture for employees, and (2) the United Way drive would be starting in two weeks.

When you send memos and telephone calls to influential people, they rarely respond. When you do get through on the telephone, the executive responds to your message in a noncommittal way. The most enthusiastic response you receive is "I might give that some thought."

Top management in your division is viewed as a bunch of losers. You are likely to be tarred with the same brush, and asked to leave along with the executives running your division. The new owners may decide to do a thorough housecleaning in order to revitalize your division.

Your performance-appraisal is long overdue. If your boss can legitimately state that your performance is substandard, your review will probably take place on time. If your boss cannot honestly condemn you in a performance appraisal, the review may be postponed indefinitely. It is embarrassing to fire someone who recently received a good performance appraisal. This is particularly true if your were squeezed out for reasons other than your job being collapsed to save money.

If you receive one or more of the above messages, it could mean you are soon to be terminated. However, *could* does not mean always. Express your concerns to your boss or another higher up. Explain that it appears to you that your contribution is no longer valued, but you would like clarification. Emphasize that you want to survive the take-over (or any other shakeup) and make a big contribution. In some organizations you might get an honest answer. Tom, a middle manager in a recently taken-over pharmaceutical firm, received a refreshing response to his confrontation about being out of the loop. He was told by his boss, the vice president of research and development, "I apologize for ignoring you. Ever since the acquisition, we've been running around in a state of confusion. Don't take the neglect personally. We need you around here."

Bouncing Back Characteristic 16: Maintain a High Profile

Enough of the pessimism about reading the handwriting on the wall. Next, assume the optimistic position that you will be fortunate enough to escape the cost cutter's axe after a merger, purge, or leveraged buyout (LBO). Pretend that under the new regime, nobody's job is secure. Survivor's will have to convince the new management team that their present contribution justifies being asked to stay. Demonstrate that letting you go would be a costly mistake to the organization.

Staffing decisions after a merger are made quickly, and are often based on sketchy information. You can be out before you have had time to adapt to the new regime's method of operation. Nevertheless, some managers will take a laid-back posture, and wait to see what position they are offered in the new combined firm. It is much better to maintain a high profile immediately after the takeover.[2]

Sizing Up Your New Corporate Culture.   The first important step is to size up the culture of the acquiring firm. Determine what types of behavior are valued by the new owner. Also, be on the alert for behaviors and attitudes that are frowned upon or considered less desirable.

Acting According to Your Findings.   The next step would be to emphasize the valued behaviors, and deemphasize or bury the unwanted behaviors. The "in" and "out" behaviors are revealed through your reading of the corporate culture. Speak openly to several people about such things as "what top management really thinks is important."

In most acquired companies, for example, you will be part of the in-group if you present detailed financial analyses of the consequences of all your actions. Don't describe your plan for parental leave in terms of its contribution to morale and helping to resolve family versus work crises. Instead, translate the parental leave plan in terms of its cost effectiveness. Focus on earnings per share, because most corporate deal makers are primarily concerned with shareholder value and stock prices.

In some takeovers, the new owners want to hear about your contribution to customer satisfaction, product enhancement, and good will. In these cases, you can best maintain a high profile by not presenting computerized analyses of return on investment, cost effectiveness, and the like. Instead, talk glowingly about how your efforts are helping the company get closer to the customer, build a better product, or create a reputation for high quality.

Taking the Initiative in Problem Solving.   An effective way of warding off the potential adversity from being part of a takeover is to maintain a high profile through an offensive maneuver. You take the initiative to help the organization deal with its rampant problems.

Comeback Scenario 10: Tanya Bridges, Human Resources Specialist

Tanya, a human resources specialist in a company taken over by a larger food company, did just that. After the takeover, the edict was out to downsize the organization by 900 jobs, and to reduce general operating costs by 15 percent.

Nobody's job was sacred, including Tanya's. The acquiring company had a full complement of human resource workers. Instead of bemoaning her fate, Tanya surveyed the damage to the organization and then asked for an audience with the new vice president of human resources. She first presented him with an oral summary of her observations, and then followed up with a written report.

> What I focused on was the havoc the downsizing was creating and what the company could do about it. I had done my homework by reading certain articles in personnel magazines. They dealt with what human resource specialists can do to soften the impact of downsizings. I explained to my boss that we had plenty of problems. Our photocopying costs were skyrocketing as hundreds of people were getting their resumes updated. Important work was going unattended as people were chasing down job openings in other companies and calling personal contacts.
>
> I volunteered to head up a survivor assistance group that would help calm down the people who were being asked to stay. First, we would have sessions with about 30 employees and one member of

top management explaining when the cuts would end and how jobs would be changed. In the weeks following we would conduct voluntary group sessions with employees who wanted to express fears and concerns about their jobs.

I presented some evidence that survivors after a major downsizing often suffer guilt. They feel bad about being the lucky ones. We would have trained counselors from the employee assistance program to help with these sessions.

I emphasized repeatedly that with a little time and effort, the company could stop the hemorrhaging in productivity and morale created by the downsizing.

My efforts quickly received the attention and support of top management. The president wrote me a letter saying that I was a valuable contributor to the new combined company. My job became secure for now. Also, I felt an inner glow based on the fact that I was really helping the employees in my company and their families.

Tanya enhanced her job security during a takeover because she identified and tackled a major corporate problem—managing the turmoil created by downsizing. If you are caught in a takeover, take the offensive to show how critical your function is to the overall enterprise. Get involved and showcase your contribution.

Bouncing Back Characteristic 17: Sell Yourself to the Retention Interviewer and Major Customers

Selling yourself to top management by maintaining a high profile is important, but further work may be needed. Management consultant Robert Bell advises that after a takeover you also need to impress the retention interviewer and get major customers on your side.[3]

Convincing the Big Customers. The new owners will listen carefully to major customers as to which managers in the acquired company are making an important contribution. If you have access to customers, getting them to vouch for you could be a winning ploy. The more astute customers are likely to be concerned about how well they will be taken care of after the merger. They are aware of the posttakeover turmoil that often results in poor customer service.

Take the initiative to convince your customers that your company should now be able to serve them even better because of increased efficiencies in the new combined company. If you have a warm relationship with high-ranking customers, gently ask them to contact your employer and express their satisfaction with the service you have been providing. A good word from a customer is the best possible reference.

You do not have to be in marketing or sales to get customers on your side. Customers would probably be receptive to a visit or phone call from the manufacturing, engineering, or quality control department of a vendor.

Convincing the Retention Interviewer.   One of the most difficult ordeals facing the posttakeover manager or professional is the retention interview. The interviewer's role is to make recommendations to the new owners about which people should be retained in the combined company. The retention interview is thus a job interview for the purpose of holding on to the job you held before the takeover. (Dealing with the merger consultant, as described later, is a variation of dealing with the retention interviewer.)

All you have learned about conducting yourself in a job interview applies to the retention interview: dress well, appear healthy, speak positively, have up-to-date facts at your disposal; smile frequently; be enthusiastic; and retain your composure. In addition, come to the interview with a rehearsed list of all you have accomplished for the company. If you can, dredge up 25 accomplishments. Also work into the interview your plans for further increases in productivity and cost savings. Explain unequivocally how you want to be part of the new enterprise and how you can help it achieve its goals. The burden of proof is on you to justify keeping your job.

Bouncing Back Characteristic 18: Develop a Lean and Mean Operating Style

After a takeover, inevitably a big push develops for improving productivity with an emphasis on trimming costs. If you want to fall into grace with the new management team—and perhaps save your job—demonstrate a lean and mean operating style. In other words, you get your work accomplished with fewer employees than you or your predecessors required in the past. Perhaps you can get *more* work done with fewer people. This is a more effective strategy than finding ways to beat the system and run with a "fat and good-natured" operating style.

Developing a lean and mean operating style is essentially a question of raising your awareness to accomplish more with fewer resources. Whenever possible, publicize your efforts of operating with a tight budget. However, avoid spending so little money that it is expensive. For example, do not attempt to save money by sending a crucial shipment to a customer by parcel post. Here is a starter kit of maneuvers and suggestions that could enhance your image as a lean and mean manager:

Instead of replacing a product design specialist who quits, suggest that the company subcontract the specialist's work on an as-needed basis.

Make shipments of your company's merchandise in boxes you save that contained shipments from your suppliers. (However, use a fresh mailing label.)

Conduct a national sales meeting in a budget motel in a medium-size city rather than at a luxury hotel in a major city.

Conduct small breakfast meetings at a Perkins or a diner, rather than in hotel restaurants.

Delay performance appraisals by an average of three months, thus postponing salary increases, and saving the company oodles of money. (Be aware, however, that this maneuver may torpedo morale.)

Recommend that your division relocate to lower-priced office space, or that departments be consolidated to enable the company to sublet some excess space.

Delay accounts payable as long as possible. At the same time, apply pressure to shorten the collection time for accounts receivables.

Cancel orders for regular shipments of fresh flowers for the reception area. Instead, suggest that the employees who have gardens bring in their own flowers to decorate the office.

Demand that every employee under your jurisdiction take no more time for lunch and rest breaks than required by law. Theoretically, the additional hours recaptured by this maneuver will lead to increased productivity.

Work closely with the office manager to control the slippage of office supplies for home use. Put up a poster reminding workers to empty their pockets of company pencils and ball pens before returning home.

Compose a list of suggestions on how the company can save water, such as eliminating the watering of lawns and decreasing the frequency of car washing.

Despite low profits or a high budget deficit, never suggest ways to economize by lowering top-management compensation. If somebody else makes such a suggestion, present an analysis showing that executive pay is a minuscule proportion of the total operating budget. (Watch out, however, for developing a reputation as an unctuous office politician.)

Bouncing Back Characteristic 19: Avoid a Them-Versus-Us Mentality

When one firm engulfs another, antagonisms often develop among employees of the two firms. Managers are more often in combat than other workers because they come into direct contact with clashes in policies and procedures. The antagonisms tend to be more intense when the takeover is hostile and forcible. It is not surprising that conflict should take place between the two firms. Of major significance, the two cultures clash. The accompanying table illustrates how two companies can differ in culture.

Contrasting Corporate Cultures

Company A	Company B
Key people are adventuresome, risk taking, and free swinging.	Key people are conservative and risk-avoidant.
Compensation quite generous and linked to performance.	Compensation low and based mostly on seniority.
Systems and procedures aimed at giving information and solving problems.	Systems and procedures aimed at tight control over people.
Emphasis on customer satisfaction.	Emphasis on well-engineered products.

With so many potential conflicts between the acquiring and acquired firm, a "them-versus-us" mentality may be pervasive.[4] Harboring such a mentality may be politically unwise, and might intensify your adversity. It may peg you as narrow-minded and unreceptive to change—hardly good credentials for retention or promotion.

Self-Defeating Scenario 2: Grant Lancaster, Department Store Manager

Grant, a manager of a large department store, fell into such a trap. For ten years he had helped his company become the leading downtown retailer in his city. One spring, the store Grant managed was bought by a large retailer from out of town.

When Grant's store was acquired, the new owners made the usual pledge of leaving management intact and making few changes in the operations of the business. Within three months, however, substantial changes began to take place. As a starting point, the new owners demanded that Grant decrease the number of floor personnel by 25 percent. According to their analysis, customer service could be maintained by operating with a smaller staff of better trained sales associates.

Customer complaints about shoddy service began to arrive in Grant's office. The new owners insisted that as soon as the associates completed their training, they would be Able to please customers. As a result, they predicted, complaints would decrease. Besides, they argued, the increase profit margins were a few isolated complaints. The next big changes imposed on Grant's store stemmed from a change in merchandising philosophy.

The new owners insisted that the store carried too much high-priced, stodgy clothing. Based on the advice of merchandising consultants, the new owners demanded that Grant's store carry a wide variety of flashy, but inexpensive clothing. Large numbers of established customers soon began drifting away from the store. They were replaced in part by youthful bargain hunters who bought mostly sale merchandise.

Grant became increasingly perturbed by the changing nature of his store, and the insensitivity of the new owners to the problems they were creating. Gradually, Grant began to express some of his hostility toward the new owners to the department managers in his store. One day the women's wear manager asked Grant when the new owners would be reviewing the upcoming fall line with them. Grant replied, "Oh, the Champions of Schlock will be getting to that right after they figure out how we can cut some additional costs."

Another day Grant visited the children's wear department. He noticed that many customers were serving themselves, unassisted by any store representative. Grant asked for an explanation from the manager. She explained that the new owners emphasized self-service. Angered, Grant said, "I don't care what *they* say. Here is how *we* treat customers." Without realizing it, Grant began to make more frequent references to the new owners as "them" and his store as "us."

Grant's feelings encouraged them-versus-us attitudes throughout the store. Soon store employees at all levels began to exchange derogatory jokes about the new owners.

Two Examples

   QUESTION: Why have the owners and their spouses been able to avoid the "Ten Worst Dressed" people list for so many years?

ANSWER: Because they never shop at their own stores.

QUESTION: Can you give me an example of the new owner's flair for new concepts in merchandising and cost savings?

ANSWER: I sure can. Starting this spring, we are offering one-size-fits-all shoes. In this way we capitalize on economies of scale, and we will never be out of any customer's shoe size.

Word soon got back to the new owner's management team about the recalcitrant attitude so pervasive at Grant's store. Shortly thereafter he was replaced by a new store manager from the parent company. Grant was not fired. Instead, he was offered the opportunity to become the manager of the furniture department, at 75 percent of his current pay. Muttering to himself that "they" were SOBs, Grant decided to accept the position and coast until he would be eligible for retirement in five years.

Grant fell into the trap of letting his hostility toward the new owners adversely affect his work. The lesson to be learned is to avoid becoming a "Black Belt in Sarcasm" when being managed by new owners. Such behavior is self-defeating.

Bouncing Back Characteristic 20: Avoid Displaying Bitterness

The corporate takeover binge has led to the trading of workers along with other corporate assets. As a result, many jostled workers feel bitter and alienated.[5] Even survivors feel bitter, particularly those who have been demoted, placed on special assignment, or watched productive associates being booted out the door. A good deal of bitterness also takes place when the new owners skim the surplus from the employee pension fund.

Suppressing Your Bitterness. To survive and prosper after a takeover, it is important to suppress your bitterness on the job. Let your bitterness out in the company of family members and friends who have no connection with your employer. But on the job, appear cheerful and grateful. Such a facade can help you preserve your job.

Several years ago, Paul Bilzerian acquired Singer Co., the defense contractor, provider of educational products, and former sewing machine maker. He purchased the conglomerate for $1.1 billion when the company's stock nosedived during the 1987 crash. Singer was renamed Bicoastal after Bilzerian sold eight of the twelve divisions to help pay $120 million in annual interest payments. (The company, of course, also needed cash to make principal payments.) Although most former Singer employees were able to keep their jobs when their divisions were sold, about 7,000 of them were given pink slips.

Bilzerian was sentenced to four years in prison for violating tax and securities laws in previous takeovers, and his appeal was overturned. Bicoastal was later forced to seek bankruptcy protection, as its level of debt proved unmanageable. Several of the remaining divisions became less profitable than expected, in large measure because of the demoralization of the workforce.

Comeback Scenario 11: Brian Pawkowicz, Project Coordinator

Brian, one of the survivors, explains how he made it through the stormy days following the takeover, while many others around him became casualties:

> Our division of Bicoastal made hardware and software for military training. Bilzerian attempted to sell our division but was unable to get the price he needed. Company presidents have become leery of paying too much for firms that sell primarily software. The problem is that these firms are only as good as their software engineers. If the software people don't like the new owners, they may leave. The firm is then left with very little to sell in the future.
>
> So there we were, stuck as a division the owner would have rather sold. We felt as if we were a child the parents couldn't wait to kick out the door when the time was right. It seemed as if Bicoastal was seeking revenge because our division couldn't be sold. In the old days of Singer, we received excellent support services from the corporate group. They prepared our taxes, helped us with financial reporting, provided data processing services for payroll, and assisted us with recruiting. All these support services were dropped after the takeover.
>
> After a massive cost-cutting drive, we became understaffed. Our profit goals were increased by the corporate group to almost unrealistic heights. Our managers and professionals were routinely putting in 60-hour work weeks to survive.
>
> Employees in our division became angrier with each passing month. Some of us resented a wealthy person like Bilzerian expecting us to economize in chintzy little ways like freezing the salaries of office help. We were working under a climate of uncertainty, not knowing if our division would be spun off at the first opportunity. A good number of the staff became embittered. As software professionals they felt they shouldn't have to worry about their employer collapsing.
>
> My decision was to maintain a positive outlook. Instead of bitching, moaning, and groaning, I dug in and did what was necessary to survive. When my boss asked me how things were going, I

told him that I thought the division was soon going to overcome its problems. I explained that the worst of times were behind us, and that we could move forward.

My strategy worked. When the next round of personnel cuts were made, my responsibilities increased. I was promoted from project co-ordinator to program manager, a one-step promotion. The vice president of software development told me that I was one of the few people the division regarded as entirely loyal. I guess my survivor instincts had prevented me from expressing my true feelings about Bilzerian.

As I think back, I doubt that Bilzerian is any worse than most of the corporate raiders. He was just playing a game he certainly didn't invent. Even if I didn't agree with Bilzerian's business philosophy, why should I have let my feelings sabotage my career? My career is on the upswing. And I haven't burned any bridges that will come back to haunt me should I want to make a move.

Brian survived by maintaining a positive outlook. Instead of dragging his heels, he directed energy into achieving corporate goals. Should you be caught in a takeover headed by a gluttonous executive, we recommend you follow Brian's lead.

Bouncing Back Characteristic 21: Deal Positively with the Merger Consultant

The statement, "Your check is in the mail" is now rivaled in sincerity by "Don't worry, very few changes will be made after the acquisition. We intend to leave everything intact. No personnel changes are anticipated." Shortly after a takeover, the acquiring company typically hires a merger consultant. The consultant's role is to assess the contribution of various departments and to make suggestions for excising noncontributing or redundant operations.

Staffing decisions are likely to be made quickly, based on sketchy information. You have to think and act rapidly if you want to be one of the survivors. Many people err by taking the passive approach of waiting to see what happens. Consultant Price Prichett offers a few survival pointers for dealing constructively with the consultants invited in to study your operations.[6]

Decide if you fit in with the new corporate culture. Before even worrying about what to tell the consultant, decide if you are compatible with the culture of the acquiring firm. Beware if you are truly incompatible with the new regime. Staying could result in a frustration level that would damage the quality of your life and career. However, exiting too quickly can be a mistake because you might lose out on a generous severance package given during postmerger shakeouts.

Retain your composure. When discussing your organizational unit with consultants, avoid being defensive, argumentative, or panicky—at least visibly. Instead, offer a balanced evaluation of your department. Cover its strengths, areas for improvement, and potential. Explain how your unit can be made more productive to meet the demands of the new owner. Also point out that the team members are willing to support you in making necessary changes.

Explain how your unit is contributing to the organizational strategy. Consultants get turned on by "strategic thinking." In practice, this means explaining how your unit fits in with the master plan of the company. If you are managing a customer service department, explain how the company philosophy emphasizes the importance of satisfying customers. Also show how your group makes an everyday contribution to the quality of customer service. Emphasizing quality is important because by now virtually every company includes quality as part of its strategy, (Whether or not the strategy is working should not deter your thinking.)

Present as many facts and figures as you can about the productivity of your unit. As the customer service manager, you might display a graph of the increasing number of customer complaints handled by your department over a period of time. Prepare a scrapbook of thank-you letters from customers you have helped. Above all, gather some figures about the annualized financial contribution of your unit to corporate profits. The consultant is likely to incorporate your data into the report submitted to management.

Avoid a cover-up. If you know deep down that your position or unit is redundant—and therefore likely to be eliminated—frankness may help. Suggest that the company should consolidate your unit with the duplicate function or eliminate one of them. Your candor may help your unit become the survivor. Discuss with the consultant what other positions you think you could handle should your unit be sacrificed. Avoid appearing bitter or angry—just keep focused on your organizational contribution, not on your job security.

Comeback Scenario 12: Neil Cohen, Manager of Quality Assurance

Neil, a manager of quality assurance, in an acquired company knew that his function duplicated a similar department in the new parent company. He was confident he could find a suitable position elsewhere, but wanted to avoid sacrificing his ten years of seniority and pension rights. The pitch Neil made to the consultant investigating his department centered on the theme that he wanted to make a contribution to the organization. He felt he was prepared to work as a "turnaround manager," one who takes over a troubled unit and returns it to profitability.

Because the acquiring company wanted to squeeze as much profitability as possible out of the combined company, the consultant listened attentively. When the consultant discussed his analysis with top management, he recommended that Neil be given an opportunity to turn around a small troubled division of the larger company. Neil jumped into the assignment gleefully. Within two years the troubled division became profitable. As a result, Neil's stature and job security were enhanced. Eventually he left the company to join a consulting firm of turnaround managers. The difference was that he left at his own convenience, rather than the company's.

Neil Cohen's strategy is a variation of a key one that surfaces many times in this book. In times of organizational turbulence, focus on what you can do to help the company perform better. Take the offense instead of taking a self-protective posture.

Bouncing Back Characteristic 22: Show that You Can Adapt to the Changes

A takeover usually creates more change than most people want to handle. Often the turmoil is so intense that many suffer from too much stress. The people who rise to the challenge of change will usually create a positive impression on the new owners. The heel draggers may face an early demise. one of the major changes occurring in the post-takeover period, is a new approach to doing business.

Comeback Scenario 13: Kerry Madison, National Sales Manager

A national sales manager for a line of young women's clothing, prospered by changing her *modus operandi:*

> Kerry Madison's line of merchandise had met with great success during the 1980s and early 1990s but her company was conducting business in a 1950s mode. Management relied almost entirely on intuition in conducting business. Long-range planning rarely went past

one season. The company record keeping was so shoddy it rarely had accurate picture of our cash flow. Most of the company's really useful information about customers was kept in the head of managers.

Kerry recalls: "New management came in waving a sword. They told us to clean up our act or our entire management team would be replaced. Another alternative they mentioned is that we would be dissolved as a separate corporate entity if we didn't become more professional. Several members of our management team snorted fire through their noses. They believed that imposing bureaucracy on our creative souls would ruin the company."

Kerry took a different tack. She tried to serve as a model of how a sales manager in a creative business could still operate in the mode of a professional manager. She bought into all of their systems of managing people and money. Her group began a tight program of planning and goal setting. She asked for a member of their information systems team to help her company upgrade its record system. Kerry also requested that their corporate marketing staff help them conduct market research about new fashion trends in the youth market.

Kerry's willingness to change put her on the new management's good list. The new owner's marketing VP took her to lunch to express appreciation for her willingness to go along with corporate systems and procedures. Not coincidentally, the three members of our management team who resisted the changes are no longer with us. one was forced into early retirement; one was fired outright; and one was demoted to fashion coordinator.

Kerry Madison's comeback scenario carries an important message. Showing a willingness to accept the new owner's way of doing business can prevent a career setback.

Bouncing Back Characteristic 23: React Positively To Your New Boss

After any type of corporate shakeup, you are likely to have a new immediate boss. How you relate to that boss at the outset is very significant. It could determine how pleasant life will be for you in the present and future. For example, suppose you tear into the new boss with complaints about the injustices of the layoffs and your former boss being replaced. You are then likely to be viewed as a troublemaker and therefore unpromotable. The suggestions presented next are aimed at helping you present a positive image to your new boss.

Taking the Initiative in Getting to Know Your New Boss. A professional-style manager will routinely schedule an appointment with key members of the department shortly after moving into the position. Not every manager is so professional, and because of this your new manager may not think of scheduling these get-acquainted sessions. If this is your situation, take the initiative to have a formal session with the new boss. Explain to the boss's assistant that you would like to be given a 20-minute appointment with the boss for a general discussion. Consider these suggestions:

- During the session be as nonthreatening as possible. Mention that you would like to get acquainted, and describe your function within the unit.

- Congratulate your new boss on his or her new appointment and pledge your support. Rehearse your words of congratulation and support in advance of the meeting. Otherwise it is easy to appear too political. A sincere-sounding statement along these lines is, "Congratulations on becoming our new department manager. If there's anything that I can do to help you and our department, let me know. I want to be considered a contributor."

- After about ten minutes of conversation, gain control of the situation by asking for another meeting to discuss what you perceive to be the biggest challenges facing the department. Mention that you would also like to discuss your plan for meeting these challenges. All but the most insecure or inept boss will welcome your ideas. Citing problems and recommending solutions is a great way of enhancing your relationship with the boss. A curious boss will often request your preliminary thoughts right on the spot.

Comeback Scenario 14: Sandy Okata, Customer Service Representative

Sandy, a customer service representative, explains how she took the initiative to identify major problems within the department:

> In my first meeting with Casey (her postrestructuring boss), I gingerly asked if he would be interested in hearing my analysis of our biggest problems. The amount of his enthusiasm shocked me. Casey invited me to have lunch with him the next day to review my findings.
> During lunch, I explained that our company's philosophy empha-

sized customer service. Yet we had a constant ten-day backlog of Un-resolved customer complaints in our subsidiary. I suggested that we needed to increase the number of customer service reps, and de-velop a set of guidelines and procedures for resolving complaints. As things stood, customers with similar complaints would receive very different treatment depending on the representative they dealt with.

I also explained that the other customer service representatives and I needed more direct access to a supervisor. Our function was now reported to Casey, but he also had other functions to manage. Further-more, he was frequently away from the office tending to business.

The bottom line was that three weeks later I was appointed as the customer service supervisor. Two new reps were added to the de-partment. Both were transferred from less essential jobs. You could say that my advice to Casey was self-serving. But it also helped take care of an important company problem.

Sandy's assertive approach to identifying important challenges within her organizational unit served to highlight her contribution. Try the same approach when a new boss takes over your department. The new boss may be so impressed with your professionalism that the new re-porting relationship enhances your position.

Be careful about giving advice. The tactic just mentioned suggests that you give advance notice about solving an organization problem that *you* have identified. In contrast, move slowly in giving advice when the new boss has an idea for making changes. The new boss may be really asking you to put a seal of approval on a decision he or she has already made. If you make any suggestions you run the risk of interfering with your boss's hidden agenda.

Before responding to the new boss's suggestions, ask questions to learn more about his or her view of the situation. Figure out if the boss has already made a decision, or is genuinely looking for fresh input. If your manager presses you to present an opinion, offer suggestions but show that you can adapt to decisions that have already been made.[7] As-sume that your boss asks for your opinion about the usefulness of cen-tralized purchasing. In response, you ecstatically describe the benefits of central purchasing, such as better pricing because of volume pur-chases. With a shrug of his or her shoulders, your boss then explains that the policy of most decentralized purchasing will remain.

Slowly extracting your foot from your mouth, you respond, "I see your point of view. Some companies find decentralized purchasing quite effective, while centralized purchasing works for others. There are distinct trade-offs for both philosophies. I guess the important thing is how well we monitor our decentralized purchasing."

Bouncing Back Characteristic 24: Obtaining Your Share of Resources During Downsizing

A common form of managerial adversity is to suffer a drastic cut in resources. Yet during lean and mean times not every organizational unit is severely cut back or eliminated. Some managers are able to obtain enough resources to keep their units staffed and supplied. These managers thus ward off adversity before it occurs. An executive newsletter offers some useful suggestions for obtaining a healthy budget during lean and mean times.[8]

Make top management's uncertainty work for you. Top management knows they can make mistakes. In fact, many employers have eliminated so many managers and professionals in recent years that innovation and customer service have suffered. Also, many good opportunities go unexplored while the remaining members of management scramble around putting out fires. A chance therefore exists that members of the executive suite are worried about having thinned down resources too much.

Fill in the information gap. Keep your immediate manager informed of your day-to-day operations. Yet avoid being a constant bearer of bad news. If you communicate mostly good news, management will be more receptive to coping with occasional bad news. Useful information can be fed to management in several ways:

- An FYI (for your information) memo may seem like a cliché. Nevertheless, it is still a standard communication tool. FYIs are especially good for passing along information that compliments your group or describes unusual activity. An FYI memo is also effective because you are not asking anybody for a decision; you are simply taking the initiative to keep somebody informed.

- Ask your team members to put their cost-saving and dollar-earning suggestions in writing and then pass these along to upper management. Dollar-earning suggestions are noteworthy because about 98 percent of employee suggestions deal with cost savings. Suggestions for earning money (such as holding a garage sale on obsolete equipment and office furnishings) are a welcome relief.

- Staff meetings can serve as another way of communicating useful information to top management. If you anticipate an exciting meeting that reflects well on the productivity of your department, invite a powerful executive to attend. Prepare in advance for the dog and pony show by gathering the most impressive news about the department's activities. For instance, how your group is solving an important public relations problem or attracting a major new customer.

Develop an employee newsletter, prepared monthly by your assistant. Useful topics include notable projects being carried out by team members, significant achievements, and plans. Avoid making the newsletter so elaborate that it might appear expensive and time consuming to produce. A deft touch is to have the newsletter reprinted on recycled paper. It adds a hint of cost-consciousness to your thinking.

Make your bulletin lively with interesting information and news clips related to your unit. Update it frequently, and be extra careful not to keep bulletins posted that have yellowed with age. Find a spot for the bulletin board that is likely to be seen by top management.

Update your boss weekly on projects completed, those under way, and new ones undertaken. So long as you don't become perceived as a pest, you will appear to be a vital contributor to the company's well-being.

Air your legitimate gripes. When the boss attempts to squeeze even greater productivity from your people, allude to the heavy workload they are already enduring. Ask, for example: "Should I tell Jessica to push back the date for the completion of her investigation of our new inventory control system?"

Keep pressing for more resources. Keeping top management informed of your constructive activities offers another benefit. It becomes easier to contend that if you had more resources, you could make a bigger contribution. An example: "With just one more field investigator, we could collect another million dollars in taxes owed the government. I know that members of Congress would be interested in a return on investment of that magnitude."

Translate requests into their financial consequences. As just implied, translating demands into their dollar consequences is favored by executives. When requesting additional resources, talk in terms of return on investment, increased earnings per share, increased sales forecasts, or ultimate cost savings. Be sure to express your requests in a helpful rather than a complaining mode. Don't complain about a filthy warehouse being unsightly. Instead talk about how refurbishing the warehouse might improve employee morale and enhance the image of the firm to visitors.

Bouncing Back Characteristic 25: Remember That There Is Life after Termination

The worst-case scenario visualized by most managers caught in a merger or purge is termination. Although the thoughts of losing your job may send shock waves through your body, there is room for optimism. An executive search firm in Chicago estimates that 90 percent of discharged managers land good jobs somewhere else, often with higher pay.[9] We suspect the placement rate for laid-off staff professionals is even higher. One potential problem, however, is that about one-third of new jobs for managers and professionals involve relocation.

More vacancies exist in small than large firms. Shifting to a smaller company requires adapting to some major changes. In a smaller company, job descriptions are likely to be loose (or nonexistent), not much support is available, and you are more likely to wear several hats. Also, your starting salary might be lower than your previous level of compensation. However, a small firm might offer stock options and a greater chance to become a vice president.

Comeback Scenario 15: Marty Dandridge

Marty describes his new life after having been part of a reduction in force at AT&T:

> It was tough leaving a well-oiled machine like AT&T. When I needed something done, I would simply make a phone call or write a memo. There were always people around to help you get a project completed on time. I wound up in a manufacturing manager's position in an electronics firm with 200 employees. Now, I even word process most of my own memos.
>
> The biggest difference in my work life, however, is that I scramble everyday. At my division of AT&T, there were still too many people around who thought they were the only game in town. If a customer didn't like the service, they could send messages by carrier pigeon. They couldn't shift their thinking to the realities of the present. In my new company, everybody has a competitive spirit. I'm working harder at lower pay, and taking more work home. I feel that my future is now more under my control. To top it off, I'm having fun.

Marty learned that there was life after termination because he was willing to risk working in unfamiliar territory—a small company. A similar risk-taking spirit may be just what you need to get moving when your career is pushed back.

Action Tips

Many different ideas for handling yourself after the merger or takeover have been presented in this chapter. Use the key ones as a checklist of action items should you be part of a merger, acquisition, takeover, or downsizing. Respond to these questions:

1. Have you read the handwriting on the wall?
2. Are you maintaining a high profile?
3. Have you sold yourself to the retention interviewer and major customers?
4. Have you developed a lean and mean operating style?
5. Have you avoided a them-versus-us mentality?
6. Are you avoiding displaying bitterness?
7. Are you dealing positively with the merger consultant?
8. Have you shown that you can adapt to the changes?
9. Are you reacting positively to your new boss?
10. Are you obtaining your share of resources during downsizing?
11. Have you remembered that there is life after termination?

3

Handling the Emotional Turmoil

If adversity were not brimming with emotional turmoil, this book would not be necessary. Instead, we might prepare a checklist of 12 things to do when adversity strikes, much like the list of actions to take when the alert signal keeps flashing on a computer printer. What makes it necessary to mull over techniques for handling setbacks is that adversity has enormous emotional consequences. The emotional impact of severe job adversity can rival the loss of a personal relationship or attending the funeral of a close friend.

Adversity Has Emotional Consequences.   The primary reason adversity has such emotional consequences is that in large enough doses it creates negative stress. Faced with adversity, most people experience a wide range of stress symptoms from physiological disturbances to errors in concentration and attention, and frequent forgetting. If not checked, the stress from adversity leads to a cycle of adversity followed by stress, followed by more adversity. A vending machine sales representative who lost his major account explains the cycle in these terms:

> During a period in which times were mediocre in our industry I lost my largest account, one that generated about 30 percent of my commissions. Losing the account really hurt. The company was on my back and accused me of being negligent. There were even hints that I might lose my job. Another problem was that I couldn't withstand the loss of 30 percent of my commissions and still meet all my expenses.
>
> I panicked a little, which only made things worse. I started pushing my smaller accounts to install more vending machines than they

needed. Soon a few complaints were trickling back to the office. I was getting in deeper trouble. Two of the receptionists at my accounts even told me that I was looking bad. I felt I was going downhill faster than I could handle.

Adversity Is Associated with Failure.   Another reason adversity creates so much emotional turmoil is that people often associate adversity with failure. For example, being fired, losing a major account, or having chosen a business partner who robs you are often seen as personal failures. All failure, in turn, involves a sense of loss. The losses may be of three kinds: self-esteem, money, and social status.[1]

The vending machine sales representative just mentioned experienced all three types of losses. Losing his major account made him feel less worthy; his income was drastically cut; and he lost status among peers because he was no longer such a high-producing member of the sales force.

Whatever the root cause of the emotional turmoil associated with a person's adversity, an incontestable fact must be recognized. If you are trying to make a comeback, you first have to deal with the emotional aspects of the adversity that made the comeback necessary. Here we look at some of the actions and attitudes that help one deal with the emotional turmoil surrounding adversity. In the next chapter we describe the uses of a support network to work through the emotions associated with setback.

Bouncing Back Characteristic 26: Accent the Reality of Your Problem

Dealing constructively with the emotional aspects of crisis does not mean denying the reality of your adversity. An executive newsletter offers this advice to the manager who is attempting to help an employee work through an emotional crisis:

> It may seem comforting to minimize or deny the impact of the trouble. To help the employee come to terms with what has happened, you are in a position to provide a helpful perspective, especially if you have suffered a similar personal crisis, or if the crisis is work-related. However, don't offer hopes that may prove false. There can be nothing more annoying to someone in pain than to be fed optimistic clichés such as: "A month from now you'll see it all in a much clearer light," or "You've got to take hold of yourself."[2]

The same advice should be applied to yourself. A resilient manager is likely to self-admit, "My problems are real. My crisis is a biggie. I'm hurting inside, and I deserve to hurt. Life is temporarily a mess, and after I lick my wounds I'm going to do something about the mess."

Bouncing Back Characteristic 27: Do Not Take the Setback Personally

When adversity strikes, many people take the setback personally. They feel they are being punished for wrongdoing or incompetence. In the midst of adversity it is sometimes difficult to realize that you have been set back because of forces outside of yourself such as political favoritism. As mentioned previously, some self-blame is healthy, but too much is self-defeating. A more constructive attitude is that setbacks are inevitable as long as you are taking some risks in your career.

Comeback Scenario 16: John Poduska, Chairman of the Board

John William Poduska Sr., chairman of the board of Apollo Computer, was fired three times before he founded his own company. Although he was personally hurt by being fired, it was a constructive force toward his founding Apollo in 1980. Poduska was not overly concerned about the financial consequences of entrepreneurship. "The dollar risk of failure is almost nothing," he says. In a new business backed by venture capital, the investors assume the financial loss. Poduska believes that you can anticipate some failure. "It's like skiing," he says. "If you ski all day and don't fall once, then you're not skiing hard enough."[3]

Setbacks Are Inevitable. The inevitability of setbacks among successful people is a major reason that setbacks should not be taken personally. And not personalizing setbacks helps reduce some of its emotional sting.

Comeback Scenario 17: Bill Stevens, Company President

Bill Stevens is another example of the inevitability of a severe setback in the career of a successful entrepreneur. He retains a vivid memory of being fired on a Thursday as president of a California company that manufactured disk drives for computers. On Friday he emptied his desk, and on Saturday he rented office space of a new company he planned.

For a year and one-half he withdrew from his savings, and lived on one-third of his previous income. He recalls, "It probably took a year or two to really get over the trauma. I wasn't ashamed. I was never timid about it. I felt I had done a pretty good job. Plus, I learned a lot. Emotionally, the lesson was not to let yourself get identified with a particular position." Stevens founded Triad Systems, a company that produces computers for small business that later became quite successful.[4]

Bouncing Back Characteristic 28:
Treat Failure as a
Temporary Setback

Many of the successful people we have interviewed do not even use the labels "failure" or "defeat" to describe the adversities they have experienced. Instead, they treat failure as a temporary setback on the journey toward what they really want to accomplish. Treating failure as a temporary setback is more than semantic game. By looking at adversity in a more favorable light, some of its emotional intensity is decreased. Just as failure or rejection is treated only as a temporary setback, stumbling blocks are treated as steppingstones.

Comeback Scenario 18: Paul
Walworth, Architect

Paul, an architect with a national reputation, worked as a department head for a large firm of architects. His job duties included supervising the work of other architects and drafting technicians, preparing budgets, handling a few technical assignments of his own, and attending staff meetings. Paul held this position for five years and then one day faced a turning point in his career. With a mixture of joy and sadness he recollects what happened:

> My official job title in those days was chief architect, a position I considered ideal for me. I had hit the right balance between doing creative work myself and performing administrative tasks. When I was promoted to the department head position, I had 15 years of experience at full-time work as an architect.

Since my profession is architecture, I enjoyed the work. However, there is a burnout factor even in a creative field like mine. So, I jumped at the opportunity to combine administrative work with professional work. I particularly liked the idea of helping less experienced architects and technicians develop their skills.

The job was even better than I anticipated. My boss, one of the managing partners in the firm, thought I was doing an outstanding job. The people whose work I supervised were pleased to have me as their boss. And, a surprising benefit of my new job was that administrative work actually helped my professional work. Because my professional work was now about 50 percent less, I enjoyed it even more. One of the buildings I designed while I was chief architect received a national award, resulting in favorable publicity for the firm.

At the end of my third year on the job, a new senior partner was brought into the firm. He was basically the president of our firm, and my boss reported to him. I regarded him as more of a politician than someone who was committed to architecture, yet I did like the man. Gradually, I developed the feeling that he was on my case. He would make frequent innuendoes in these meetings that I was not doing a proper job as chief architect. For instance, he would hint that we were not hiring the right kind of new talent in the firm, or that I was spending too much time as an architect and not enough time as a manager.

My suspicions about the senior partner being on my case were verified when my salary was reviewed. Although he was not my direct boss, he had things set up whereby he made final decisions about the salaries and bonuses for other administrators in the firm. For two consecutive years my percentage increase and year-end bonuses were much lower than I had received in previous years. When I asked the senior partner why my compensation was slipping in comparison to others in the firm, he explained that I was not getting the most from the people in my department. He claimed that the group wasn't clicking, that synergy wasn't taking place under my leadership.

One day I received a call from the senior partner's secretary. She asked me if I could meet with him at two o'clock next Tuesday afternoon. The explanation she offered me was that she needed some additional information for evaluating my performance. After a two-minute warm-up conversation about his recent trip to Paris, the senior partner said he wanted to get to the nub of the matter. He asked me to resign from my position as chief architect and department head and return to full-time work as an architect.

The reason he offered was that I was neglecting my managerial responsibilities in favor of my professional work. Stunned and disappointed, I refused to resign. I told him that he would have to reassign me, because I would not resign from a position I considered to be ideal from my standpoint. Naively, I then asked if we could negotiate the matter about my not doing the job he thought needed doing. No negotiation was possible. The senior partner had made up his mind and had already chosen my successor—a younger woman I had recruited into the firm.

For the next two weeks my mind was spinning and my insides were churning. I had been forced out of a job I found to be ideal despite my differences with the senior partner. I didn't want to return to full-time work as an architect. But even more strongly, I couldn't hack the loss in status and prestige that I associated with being a chief architect. In talking things over with my wife one night, a flash of insight hit me. If I enjoyed being a boss so much, why not open my own firm? I knew that it could mean a substantial drop in income, but since my wife had a career of her own, we were in a position to take risks.

Two months later, I founded Paul Walworth Associates, Licensed Architects. Within about one year I was making about three-fourths of my former income. The big difference, however, is that I was now liberated. No bureaucrat could tell me I wasn't right for my job. If I couldn't find clients or if competent people didn't want to work for me, that would be the failure of my own doing. No longer could my career be governed by the whims of an arbitrary boss.

Paul Walworth thus used the rejection he experienced from the senior partner as a steppingstone toward greater personal fulfillment. His willingness to take the sensible risk of opening his own firm also contributed to his comeback. The next time you experience significant rejection, ponder how it could be turned into a good professional opportunity.

Bouncing Back Characteristic 29: Put Life Into Perspective

The emotional turmoil associated with adversity can often be softened by putting one's life into proper perspective. In the midst of adversity, it is easy to exaggerate the magnitude of one's loss. Paul Walworth, for example, might have been drawn into the negative thinking that he had lost a major chunk of his life. In reality, he had lost only a position that he favored. He was still a talented architect with administrative experience and a good reputation. Paul's family and health were also still intact.

A job loss has a large potential for making one lose perspective because a job is such a big part of one's self-image. Career advisor Tom Jackson has developed a technique for helping the unemployed person put life back in proper perspective. He claims that when he is hired as an outplacement consultant, his first task is to get the laid off workers to "change their language about themselves." Changing one's label helps one regain perspective. In Jackson's words:

> When a steel mill is forced to shut down, think what happens to the worker who has spent his or her whole life at that plant. The chances are the worker looks in the mirror every morning and says, "I am an unemployed steel worker." Just by the name the steel worker calls himself, he is telling himself he is a failure, and how do failures operate? By failing.
>
> If we can get him to look in the mirror and say, "I'm not an unemployed steel worker—*I'm a human being with options*," then I have set him free in a powerful way.[5]

Putting life into proper perspective can also encompass swallowing pride. In rebounding from adversity it may be necessary to settle for less than one had before: less expensive housing, owning one automobile rather than two, postponing vacation trips, or occupying a less prestigious job.

Comeback Scenario 19: Jim Warner, Engineering Manager

Jim Warner's story illustrates putting life into proper perspective. He recounts:

> I first came to work for Xerox after being laid off by General Dynamics. I joined GD after I graduated from college and was there for over 20 years. My first job was as a design engineer. In my last position in the company I was in command of 350 people. When General Dynamics closed, I was lost at first. I moped around for a short time, but my wife wouldn't have much of that. She convinced me that 47 wasn't too old to do something else.
>
> I was used to working at a big place, so I applied to a few big companies. Xerox called me pretty quickly. After a couple of interviews, they offered me a job in telecommunications as a senior analyst, not a manager. I think they were testing me to see if I was willing to work hard and start all over. I didn't think that I was in a bargaining position, so I grabbed the opportunity.
>
> My starting position was at the top nonmanagement level. I worked my butt off for a year, and then they moved me into a management job. Four years later, I was promoted to department head. So here I am today.
>
> I think I bounced back because I didn't get fat and lazy. I would have been perfectly happy to retire at the level I had reached at General Dynamics. But to start over, I had to forget about that cushy po-

sition. I have much less power now that I had in the past, and I don't think I'm going much higher.

Right now, I'm having fun. My job is challenging and I like the people. So the moral of my story is swallow your pride if you have to, but don't give up. It may sound corny but it's true.

Jim Warner recovered from his setback adroitly because he was able to put his lowered status into proper perspective. Sometimes being too status conscious can interfere with finding a position that truly fits our talents and interests. Keep the preceding point in mind should you experience a loss in status after a job change.

Bouncing Back Characteristic 30: Do Not Use Your Crisis as an Excuse for Giving Up

Self-Defeating Behavior 3: Garth Benton, Economics Professor

Garth Benton was an assistant professor of economics at a college of business and management located in a small town. His wife was the branch manager of an on-campus bank. Garth, his wife, and their two children lived in a house they purchased two years after moving to the university community. The family enjoyed their lifestyle and looked forward to becoming permanent residents of the university community.

Toward the end of his fifth year of employment at the college of business, Garth applied for tenure—a condition of relatively permanent employment indicating that a faculty member's work meets with strong approval from colleagues. To not receive tenure is to be considered unwanted. The faculty member who fails to receive tenure is offered a terminal contract of one more academic year. Garth busily prepared a dossier of his published research, his effectiveness as a teacher, and his service to the college (such as serving on committees).

Four months after Garth submitted his application for tenure, he was called into his department head's office to be informed of the decision. The tenure committee had voted five to four against his receiving tenure. A key point against Garth was that although he had published a sufficient number of papers during the past five years, only one of his papers was published in a scientifically rigorous journal. A sense of rage, anger, and shame rushed through Garth's body as he heard the verdict. With tears in his eyes, he exited quickly from the department head's office. Garth wondered how he could face his wife, children, and colleagues.

Late that afternoon, in an explosive mood, he informed his wife of the committee's decision. Garth blamed his wife and children for having made too many demands on his time for him to have produced high-quality work in the last several years. He then went into a tirade about his wife having pushed them into purchasing a house, a decision that should be postponed until a faculty member receives tenure.

For the next few weeks, Garth was volatile and touchy. He canceled social appointments, did not interact with his colleagues, and put aside his current research project. He spent much of his time watching television or brooding. When asked by his wife if he had started looking for a new position for the following academic year, Garth would snap at her with comments such as "bug off."

Next, Garth's classroom behavior began to deteriorate. He would show up late for class, arrive unprepared, cancel exams, and dismiss class early. When asked by a colleague if he was facing any problem that she could help with, Garth retorted, "How do you expect me to act when I've been screwed by my own colleagues?"

Garth ultimately landed a faculty position of less stature than the one he presently held. His new position was at a community college 200 miles from his present location. The job paid less and offered him very little time to conduct research. Garth's relationship with his wife had deteriorated to such a low point that she and the children did not relocate with him.

Faced with the emotional trauma of being denied tenure, Garth disintegrated emotionally. His behavior changed from rational to irrational, from constructive to self-destructive. Julius Segal, a psychologist specializing in overcoming trauma, believes that people such as Garth do not have to use crisis as an excuse for giving up. He observes, "There is, in contrast, an infinitely more healing response to our pain and suffering. We can use the crises we endure not as excuses for regression but as opportunities for growth."[6]

Reexamined in this light, Garth overreacted to his not receiving tenure. Thousands of faculty members, including professors who have achieved national celebrity, do not receive tenure. Garth was entitled to be angry and to brood for a short period of time. But he erred on the side of allowing a substantial setback overcome him. If he had not surrendered to his self-defeating emotions, Garth could have done what most economists recommend: attempt to maximize personal gain in a given situation. He could have searched for a faculty position in a college that did not have quite as high publishing requirements as his present university. While conducting his job search, he should have done his best to perform adequately as a teacher and researcher.

Garth used his anger and subsequent depression as an excuse for giving up. Guilt is another emotion that sometimes prompts people to lose

their determination to bounce back from adversity. Self-blame motivates them to think that the crisis they are facing is a deserved punishment. If they continue to stay trapped in the misery of the crisis, they
will be deservedly punished. In Garth's case, he might have felt guilty
for not having upheld the academic ideal of publishing in top-quality
journals. His guilt would seem pointless to others who perceive no particular merit in getting obscure, esoteric articles published in journals
read by only a handful of scholars. Nevertheless, if Garth allowed guilt
to overcome him, obtaining a lesser job and alienating his family made
for a powerful form of punishment.

Bouncing Back Characteristic 31:
Use Grit Instead of Guilt

In place of guilt, a gritty response to adversity is vital for anyone struggling to find his or her way back from trauma. A friend of mine, Sheila
Middleton, illustrates this tactic.

Comeback Scenario 20: Sheila
Middleton, Investor

Sheila made a bad investment decision. At the advice of a securities sales
representative who telephoned her one night, she bought 5,000 shares
of a stock selling at $2.50. The broker advised her: "We expect this
stock to hit $6.00 per share within 45 days." Sheila paid for the stock
with a check written on a line-of-credit account, thus making the purchase with borrowed money.

Within one week the stock surged to $4.10; within two weeks it
plunged to $.75 per share with virtually no takers even if Sheila wanted
to pitch out. She now had to make monthly payments on a $13,500 loan
(stock plus commission). The $350 monthly payments put a severe
crimp in Sheila's budget. She was unable to purchase holiday gifts for
her daughter and friends, and she had to postpone getting crowns on
two of her teeth.

At first Sheila felt guilty about having speculated with borrowed
money, thus jeopardizing the financial well-being of herself and her
daughter. Sheila did not have the luxury of turning to her former husband to bail them out, because of pride and the fact that he was experiencing financial problems of his own. Sheila's guilt intensified as she
realized that she would soon have to borrow money from her credit
card to cover her line of credit payments—a quick path to bankruptcy.

Sheila's guilt quickly turned to constructive energy. She told me, "I've been duped, but why be ruined?" Sheila promptly found a part-time position selling home improvement products that paid enough to cover her $350 line of credit payments. Despite the time it took away from leisure and family time, Sheila stuck with the job for six months. Finally, her stock hit $3.25 per share, and the broker was able to locate a buyer. Sheila sold, and used the $8,050 (net proceeds after commissions) to reduce her loan. She planned to keep the part-time sales position until the balance of her loan was repaid. However, Sheila became so proficient in home improvement sales that she decided to continue to sell about five hours per week. Sheila, indeed, substituted grit for guilt.

Sheila's experience provides an important lesson. Instead of wallowing in guilt over having made a bad investment decision, she swung into action to overcome the problem. The grit she applied to her problem worked so well, that Sheila developed a new part-time occupation. The next time you feel guilty about a mistake, try grit instead.

Bouncing Back Characteristic 32: Don't Panic

Panic overcomes many people when they experience emotional trauma. Instead of using the coolly rational process they rely on when faced with tough business decisions, many managers and professionals panic. Panicking is understandable because it is a normal human response to trauma; however, because it is normal it does not make panic useful.

Self-Defeating Scenario 4: Larry Chavez, Sales Promotion Manager

Larry Chavez, a manager of sales promotion in a consumer products company, provides an example of the counterproductivity of panic. The company he worked for was bought by an industrial company whose managers were not highly knowledgeable about consumer products. After six months of leaving Larry's company in tact, the new parent company decided that costs would be reduced and profits increased if some departments were consolidated. The vice president of administration of the parent company decided that the consumer products company did not need both an advertising and a sales promotion department. Shortly thereafter an edict was issued that the advertising and sales promotion departments would be consolidated.

Larry was filled with a sense of panic. Although his job was terminated, he would be demoted to a sales promotion coordinator. In his new job he would perform less administrative work but would still spearhead sales promotions such as consumer rebate programs. To ward off what he perceived as a career disaster, Larry sprung into action. He wrote the company president a letter explaining why the company needed a separate sales promotion department. He sent messages throughout the company's electronic mail system criticizing the merits of the consolidation. Larry also attempted to discredit the advertising manager to top management, hoping that he would be appointed as the manager of the new combined department.

Larry's panic-ridden action almost led to his dismissal. He calmed down in time to save his job but not his reputation. A note was placed in his personnel files that he should no longer be considered promotable to management.

How could Larry have handled this situation better, even though strong emotions were shaping his actions? Most importantly, he should have said to himself, "I'm experiencing heavy stress now, so I had better watch out. People can do crazy things when they are stressed out." He also might have listened to his wife who asked him repeatedly, "Are you sure you are all right?" If Larry had overcome his sense of panic, he could have begun the long hard route back of performing well in his new position in order to qualify for a future promotion. Or he could have performed well while patiently searching for a new position in another company.

Most of Larry's panic occurred around the time his career crisis hit. Panic can also occur as the person works through alternative solutions to the crisis. Again, if the person can keep from panicking, he or she is more likely to make a comeback. When one alternative after another does not cure your problem, keep in mind that you are now one step closer to a solution. At least you have tested one approach and know that it must be improved.

The origins of this strategy trace at least as far back as Thomas Edison. He was once asked by a friend why he kept on trying to make a new type of battery, when he had failed so often. Edison replied: "Failure? I have no failures. Now I know fifty thousand ways it won't work."

Bouncing Back Characteristic 33: Don't Get Mad, Get Even

The right cliché can help you deal effectively with the emotions accompanying adversity. A key one is "don't get mad, get even." Uncontrolled anger is generally counterproductive, while anger channeled into constructive action can facilitate a comeback. Instead of venting your anger toward the person or persons who created adversity for you, it is better to use your inner fire to plot your revenge. What we have in mind is an ethical and legal retaliation.

Comeback Scenario 21: Paul Walworth, Architect (Again)

Remember Paul Walworth, the architect who was demoted by a senior partner, and then established his own firm? He describes how he got even, rather than staying mad:

> One year after having started my own firm, the sting of the demotion lingered on. I still felt it was unjustified. My firm was doing fine, but I still had unfinished business to take care of. A prospective client was inviting bids for the architectural work needed for an office building to be located in a new waterfront complex. The client told me his company would be inviting bids from two other firms for the same work. I found out that one of these firms was my old firm. A building of this type is a high-status project for the architect, builder, and developer.
>
> Armed with intimate knowledge about how my old firm would price its bids, I came in with a bid that would most likely be 15 percent less than their bid. If our bid was successful, our profit margin would be quite slim. However, that wasn't the issue with me. I wanted professional revenge. My new firm, Paul Walworth Associates, did get the bid. I heard that my old senior partner was quite disturbed about the turn of events. I couldn't have been happier. My intentions are to outbid them again at the next opportunity.

Paul ultimately found revenge against his old firm and the senior partner who demoted him. His revenge took the constructive form of winning a competitive bid against his former firm. If Paul had been consumed with anger he might not have been able to think rationally and creatively enough to have obtained revenge. Anger typically interferes with creative problem solving.

Bouncing Back Characteristic 34: Say Goodbye to the Past

Lingering feelings about past hurts make it exceedingly difficult to overcome adversity in the present. The person who is still angry with a former business partner who cheated him out of a fair share of the profits will have a difficult time entering into another business relationship. And the middle manager who still hurts from being dismissed from a job she valued will find it difficult to properly focus her energy on a new job.

The importance of saying goodbye to the past for overcoming business adversity can be more clearly understood when an analogy is drawn to personal life. If you still are deeply attached to a person from your past, it is difficult to be satisfied with a new relationship. The new person is competing against a glorified memory of an old relationship. As one man expressed it:

> I haven't had a decent relationship since I made the mistake of leaving Katrina 14 months ago. The pain became so great that I tried to get back with her. But it was too late. Katrina got even in the best way imaginable by getting involved with one of my old colleagues. When I found out they were engaged I was crushed. I know I need to get over Katrina, but I don't know how.

An important part of saying goodbye to the past is knowing when you are still emotionally involved with past relationships. One sure indicator is when the old relationship—whether a business or personal one—still triggers an internal physiological response. For example, seeing an old lover or reading about your former company in the newspaper might create a rapid increase in your heart rate or a shortness of breath. Another important indicator of unfinished business is when you are preoccupied with the memory of a past relationship. The preoccupation often manifests itself in a disturbing amount of daydreaming about the past relationship or business situation that created the adversity.

One way of getting rid of the emotional debris from the past is to confront the past situation that still stirs in your mind. Part of the confrontation is to clearly express to that person how you feel.[7] The conversation with, or letter to, that person serves as a ritual to finally terminate the relationship. Your conversation should include an explication of how you felt about the situation. The cheated business partner might say to the partner at fault:

> I was so angry when I found out you had cheated me out of $15,000 in profits owed me. I felt revulsion for you. I was crushed to be betrayed by my own partner. Now I have come to recognize that you were facing heavy financial pressures at the time. That fact has helped me become a little more tolerant of the situation. I really don't wish you any harm for the future.

Retrieving Valuable Lessons. Another way of saying goodbye to the past is to retrieve its valuable lessons, and change your behavior accordingly. You will recall John, the executive who was derailed because of his bullheaded approach to people. An important part of his recovery plan was to remember the reason why he was derailed, and then behave differently in the present. For example, when John was in a marketing meeting he held back from imposing his solution on the other group members. Instead, John was more diplomatic. He allowed the others to express their opinions before making his presentation.

Don't Stay Depressed.   Another mechanism for saying goodbye to the past is to convince yourself that it is not worth staying depressed permanently. A 24-year-old man went blind as a result of diabetes. New medical treatments were successful in restoring his sight and enabling him to reenter the work force as a laboratory technician. He believes he has been given a second chance not only to see but to enjoy life. According to his analysis, "An experience like this makes you grow up fast. You realize that whatever happens, you can't spend the rest of your life being depressed about it. You have to pick up your life and go on."[8]

Leading a very enjoyable life is another way of mending old wounds from the past. As many people say, "Leading a good life is the best revenge." One happy day after another helps dissipate the disturbed feelings about a business or personal relationship that created turmoil for you in the past.

Comeback Scenario 22: Tony Larkspur, Headquarters Executive

Tony Larkspur, a home office executive in Los Angeles, was a victim of a corporate takeover. After the takeover the predator company decided to consolidate the headquarters of both companies, and eliminate many positions in the process. Tony escaped losing his job but was asked to relocate to a plant in Indiana as an operations manager. The new position he was offered was lower in rank than his present one, which alone did not constitute much adversity. However, Tony's wife and daughter rebelled at the thoughts of leaving California and their friends. Tony had 60 days to make a decision. During that time he was unable to find a suitable new position in Los Angeles, so he accepted the position in Indiana.

The trauma for Tony was that refusing to relocate could mean that he would be temporarily unemployed. Yet if he did relocate, he would jeopardize his relationship with his wife and daughter. A series of heated family communication sessions finally led to a workable compromise. Tony would relocate in February, and his family would join him in June after his daughter graduated from high school.

Things went unusually well for the Larkspur family in Indiana. Tony's job proved to be more exciting than the one he held in Califor-

nia. Tony particularly enjoyed being back in operations after his tour of
duty as a home office executive. The Larkspurs were able to purchase a
much more elegant home for a lower price than the one they owned in
California, and they readily made new friends in Indiana. Tony commented, "All that craziness about demotion and relocation is behind me
now. I'm truly much better off."

Bouncing Back Characteristic 35: Maintain an Identity Separate from Your Job

The people who respond best to career adversity are those who do not
put all their emotional eggs in one basket. When a job crisis hits, they
still have their family, friends, community activities, hobbies, or outside
business interests in which to invest emotional energy. In contrast, others are particularly hard hit by a job crisis because so much of their
identity is tied up with their employer or their one business. Diversifying your emotional portfolio is thus a way of preparing in advance for
the emotional aspects of a career catastrophe.

Comeback Scenario 23: Ray Doig, Venture Capitalist

Diversifying your emotional portfolio is closely tied in with maintaining
an identity separate from your job or employer. When Ray Doig, venture capitalist and former Twentieth Century Fox executive, was first
coming to terms with his falling out with Fox, a friend recommended an
exercise that can help differentiate a person from his or her job. As applied to Doig, it worked this way:

> Imagine that we took you and threw you out in the middle of the
> Mojave Desert. Then we took all your clothes away from you, as well
> as your Mercedes, your expensive watch and everything else. You're
> standing in that desert, stark naked, and a big voice from above
> comes down and says, "You, there, who are you?"
> Your response should not be, "I am vice president of Fox." It
> should be "I am me. I am a person. Whether I sit in an executive
> office, or I drive a gasoline truck or I'm stark naked out in the mid-
> dle of the desert, I'm me."

In addition, points out Doig, "Don't let the things you acquire be you.
Don't let that job you achieve become you, because it can be taken away
from you. The only thing that can't be taken away from you is your life.
As long as you're up and moving, you're you."[9]

Bouncing Back Characteristic 36: Pamper Yourself

Pampering yourself is a proven technique for recovering from the emotional hurts associated with adversity. Pampering involves finding little ways of doing nice things for yourself. It could take the form of buying yourself a new outfit, getting your hair styled, enjoying a massage, taking a weekend vacation, eating your favorite snack at midnight, sleeping until noon, or having your car repainted. The form of pampering you choose will depend on your cash flow and preferences.

Comeback Scenario 24: Jeff Albert, Vice President

Jeff was accused of sexually harassing a male maintenance worker. The charges brought against him were later found to be groundless. Nevertheless, Jeff was advised that his name was being withdrawn as a candidate for a promotion he wanted. To add to his discomfort, the company president began to give Jeff the cold shoulder, and rumors circulated that Jeff was gay. After thinking through his options carefully, Jeff decided that his best course of action was to leave corporate employment and purchase a franchise. Jeff suspected that if he sought employment with a large company, the sexual harassment charges might surface in a reference check.

Before getting fully involved in searching out the right franchise opportunity, Jeff decided to pamper himself and to include his wife, Laura, as a "pamperee." Jeff was deeply appreciative of the emotional support he received from his wife during the investigation of charges. She told him that she found the allegations less threatening than if he had been accused of harassing a woman. Jeff and Laura spent a weekend in a downtown hotel. They ate exotic foods, shopped for frivolous trinkets, spent several sessions in a whirlpool bath, and watched an X-rated movie in bed.

Overcoming adversity usually involves more than one characteristic or tactic. Jeff, for example, is putting things into proper perspective and pampering himself. Notice that he pampered himself in the early stages of his recovery. Pampering will help you overcome the initial shocks of a setback.

Bouncing Back Characteristic 37: Look for Signals of Good News

A curious, almost mystical, way of bouncing back from the emotional hurt associated with job reversals is to receive telltale signals from the outside world. The right signals will provide you with a burst of optimism that can help ward off the depressive elements of a crisis. If you keep your mind finely tuned to the world around you, you will be able to notice these signals. Once they appear, you can face others with renewed confidence and realize that good news is imminent. Just as a bird's chirping signals the end of a heavy rainstorm, the world of work offers its own indicators of good times ahead. Not everybody gets the same signals, but here are a few that could mean the turning point for you:

- The Internal Revenue service informs you that they recalculated your tax return. You and your tax advisor had erred in favor of the IRS. Therefore, a check for $584 is enclosed.

- You have been trying to get an appointment with a key executive for two weeks. one morning her assistant phones you and says, "Ms. Evans will be able to see you at 11:15 this morning."

- A manager whom you insulted in a meeting last week smiles at you with forgiveness and invites you to join her for lunch.

- A prospective customer of a large account returns your phone call, asking to learn more about your product.

- Your request for additional staff support is approved.

- Your name is included on the distribution list of an important company document.

- Your rival for promotion resigns.

- A takeover bid fails, and your company will be left intact with no unusual debts to repay.

Action Tips

In overview, you have to handle the emotional turmoil associated with adversity before you can make a successful comeback. Keep these action tips in mind:

1. Accept the reality of your problem.
2. Do not take the setback personally.
3. Treat failure as a temporary setback.
4. Put your life into perspective. (Think through what is really important to you.)

5. Do not use your crisis as an excuse for giving up.

6. Use grit instead of guilt.

7. Don't panic.

8. Don't get mad, get even.

9. Say goodbye to the past.

10. Maintain an identity separate from your job.

11. Pamper yourself.

12. Look for signals of good news.

4
Getting Help From Your Support Network

Asked how he put the pieces back together again after his company went bankrupt, and his wife skipped out on him—both in the same month—Al replied, "It was rough, but I talked over my problems with my best friend and my children. Even though it seemed that the rest of the world had deserted me, they hadn't. Talking to my friend and my kids gave me the strength to figure out what to do next."

Al's matter-of-fact statement points to a truth about overcoming setback: Relying on others for emotional support is necessary to survive the trauma. A team of stress researchers supports the observation just stated. Many heroes, such as Lee Iacocca, appear individualistic and independent. Yet such people in reality depend on a host of others in their public and private lives. "Consequently they achieve success while not being torn apart by the accompanying demands and stresses. Their attachments to many people through their public and private support networks enable then to sustain success and manage heavy demands and stresses with a minimum of distress."[1]

The key role of emotional support in overcoming adversity is even better documented in personal than work life. A representative line of evidence is provided by psychologist James Pennebaker. He pulled together the results of studies of more than 2,000 people who had suffered crises such as physical abuse, rape, or the death of a loved one. He observed that survivors were physically and mentally healthier if they took the opportunity to confide in someone about their crisis. People who had not discussed their traumatic experiences developed more illnesses such as headaches and lung disease.[2]

Bouncing Back Characteristic 38: Knowing How to Ask for Help

Some people find it natural and easy to ask for help when faced with a career crisis. These people will do something as direct as picking up the phone, calling an old friend, and saying, "Hello, this is Lillian. The reason I'm calling you is that I feel as if I'm lying down in the desert sun and the buzzards are flying overhead. My three biggest clients have chosen not to renew their contracts with me. My fourth client is vacillating. What is the earliest date we can get together for a drink or dinner?"

Because not everybody is adept at asking for help in time of crisis, several suggestions have been formulated to deal with this sensitive issue.[3]

Step 1.   Be specific about what you want. By saying to someone that you are in big trouble and have no idea what to do next, you hand him or her a complex problem. Its immensity may frighten your potential confidante. If the person agrees to talk with you, suddenly there you will be dumping on him or her in an emotionally charged way, asking for advice the person may not be prepared to give.

A practical way of being specific in asking for help is to point to exactly the type of help you need. You might say to a friend, "I'm beginning to conduct a job search, and I want you to listen to my plan of attack." A similar approach would be to point out exactly what you want the person to do such as, "I wonder if you could give me the names of a couple of people who might know of job openings in my field."

Step 2.   Be as positive and self-confident as possible. Instead of stating that "Everything is caving in on me," mention that "I'm faced with a couple of important problems to solve, and I want to get your input on how well you think I'm juggling my priorities." (One problem with this recommendation, of course, is that at your low point you may not feel positive and confident; this is precisely the reason you are requesting help.)

Step 3.   Translate your request for help into an even exchange of ideas. A suitable expression widely used in business is, "I would like to exchange some ideas with you on a problem I'm facing." An equally useful approach is to ask, "Would you be willing to brainstorm a few ideas with me about some problems I'm working on?" Even if you really want some specific advice on solving your problem, presenting your request in a way that emphasizes an even exchange makes both parties feel more comfortable.

Step 4.   Flatter the person from whom you wish to receive support. Casually mention that "the reason you want their advice is because you respect their thinking, their accomplishments, their judgment; you truly value what they have to say."[4] Although this approach may sound obsequious, it is effective. Virtually everybody likes to hear that his or her judgment is valued.

Step 5.   Follow up any form of help with a short note of appreciation. A person who has tried to help you has invested something of himself or herself in your life, and the person may want to know how the investment has paid off. Also of significance, networking is sometimes overdone. The same person might be called on to help many people and thus become irritated with offering so much help and receiving so little in return. A note of appreciation, and an occasional progress report, might be a much needed reward for the helpful person in your network.

Bouncing Back Characteristic 39: Call on Friends in High Places

The key role of people in your support network is to give you an emotional boost and perhaps some advice. Members in your support network can also help you make a comeback by providing you clout and resources.

Comeback Scenario 25: Vaughn L. Beals, Jr., Motorcycle Executive

Beals, the chairman of Harley-Davidson, called on friends in high places to facilitate the comeback of his company—and therefore himself.[5] In the early 1980s, Harley-Davidson was almost put out of business by Japanese competition. Beals and his management team bought the company from AMF in 1981 with borrowed money. Since that time they have scrimped and saved to convert heavy losses into modest profits. An important aspect of Harley-Davidson's comeback was financial maneuvering. A large stock offering in 1986 enabled Beals to refinance debt that has retarded the company's growth and made its motorcycles vulnerable to competition.

Beals and the other members of his team had made substantial progress on their own in turning around the fortunes of the company. A turning point, however, came in 1983, when Beals enlisted the help of powerful people in his support network. He convinced Ronald Reagan and key members of the U.S. International Trade Commission that the Japanese were selling excess motorcycles below cost in the United States. President Reagan responded with a special five-year tariff on heavy motorcycles that diminished gradually over the five-year period.

The protection eased competitive pressure enough for Harley to earn healthy profits by 1986 and to regain some of its lost market share. Beals said proudly, "Early in 1987, we decided to stand up and show the world how far we had come. We took the unprecedented step of asking the Reagan administration to drop the protective tariffs—a full year before they were due to expire." By 1991, Harley was headed toward its eighth consecutive year of profits.

Because Beals and twelve other Harley executives bought the company in a leveraged buyout, the company's comeback was also a personal triumph. Part of this comeback can be readily attributed to the support Beals received from Reagan in his patriotic appeal for the survival of Harley-Davidson.

You may not be able to call upon a world leader to help you overcome adversity. However, you can seek the assistance of your highest-level contact.

Bouncing Back Characteristic 40: Use Self-Help Support Groups

So many people face emotional trauma that a wide variety of self-help support groups have sprung up to help them cope. A *self-help group* is a mutual help group in which the members listen to and provide each other support and encouragement. They are modeled after Alcoholics Anonymous in which members candidly divulge their problems and their strengths to each other. The AA members agree to call on each other when they need help acutely.

An estimated 12 million people currently help themselves and other troubled people by participating in approximately one-half million self-help groups. The groups are usually organized around a central problem faced by people such as food abuse, drug abuse, alcoholism, gambling, being lonely, or being bald. Many cities also have self-help groups for displaced managers, such as Forty Plus. Frank Riesman, the founding director of the National Self-Help Clearing House (33 West 42nd

Street, New York, NY 10036) claims that self-help gives you control of your own life. The idea of self-help is now widely accepted.

The California Self-Help Center has established 198 categories to classify the state's 3,300 groups and divided them into four broad types, those for:

1. Physical and mental illness
2. Changing addictive behavior
3. Coping with a crisis of transition
4. Friends and relatives of the person with the problem

The person attempting to recover from a career crisis would ordinarily join a group designed to ease transitional problems.

Comeback Scenario 26: Steve Gladieux, Chief Engineer

Fifty-five-year-old Steve was laid off from his position with a machine tool company during an industry downturn. The only help the company offered Steve was three months' severance pay. In a state of anger and confusion, Steve made a poor start in conducting his job campaign. His sense of desperation quickly burned up his two valid leads for a new position. Thumbing through a suburban newspaper, Steve read about a support group for unemployed executives being conducted at the counseling center of a local university. Steve made a phone call and found out that the group was being launched on a trial basis, with an initial scheduling of ten sessions. Steve attended all ten sessions, and describes his experiences in these terms:

> I attended the first session with a positive attitude. I knew I needed some kind of help, and the support group sounded like a good idea. The leader of the group was a kindly young counseling psychologist. She told us that we were going to do all the work, and she would act as a facilitator. A few of us joked that we didn't know we were signing up for group psychotherapy. Yet underneath we knew that this woman was going to help us.
>
> At first we took turns telling the other group members what had happened to us and how we felt about it. I told the others that I was angry and crushed. I had worked for the same firm for 20 years and had received satisfactory or better performance appraisals for all of those years. The company decided they could do without my managerial talents since they were in a financial bind. The president planned to run the company without a chief engineer for a while.
>
> When it was my turn to talk, I told the group how frightened I was

to be out of work at my age. If I began drawing on my pension at age 55 it would only amount to a few hundred dollars per month. Social Security wouldn't kick in for another seven years, I also told the group that I had too much to offer the machine tool industry to retire just yet.

The group helped me considerably by agreeing with me that I still had a lot to offer my industry. The group gave me the self-confidence to begin conducting my job search intelligently. What helped me the most was that the other people in the support group were actually interested in hearing what progress I made each week. I can't say I couldn't have found a new job without their encouragement, but it was comforting to know I wasn't digging my way through the forest alone.

Why Self-Help Groups Work.   Several reasons explain why self-help groups assist people in coping with personal problems. One factor is that group members learn about *common aspects of their problem*. The predominant activity in these groups is information giving. Personal disclosures are especially important. Relatively few statements of support and sympathy are found.[6]

A second reason is that members often come to *attribute their problem to another cause* and thereby change their behavior. The new ideology about what caused their difficulty leads to a "cognitive antidote" to the problem. In everyday language, the person in crisis develops a new perception of the nature of the problem. A distraught manager who was laid off might come to believe that he or she was not at fault; it is the short-range, gluttonous thinking of management that has lead to a paring down of the organization.

Strong acceptance by the group is another important-reason for the success of self-help groups. This was clearly the case with chief engineer Steve. Sharing a previously undisclosed problem with group members is yet another reason underlying the contribution of self-help groups.[7] It has long been recognized that putting feelings into words is a healing experience. Steve, for example, openly told the group about his feelings of anger and confusion. He felt better as a result, and was therefore in a better position to take constructive action in his job search.

Bouncing Back Characteristic 41: Getting Support through Outplacement

Mergers, acquisitions, and corporate cutbacks are the source of approximately two-thirds of the job losses handled by outplacement firms. The support received includes help with the mechanics of job finding such as tips on marketing oneself and desk space, along with encouragement from both counselors and other job seekers.

Comeback Scenario 27: Ellen Godwin, Marketing Executive

Godwin explains how she received help from an outplacement firm:

> Life looked pretty grim for me that unforgettable day in November, just last year. I was one of the task force members to help our company to decide whether or not to purchase the midwestern group of stores. My argument against the acquisition was that we would be diluting our strengths by purchasing stores that would serve the same markets we were already serving. I thought we would be better off rejuvenating some of our existing outlets. Maybe my negative vote put me on the hit list. Whatever the true reason, the president told me over lunch that my position would be terminated December 31. He told me not to take it personally—I wasn't being terminated, just my position. Because they had no other position to fit an executive of my stature, the only sensible alternative was to dismiss me.
>
> Unfortunately, at age 51 I still needed every penny of my salary and bonus. With a condo, two children, and a BMW, I could not live on unemployment insurance or a minimum wage job. I had to find another top-level merchandising position. The next two days were definitely the most difficult. I knew that this was the worst possible time of the year to find a retailing job. Hiring for top jobs in the industry would be postponed until the results from the Christmas season were known. Besides that, it was general knowledge that once you hit age 50, jobs become much scarcer in retailing management.
>
> The president told me that in addition to four months' severance pay, I was entitled to receive outplacement counseling at the company's expense. According to Gary (the president, Gary Moran) the outplacement firm had an excellent reputation. They would help me overcome the natural trauma of being without a job, and they would help me quickly regain employment. I assumed wrongly that the outplacement firm would match me up with one of many executive openings in their files. Later, I learned that finding you a job directly is not part of an outplacement firm's act.
>
> I showed up at Knoll and Houseman the following Monday morning because I didn't want to waste any time becoming reemployed. I gave the receptionist my name, assuming that she was expecting me. After a few minutes of checking, she told me to wait; that my counselor would be with me shortly.
>
> When the counselor met with me he mentioned that I looked nervous and preoccupied. Of course, I was nervous and preoccupied. I felt frightened and humiliated, thus making me appear nervous. Somewhat to my disappointment, the counselor only spoke with me for about 15 minutes. I was then ushered into a small conference

room, and told to *take a group of tests and questionnaires.* It was annoying to spend four hours taking tests because I wanted to jump right into looking for a job.

After taking the tests and answering the many questions about myself, I began to see some purpose in what I was doing. The questions about my experiences and accomplishments were particularly helpful. They made me think about who I was professionally and where I had been. Up to that time I hadn't given enough serious thought to the specific nature of the contribution I was making to my company.

My counselor told me that my tests results showed that I was an intelligent, resourceful person, with no outstanding hangups that would prevent me from becoming reemployed at the appropriate level. He also told me that the questions I was forced to answer about myself provided the raw data I needed to *prepare a good job resume.* Again, I was eager to start my job search, but I was sensible enough to realize that you need a good resume to get started.

I was referred to a slick loose-leaf binder containing models of good resumes. I found one that seemed well suited to my career, so I modeled mine after that. A resume specialist on the staff then worked with me to perfect what I had developed. Three days later, she had 100 copies of my resume ready, reproduced on high-quality paper.

Next, I requested another meeting with my counselor. His schedule was full, so I had to wait two more days. I was getting a little anxious about the days rushing by. I also knew that it would be difficult to get many job interviews with the holidays coming up soon. But I was reassured by other clients sitting around the office that a job search takes longer than most people expect. A rule of thumb I heard was that to find a job it takes about one month for each $15,000 of annual income. If that were true I could face an eight-month search. I decided to ignore that rule of thumb.

My counselor told me that he was pleased with my progress, and that I was now ready to hone my self-marketing skills. This translated into my *practicing how to speak to people over the phone* about job openings, and *how to conduct myself in job interviews* and informational interviews. The purpose of the informational interview was to speak to people about my interests but not to actually look for a job. I was pleasantly surprised to hear how well I sounded on tape, and how professional I looked on videotape.

With my pile of resumes at hand, and the practice interviews under my belt I felt ready to begin my formal job search. I asked my counselor where I should start sending my resumes. He told me that sending unsolicited resumes to prospective employers is too amateurish. Instead, he told me that I should use a cover letter to accompany each resume, and send both to qualified leads.

When I asked where I would find the list of qualified leads, my counselor told me that the leads would come through my contacts. My next assignment was to *draw up a list of every possible person I knew* who could conceivably help me find a suitable position or could refer me to someone who might help me. When I asked my counselor why I needed outplacement counseling if I generated my own leads, he replied; "Our job is to help you find a job, not find a job for you. If you're looking for leads, *write to executive search firms and employment agencies.*"

My counselor's comments sparked an important insight. The outplacement firm was a resource for helping find a new job, but it was only one resource. Fired up with that insight, I then pored over *classified ads in national and local newspapers.* I used the many directories in the Knoll and Houseman library to come up with a list of *executive search firms* who might help me. I ordered another 100 copies of my resume.

My job hunting had now become a 45-hour-per-week job. After having sent out about 50 resumes, I checked back in with my counselor to discuss my progress. He confronted me with the fact that I was taking the *easiest and least efficient approach* to finding a job. He told me to concentrate more on *telephoning my contact list and setting up in-person appointments.*

I did line up about six people who said they would speak to me. It felt so awkward asking professional acquaintances to help me find a job. I was supposed to appear cool and polished, but I felt like I was asking for handouts. A few people were cordial, but others treated me like I was wasting their time. The most painful part was watching my contacts squirm in their chairs and look at their watches.

The holiday week was the most depressing. I felt so desperate calling on people to help me find a job when most people are contemplating their year-end bonus.

Each day I checked in at the outplacement office, to see if there were any mail or phone messages for me. The first six responses to my letters of inquiry were basically form letters of rejection. The best response I received was handwritten from an old acquaintance wishing me good luck in getting back on track. Gradually I began to speak to other job seekers and Knoll and Houseman about my experiences. They were helpful in cheering me up and telling me not to be discouraged, that a good job was as close as my next interview.

My first warm lead came the day after Martin Luther King's Day. A department store in Chicago was looking for a general manager, and they thought I might qualify. They mentioned that the job would pay about $25,000 less than my last salary. Because it required a relocation and a substantial pay cut, I declined to fly out for an interview.

Thirty more days went by with no apparent progress in getting myself reemployed. I received about 25 more rejection letters from retail organizations I had written to, either by an unsolicited letter or in response to a classified ad. No executive search firm I contacted showed any interest in me. Several of them told me that they would never touch an unemployed executive; their clients wanted them to find people at the peak of their careers.

A promising lead finally turned up from an unexpected source. When my counselor practically forced me to contact everybody I knew, I scheduled a luncheon date with the former personnel director of our company who had since taken a job at a dress manufacturer. She told me that she had no leads for me at the time, but would keep me in mind should any lead turn up. As it worked out, the secretary of the president of her company called me to say that the president wanted to talk to me in a hurry about a key job opening.

I went for an interview the next day. The three top marketing people in the company had quit *en masse* to form their own competitive company. The president said he might be suing the three managers for breach of contract, but in the meantime he needed a marketing director in a hurry. I spent three hours at the company, visiting with the other managers at headquarters. I was told that if negotiations proceeded further, I would have to visit the company factories in Tennessee and Puerto Rico.

With great enthusiasm, I requested another meeting with my counselor. He congratulated me on my progress and told me that since I would now probably begin to receive job offers, I should *attend the negotiation workshop.* It sounded like a good idea, so I did attend the next session. We were taught how to negotiate such things as equitable compensation, perks, an employment contract, and relocation allowance if needed.

Two days later, the president did call me. He wanted to have lunch with me as soon as possible to carry our discussion one step further. During the main part of the meal, he went into great detail about the company's strengths and weaknesses. He told me the company needed an executive with a retailing background because large retailers were their primary market.

As soon as the coffee was served, the president offered me the job at $5,000 more per year than I was making at my old job. Before he could practically finish his sentence, I said I would take the job; that I would be thrilled to give the position my full professional effort. I wanted to communicate my true level of enthusiasm for the job before he changed his mind. Besides that, I didn't want to appear small minded by asking about employee benefits. I figured I could learn about those later.

The job has proved to be a challenge, and the firm had more problems than even the president knew about. The pressure is tremendous, but I feel I have grown professionally by getting executive experience in directing the marketing effort of a retailer. With this kind of experience, I might qualify for the presidency of a manufacturer or retailer in the future.

I did get somewhat frustrated with the outplacement firm and with my counselor because it didn't seem like they were doing that much for me. Yet they *did force me to make use of my contacts,* and they *helped me develop insight into conducting a job search.* Although my counselor seemed a little *impersonal,* I think he gave me the type of support I needed. He forced me to rely on my own resources. Talking things over with the other job seekers was also helpful. Knowing that a lot of other good people were seeking reemployment made my plight seem less humiliating.

> If I was forced to lay off a manager in my firm, I think I would refer that person to the same outplacement firm. Looking for a new job is too big a task to go it alone.

Ellen Godwin received the type of help she needed from an outplacement firm. Should you need to use such a service, recognize that outplacement at its best offers you the emotional support and encouragement you need to cope with the trauma of job loss. You will also receive a review of the fundamentals of conducting a job campaign. Such information can also be obtained from a book, but emotional support from a counselor is unique.

Bouncing Back Characteristic 42: Get Help from a Mental Health Professional

The marketing executive just described received the right type and amount of emotional support she needed from outplacement services. For about 10 percent of other people facing a career crisis, emotional support from a mental health counselor may be necessary. For these people, a career crisis leads to a much larger emotional crisis.

Comeback Scenario 28: Joseph W. Streit, Guidance Counselor

Streit describes how professional counseling helped him recover from a career and personal crisis:

> I've often thought about writing about my recovery but have either not had the time nor made the time. I imagine there is an inherent unwillingness inside of me to do this—an unwillingness to really deal with the topic. Perhaps part of my survival is not really looking at what took place because it is still rather painful. The episode gets me lost in some free-floating bitterness and hostility. I am both blessed and cursed with a good memory. I believe I would rather forget the entire incident. I know that I have survived for here I am working effectively and creatively as a guidance counselor.
> I believe in the philosophy that as a result of every experience in your life you are changed. You are never the same person. I know now, through this career *reversal*, that indeed one is never the same. You recover and go on, but you are not quite the same—your perceptions of yourself and the world around you are changed.
> As a young man leaving undergraduate school, I had a life plan and a strategy for achieving it. I now believe that this is a mistake. Not that planning is an error, but having plans which are carved in

stone bind you to one course of action. You are left without options. If the bottom falls out, one is left alone, often groping for a foothold to begin climbing again.

My game plan was to begin my career as a history teacher and begin studies in the evening towards an MA in counseling and guidance. I would then finish graduate school and continue to gain certification as a director of guidance, supervisor, and school principal. I would work my way through these various positions, ultimately winding up as a superintendent of schools or assistant superintendent. Perhaps I would then work for the education department at the state or federal level.

Everything worked out well and proceeded according to plan until I became a guidance director. When I became director of the department in which I worked, I was not aware that a major fraud had been perpetrated in the office for years. The individual whom I replaced was an alcoholic who actually functioned as a figurehead. He kept himself behind closed doors all the time, and had the support of cronies and others politically indebted to him. These factors, along with pluck and luck, enabled him to survive until alcohol abuse and other personal problems led to his retirement.

To make a long and horrible story short, I inherited a mess. I am generally not a subscriber to this statement. However, in this case it is true. Records were completely scattered about. The floor was used as a filing system, and school and student records were strewn about his office and other places in the school. Not only did my task become one of management and moving forward, it became a task of immediate reconstruction.

Other problems also surfaced quickly. I was faced with working for a man who to this day expounds the merits of management by intimidation. In the years preceding my holding the position he had caused at least two nervous breakdowns and resignations. Not only did he not supervise or evaluate his staff, he neglected to inform and direct when necessary.

I decided to remain in the position for two years, long enough to gain the additional certification I needed. I would then run from the position to a higher-level one in another organization. I believed that I had the intelligence, youth, stamina, and drive to survive.

The long hours I had to work were the first steps toward my demise. Despite the requests for additional staff, none ever arrived. In order to handle the workload I began working longer and longer days. Eventually I was working 18-hour days. When retirements took place in the department, temporaries were hired from other academic areas. They were shifted in and out by higher administrators without my counsel. Because computer equipment was not available, I had to compute class ranks manually. Each student was ranked four ways. I still remember one morning at four o'clock when I had finished computing a rank, and the calculator tape filled a kitchen floor and spilled down seven stairs into a recreation room.

By mid-year I faced physical exhaustion. At that point my personal life began to collapse. It was at this time that my father, who was suffering from lung and brain cancer, began to lapse into a coma that preceded his death. As an only child with a partially handicapped mother, a great deal of demands were placed on me. Concurrently with this my mother-in-law became terminally ill with lung cancer and began her agonizing death.

My wife and I had an infant son, and few relatives willing or able to assist us. I therefore found myself babysitting many hours while my wife attended to her mother. My free moments were spent at work or in my study, or attending to my father.

The pressure and confusion soon got to my wife. She began to direct her attention to social situations outside of the family. This was the beginning of a series of affairs which eventually led to our divorce.

By the end of the school year I was physically exhausted and emotionally drained. I had experienced one death in my immediate family, another death was imminent, and I was in the process of watching my marriage crumble. I was in a state of personal and professional collapse.

I felt I could no longer go on. I was at a point where I could not eat or sleep. My weight had plummeted from 190 to 155 pounds. I was at a point where I could not think.

I resigned from my administrative job and negotiated filling an open staff position in my department. However, I worked through the summer, finishing my tasks as best I could, without a vacation. I took a weekend off (staying in bed) and came back to a new school year.

I worked through that first fall semester as if I were a zombie. I was exhausted to the point that I could almost not work through the most basic problems. However, I missed no work and attended well to my professional duties. By Christmas my weight had fallen to about 140 pounds and I was hospitalized for two days for stress and depression.

At that point I entered counseling which lasted for about eight months. A wise counselor knows when he or she is in trouble, and I knew it. Through counseling I worked out my feelings about myself and my career, and put many things into perspective. My marriage could not be put in order. It staggered to its death two and one-half years later, and I became the plaintiff in divorce proceedings.

During my recovery period I became active in community affairs and party politics. This helped me use my organizational skills and management techniques. I have managed successful political campaigns on the local and state level and have twice been appointed by the Governor of New Jersey to an important committee on higher education. Later I was elected chair of that committee. I also became an elder in a Presbyterian Church. I once again picked up the clarinet and rediscovered musical and artistic abilities long forgotten.

Through these activities I regained confidence in myself and the world around me. I have learned that I have weaknesses, but these are outstripped by my strengths. I have learned that not only can I survive, I can prosper. I have learned that life does have valleys, but you must pass through these to get to some incredible peaks. And I've also learned to take the time to enjoy these summits.

I have made new friends and new relationships. I have dealt with powerful and famous people on the local, state, and national levels. Some years back, in the same month, I spoke to a friend in the Lifer's Group at Rahway Prison, and had a discussion with Ted Kennedy. How many people can have a life tapestry as beautiful and as interesting? I wonder if my life would have been as varied had I been successful in the conventional sense?

At work I am successful again. No, I am not an administrator. On the contrary, I am still on the front line. However, I am considered an elder statesman. I am also free to be an independent agent. There is a freedom in not being upwardly mobile. You have the freedom to ascertain and do what is best—not just what is best for your career.

If anything negative has come from all my adversity, I must admit that I am *reluctant to aspire again.* I am aware of the fact that I am gun-shy of career risks. I am bruised and afraid of the pain that you risk. I intellectually understand that this is wrong and can only hope that in time I will deal with it in a better way. I often feel like the person who was attacked by a dog as a child. The adult can never walk past a dog with the same warmth and trust again.

Perhaps it is not important that I try to become upwardly mobile in my career again. I am at the point where I believe that living a good life is more important. Above all you must have serenity within yourself.

I have accomplished much in my career since the hard times. I have shared the lives, fortunes, and misfortunes of hundreds of persons and families. Would I have done so as the administrator, locked in some remote office? I have built new counseling programs and seen them become successful. I have enjoyed politics immensely and through politics have refined old skills and talents and found new ones I have never dreamed of, I have regained my music skills, and discovered arts, museums, travel, good restaurants, and good times. I have made new friends who are my most valuable possessions. It sounds peculiar, but through my losses I gained everything and have become a better person.

Perhaps I should have written the account of my problems and recovery earlier. Thinking through what has happened to me has validated the statement that "There is no gain without pain." My life has been so interesting and rich, I wouldn't change a thing, and I trust there are more good things ahead.

Benefits of Counseling.   Professional counseling thus helped Joseph W. Streit recover from bone-crunching adversity, some of which was self-imposed. Counseling gave him a chance to think through his feelings about himself and put life into perspective. Another potential benefit of psychotherapy in making a comeback is that it helps you understand what is going on emotionally. Quite often the problems we face today seem so severe because they bring to the surface earlier hurts. A basic example is that severe rejection from a boss, may remind a person of being rejected by a powerful parent.

Worries of Abandonment.   Another old bell rung often by career adversity is a feeling of abandonment. The manager whose budget is severely cut, and whose staff is drastically reduced, may feel abandoned by the organization. And fear of abandonment is one of our earliest and most intense childhood concerns.

Beverly Zabriskie, a psychoanalyst, offers a useful explanation of how career reversals are tied in to childhood worries about being abandoned. She observes that often people who are the most ambitious are those who have been programmed since childhood to believe that their level of performance is more important than who they are. This programming leaves them unusually vulnerable.

Understanding what is taking place emotionally can help high achievers handle setbacks, notes Zabriskie. "When such an achiever goes through a rejection—even if it's a collective event like a takeover—the first feelings to come up are the most irrational.

"Once you've experienced the surge of anxiety that inevitably comes with rejection," Zabriskie explains, "the trick is to understand that the accompanying sense of helplessness comes from a very young age when indeed, you were dependent and could be abandoned. It takes some time to get one's footing as an adult and remember the different ways one has survived and achieved.

"That understanding is the first step toward survival. You know you are more than just those irrational feelings, and you mobilize your coping mechanisms."[8]

In short, you pull together your courage and recognize that you are an adult who has the internal resources to cope with almost any type of career adversity.

Bouncing Back Characteristic 43:
Be Prepared to Resolve
the Conflict of Others

So far in this chapter we have described obtaining support from others in order to help cope with adversity. Adverse circumstances may also require that you help others overcome their problems. As an aftermath of a merger and acquisition, for example, coworkers may become embroiled in conflict. Hybrid work groups that result from some combined operations are breeding rounds for intense conflict. It is possible for an executive to end up supervising a counterpart from the other company.

A marketing executive wound up in managing a hybrid staff, including his counterpart from the acquired firm. Several months after the new work group was formed, the staff had suffered low morale, poor cooperation, and in-fighting. Resentment and envy about who received which job were crippling the productivity of the division.

As a last ditch effort to unify the work group, the marketing executive took them to his fishing cabin for a weekend. He had hoped that some open discussions in the lake retreat would relax the angry tensions that had accumulated. He planned on discussions attempting to alleviate the destructive competition and petty bickering that was taking place. The executive believed that the group needed to express the pent-up hostilities and resentment that had been festering among them.

The discussions proved more frank than the executive anticipated. Instead of leading to reconciliation and harmony, the discussions led to a fist fight.[9] Perhaps the executive should have encouraged the people to express their feelings with him in one-on-one meetings, or with himself and the two combatants. Encouraging free-for-alls may not be the best method of providing emotional support.

Action Tips

In summary, a key adversity-fighting strategy is to get help from your support network. To obtain support, try these tactics as appropriate:

1. Learn how to ask for help.
2. Call on friends in high places.
3. Use self-help support groups.
4. Get support through outplacement.
5. Get help from a mental health professional.
6. Be prepared to resolve the conflict of others.

5
Energizing Your Comeback With Positive Thinking

Great comebacks are fueled with large amounts of optimism and positive thinking, and lesser comebacks are fueled with lesser amounts of optimism and positive thinking. At the other end of the scale, people who do not recover from adversity are often fueled by pessimism and negative thinking. This basic observation is endorsed by countless evangelists, motivational speakers, psychologists, and political figures. Winston Churchill's statement on the importance of thinking and acting as if a positive outcome will be forthcoming applies well here: "Never give up. Never give up. Never, never, never give up."

The contribution of optimism and positive thinking to overcoming adversity has become ingrained into our culture, as reflected in many clichés and aphorisms. Among the most uplifting are:

"Don't give up."

"Keep trying."

"You can succeed if you try."

"This too will pass."

"Happiness is just around the corner."

"Wishing will make it so."

"If you think you can, you can."

"Goals make wishes come true."

"Keep up your spirits."

"Believe in yourself when the going gets rough."

Simply repeating these clichés is not sufficient to accomplish a comeback. It is also important to be convinced by some hard facts about optimism and positive thinking, and to understand how others have used these forces to bounce back from adversity. Should you be caught in a merger or downsizing, this information should come in handy.

Bouncing Back Characteristic 44: Appreciate the Healing Power of Optimism

The power of positive thinking is even more effective than Norman Vincent Peale believed. Peale and many others have touted the contribution of optimism to leading a successful life. According to the research of two psychologists, optimism also has a specific beneficial effect on a person's health and ability to overcome the stress associated with adversity.[1]

"If I were lost at sea in a lifeboat, I'd much rather be stuck with an optimist than a pessimist," claims Michael Scheier, a psychology researcher at Carnegie Mellon University. "I would expect an optimist to be able to row, and for a long period of time, because that person believes it will pay off. A pessimist would lay back in the sun, taking it easy because he or she would say, 'What's the use.'"

Charles Carver, a psychology researcher at the University of Miami (Florida) observes that "People's optimistic or pessimistic orientations are not just faces we display to the world. They have lots of implications for what people do, how they feel, and potentially they may have important health implications."

The healing power of optimism is unlikely to be achieved if a person only adopts a cheerier attitude about a particular situation and remains a pessimist about life in general. A person's global perspective about life has a greater influence on health, success, and ability to overcome adversity than attitudes about a specific difficulty.

By developing a test to measure optimism and skepticism, the two psychologists were able to evaluate how peoples' attitudes influence their ability to cope with difficulties, including crises. It was found that people with a generally optimistic attitude handle stress better, recover more rapidly after coronary bypass surgery, and respond better to alcohol treatment programs. Richard Schulz, a professor of psychiatry at the University of Pittsburgh, used the same test, and charted the progress over a year of 170 people who had to care for stroke victims. He found that independent of the progress of the patient, optimistic caregivers were less depressed and physically healthier at the end of a year than their pessimistic counterparts.

According to Scheier, there is something important about positive thoughts in themselves. "If, when people confront difficulties in their lives they believe the outcome eventually will be good, they're more likely to obtain a good outcome than if they believe it will eventually be bad." A more recent analysis also contributes to an understanding of how optimism improves performance and enables people to work their way out of adverse circumstances. Based on his studies, psychologist Martin Seligman says that the link between optimism and performance is basically persistence. "Optimists keep at it; pessimists give up and fail, even if they are of equal talent. And because optimists are always hopeful about the outcome, they tend to take more risks and try new things."[2]

Optimism Must Be Combined with Action.   Optimistic thoughts alone do not enable people to conquer stress. Optimistic people are doers, and concentrate on ways to solve problems. Pessimistic people, in contrast, are more passive and believe that failure is inevitable. In the experiment with bypass surgery patients, optimists were more likely to make plans and set goals for their recovery, and were less prone to dwell on their nervousness and anxiety. Pessimists attempted to block out thoughts of the nature of the recovery experience.

The old adage that pessimists see a glass as half empty, while optimists see it as half full is only partially true. The real question is, "What are the odds of filling it up?" said Scheier. An optimist will say, "Yes we can fill that glass up." The pessimist might say, "No, it's going to evaporate and go away."

Optimists Believe that Good Things Will Happen.   Optimism is more than reading the best into a situation. It's also a matter of believing that good things will happen. It takes hard work for a pessimist to become an optimist. Nevertheless, Seligman has made important progress in teaching people how to become optimists. He has developed an optimism training program for Met Life which helps employees change the way they explain disappointments. People are taught *how to recognize negative thoughts,* and then to externalize and dispute them. This is important because a person can be quite far gone without even knowing it. Although optimism training may prove worthwhile, with a planned and determined approach, many people can acquire an optimistic outlook.

Bouncing Back Characteristic 45: Develop the Habit of Hope

In recognition of the contribution of optimism to overcoming adversity, it may prove worthwhile to develop habits of hopefulness. A major reason that learning how to hope is hard work is that hopefulness is a lifelong behavior pattern. Evidence suggests that hope develops soon after birth. A parent's first response to her or his baby's demands for food, warmth, and cuddling lays the foundation of optimism. When the response is prompt and loving, the baby becomes convinced that the world is friendly and that hoping produces results. As children mature, parents and other significant people have many opportunities to foster or discourage optimism.[3]

Alice Lake has formulated techniques that if diligently applied can enable people to become more optimistic and hopeful. These techniques, plus the others listed here, can be used to convert the outright pessimist, or increase the hopefulness of somebody who has about an average degree of optimism.

1. *Find your own silver lining.* Examine your adversity to see what positive elements can be found. If you are demoted from a managerial position, you might take the opportunity to develop your rusty specialist skills such as accounting, programming, or copywriting.

2. *Don't wallow in self-pity.* The resilient person wastes very little time commiserating over the adverse event. After his or her house burns down, the optimist says, "Time to call my insurance agent." A committed golfer, who was badly hurt in an automobile accident, refused to give in to despair. "I'm lucky to be here," he said. With a crushed arm and connecting muscles to his hand severed, his chances of swinging a golf club again appeared small. But he did not give up hope. After several operations and seven months of intensive physical therapy, he returned to the golf course despite wearing a brace.

3. *Learn to laugh.* Laughter is an antidote to misery that improves the present and raises hope for tomorrow. In addition to reducing tension associated with stress, laughter triggers the secretion of hormones that mobilize the immune system. A specific value of finding the humorous aspects of hard times is that it helps place things in proper perspective, and reduces some of the potential depression.

A lawyer who was disbarred for mishandling the funds of several clients had to drastically reduce his expenses while looking for a new occupation. He commented, "The funniest thing about this whole episode is that I sold my house and income property. I'm now renting an apartment in a building I used to own. Would you believe that I'm making the same complaints about the heating system that my tenants used to make to me?" The humorous incident helped spark his thinking about his long-standing interest in real estate. He subsequently found new employment as a commercial real estate agent.

4. *Borrow hope from others.*   The description of the type of help one might receive from a self-help (or mutual support) group endorses this same technique. Listening to others who are optimistic about recovering from their problems can often help you become optimistic. Outplacement services can be a good setting for borrowing hope from others. Job seekers typically lift up each other's spirits by sharing hope.

5. *Broaden your options.*   A key approach to developing hope and overcoming adversity in general is to find several alternative solutions to the crisis at hand. "When you have only one road to happiness and that becomes blocked, hopelessness often follows," says Lake. A surgical resident badly hurt his right hand (he was right-handed) in a gardening accident. He sunk into a deep funk until he gradually began to look at some logical alternatives to a surgical career. The option he finally chose was internal medicine, a medical specialty in which fine hand movements are not so critical. (Psychiatry would have been another alternative.)

6. *Collect optimistic information.*   If you are the cognitive type, gathering reassuring facts can give you hope about a gloomy situation. To give a personal example, my ophthalmologist and two colleagues he consulted told me it appeared that I was developing glaucoma in my right eye. The unreassuring, pessimistic fact I gathered from a household medical encyclopedia was that glaucoma is the leading cause of blindness. To counterbalance this threatening news, I gathered some hopeful facts. My ophthalmologist informed me that over 90 percent of glaucoma cases can be successfully treated with eye drops!

7. *Minimize contact with pessimistic people.*   A practical strategy for developing hope is to minimize contact with pessimists and maximize contact with optimists. The justification for this suggestion is that pessimism is mildly contagious—pessimists spread their gloom much like a virus. Gloom peddlers specialize in forcing you to develop a spirit of hopelessness. For example, the merchandising vice president who was helped by an outplacement firm (described in the previous chapter) was told by one of her friends, "You might as well look for a lesser type of job. The chance of a person your age finding a new position at the vice presidential level is close to zero." In contrast, most of the people the merchandising executive met at the outplacement firm were optimistic.

Remember, however, that gloom peddlers could use your help. You might want to donate some listening time to them in order to allow them to "borrow hope from others." Yet back off when their gloom threatens to become contagious.

8. *Practice daydreaming.*   Fantasizing about better times is a potent method that allows us to anticipate events and rehearse handling them. Psychiatrist Sally Severino says that daydreaming gives us the ideals for which to hope. Nevertheless, fantasy should not be used as a substitute for reality. It's okay for the small business owners to fantasize about having no problems with creditors, but it's unrealistic to believe that they can continue to stay in business without meeting financial obligations.

9. *Use denial to cushion despair.*   Used judiciously, denial can ignite a brief spark of hope to get us through the worst part of a crisis. For example, the account executive who loses her major account and her boyfriend in one month, and during the same period discovers she has a melanoma, may need to use denial temporarily. She might say to herself, for example, "My client will probably miss me once the new agency's campaign fails, and my skin cancer is very superficial." Denial in the long run, however, will impede the direct action that needs to be taken to make a valid comeback.

10. *Avoid exaggerating the magnitude of your crisis.*   Faced with the oppressive impact of a crisis, many people exaggerate its long-term, negative consequences. A lawyer who received a formal reprimand from her county bar association might say, "I'll never get another client in this town." One way to counter such exaggerated thinking is to marshal a few facts. The lawyer in question might conduct a quick investigation to find out what has happened to most attorneys in her town who received a reprimand. Her research might reveal that receiving a reprimand has historically resulted in a very small decrease in clients.

11. *Subdivide the comeback task into interim tasks.*   A major challenge in mobilizing a comeback is that the job seems so overwhelming. If the job were made less overwhelming, it would be easier to be hopeful. A useful antidote here is to assign yourself small "comeback tasks" that you can pursue each day. The lawyer who received the reprimand might launch her comeback on a given day by composing a letter to be mailed to all her clients. Her letter might explain that although she did not agree entirely with the county bar association she has accepted the reprimand, and it has not affected her right or ability to practice law. Similarly, the way to recover from a fire is to make a list of all the people who have to be contacted, and literally begin "picking up the pieces."

12. *Avoid panic when things seem hopeless.* We recommended pre-viously to avoid panic in order to cope with the emotional aspects of a crisis. A variation of the principle also applies when trying to generate hope. If you conserve your energy by staying reasonably calm, you may be able to develop a more hopeful attitude. Conversely, if you suffer from intense fear and despair, you are less likely to weather the crisis. Jim Montimerano was forced back into the job market at age 54, after 38 years with the same company. He told us, "One reason I kept going was that I never hit the panic button. I woke up each day and convinced myself that today was the day things were finally going to turn in my favor." (You'll read more about Jim in Chapter 8.)

13. *Take charge of your life.* If events are controlling your life rather than you controlling them, your feeling of helplessness is likely to lead to a feeling of hopelessness. A manager who is being squeezed out of power because of negative chemistry between himself and his new boss may feel hopeless. He will not begin to feel hopeful until he gains control of his power base. To accomplish this he might explore three options: (1) discuss the situation with his boss's boss, (2) find a powerful position in another corporation, or (3) enter into business himself so he can automatically have the most power in the firm.

Bouncing Back Characteristic 46: Make an Optimistic Interpretation of Events

Another way to use optimism and positive thinking to energize a come-back is to make an optimistic interpretation of events that others might interpret pessimistically. John Z. DeLorean provided a classic example at a late stage in his career.

Comeback Scenario 29: John Z. DeLorean, Auto Builder

As most business people recall, DeLorean left a promising career at General Motors Corporation in 1973. He devoted much of his work time during the next decade and a half building the DeLorean Motor Co., and then handling its bankruptcy.

During the time DeLorean was spearheading his automobile com-pany, he had been on trial for cocaine dealing, racketeering, and fraud. The company went bankrupt, his wife left him, and he fell behind in his mortgage payments. Despite these problems, in 1987 DeLorean re-ceived back $22 million in assets and the right to continue to manufacture under the name DeLorean Motor Co. By 1987, he had plans under way to build a high-performance, limited edition auto designed and built in West Germany. Called the "Isdera," the car was to have a Mercedes-Benz engine and a Porsche suspension. As reported several years later, the new auto promised to be an exotic V-12, high-performance machine, in the $175,000 range. Before proceeding further with the car, DeLorean needed to raise large sums of money from investors—a feat he was confident he could accomplish.

When asked how he felt about all the difficulties he had faced in the years since he had left General Motors, DeLorean who was age 62 at the time said, "That was just a stage I went through. The main accomplishments of my life are still ahead of me."[4] Undoubtedly, DeLorean's optimistic interpretation of past events helped give him the courage to attempt a comeback. His optimistic spirit is also part of his charisma that enables DeLorean to attract investors despite his shaky financial record.

For many people, an effective way of making an optimistic interpretation of adverse circumstances is to recognize that no matter what happens to them, their core assets still exist. A business owner might go bankrupt because he or she made some bad investments with money needed to pay employee salaries, bills, and taxes. Although that person's situation would certainly be bleak, he or she would still have the talent that enabled him or her to establish the business in the first place. Thinking of a workable idea for another business and finding creative ways to finance it would be a formidable task. Yet it could still be done using the person's core assets.

DeLorean thought in these terms when he undertook the rebirth of his motor car company at age 62. He intuitively relied on his core assets of knowledge of the automotive industry, a flair for automotive design, and an uncanny ability to attract investors to his business schemes.

Making optimistic interpretations of events that could readily be deemed pessimistic involves developing the right mental set. Studying the optimistic interpretations of adverse circumstances presented in the following chart will help you develop the right mental set for interpreting events optimistically.

Adverse Circumstance	Possible Optimistic Interpretation
You get fired.	Here is an opportunity to find a job I really want or start a new career.
You lose out in a political power play for the third time in your career.	The other players in this game are much better office politicians. Since I'm not very political, I should concentrate more on technical than managerial work.

Adverse Circumstance	Possible Optimistic Interpretation
The last 38 sales leads you pursued refused to buy.	Not to worry, in this business, you have to call on a lot of prospects to make one sale. (To use the most oft repeated cliché for handling rejection, "I'm one step closer to a Yes.")
You take over as general manager of a division that is losing large amounts of money.	After studying the situation for a month you inform your staff, "Don't be discouraged. My analysis is that we're a smooth-functioning organization internally. We therefore have the capacity to be very successful. The only thing we are lacking right now is orders. Once we get some orders we will be able to handle quite well."

Bouncing Back Characteristic 47: Develop the Iacocca Spirit

America's favorite industrial folk hero provides an excellent model for developing an optimistic attitude toward overcoming adversity.

Comeback Scenario 30: Lee Iacocca, Automotive Executive

Iacocca accomplished the most publicized corporate and personal comebacks in business history. In 1979 he made a public commitment to revitalizing Chrysler Corporation as the company approached annual losses of greater than $3 billion. He accomplished his optimistic undertaking. Lobbying congress and the president, and mobilizing labor unions and banks, Iacocca arranged $1.5 billion in loan guarantees from the federal government. Chrysler paid back the notes seven years before their due date, and Chrysler became a highly profitable company by the early 1980s.

Iacocca's personal comeback is at least equally as remarkable as the corporate comeback he directed. Many business scholars believe that although Iacocca made a major contribution to the revitalization of Chrysler Corporation, it was still a *team* effort. Iacocca was deeply humiliated by Henry Ford at the end of an intense internal struggle at Ford Motor Co. Ford finally fired Iacocca stating simply, "I don't like you." After the firing, Iacocca was relegated to a warehouse office—a cruel indignity for a man as proud and egotistical as Iacocca. Within a few years, Iacocca became one of the most revered men in America, and clearly the most visible corporate executive in the world.

Iacocca's optimistic spirit has several closely related components.

Above all it is laced with courage. As one news magazine writer put it, "His life embodies just the kind of happy ending that Americans like to celebrate: he had reverses, he fought back, and he came out on top."[5] In this regard, Iacocca is the *ultimate-resilient manager.*

High Self-Assurance.   The Iacocca spirit also includes a heavy component of self-assurance manifested by an unswerving belief that he is right. As a manager, this self-assurance leads him toward autocratic decision making. He often makes the concession of listening to staff members, but then makes up his own mind. His self-assurance comes through in his legendary ads for Chrysler cars. Iacocca's tag line was, "If you can find a better car, buy it." Although an advertising copywriter most likely prepared this ad, Iacocca approved it because it fit his spirit of self-assurance.

Iacocca's spirit includes a missionary zeal and strong personal salesmanship. Although Iacocca graduated from college as an engineer, he quickly shifted to truck sales and later became a merchandising specialist. His major contribution to the Ford Mustang was in marketing, not designing the car. His missionary zeal manifests itself in his frequent stump speeches criticizing what he believes is an inequitable American trade policy with Japan. He demands a reduction of the trade deficit and a comprehensive trade policy. In his talks to college students he tells then to "get mad" and "fight the system."

Role of the Optimistic Underdog.   In his days of revitalizing Chrysler Corporation, Iacocca played the role of optimistic underdog — a type of optimist many people (especially Americans) revere. His gutsy approach to turning around Chrysler was perceived by one observer in these terms: "It was like the underdog pool player in a high-stakes game who announces an impossible bank shot involving awkward, oblique angles and chancy ricochets, and then does it."[6]

Should you be attempting a comeback against tough odds, you might cast yourself as a gutsy underdog. Let others know of the long odds you are facing and how you are going to beat them. Implementing your comeback might be difficult but perceiving yourself as an underdog intent on beating the odds might give you the edge.

Bouncing Back Characteristic 48:
Focus on Your Major Goal

Working your way up from the depths of adversity may require a guiding light. One important purpose of the guiding light, or high-level goal, is that it picks up your spirits as you rebuild your career brick by brick, inch by inch.

Comeback Scenario 31: Bob Barbato, Small Business Owner

Bob Barbato had the major goal of becoming a successful small business owner in addition to keeping up with his duties as a professor of entrepreneurship. He had the capital and the business savvy to reach his goal. Nevertheless, he faced some serious problems.

Bob bought a restaurant adjacent to a beach that specialized in low-priced meals and snacks. After several months of operation he faced a lawsuit from a custard stand located across the street. The attorneys for the owners of the custard stand contended that Bob was violating his lease by allowing his customers to take ice cream off the premises.

A long and costly legal battle ensued about whether or not Bob's restaurant could allow its customers to take custard or any other ice-cream related product outside the restaurant. Shortly before the case was finally scheduled for court, the opposing side made Barbato a generous offer for his business. The purpose of buying out Bob was to eliminate competition. Bob's partner, however, did not want to sell the restaurant because it would mean that he (and his brother who worked at the restaurant) would be out of a job.

Bob now faced a conflict. If he sold out to the competition he would collect a handsome profit but his partner and the partner's brother would be forced to find new employment. Bob did not want to disappoint his partner, yet he reflected on what he was really trying to accomplish: "The primary purpose of my being in business is to make money. I bought the business at a low price, and I'm now being offered a high price. If I sell, I've achieved an important goal." He resolved the conflict by selling his share of the business to his partner, offering him a 25-year payback. Bob's partner was now in competition with the custard stand owners across the street.

A judge's final verdict placed almost no restriction on the sale of ice-cream products by Bob's recently sold restaurant, thus not limiting its profitability. Bob was happy for his partner, and now refocused his attention on the goal he was really trying to reach—to operate a successful small business. Bringing his major goal into focus sent Bob a message as to what should be done next. After exploring several other business ventures, Bob opened a baby furniture store, in partnership with two of his former students. The store is on its way to becoming a successful small business.

As Bob analyzes the situation:

The biggest adversity I faced was spending all that money on a pointless legal battle. It's gruesome waking up every day and have to worry about mounting legal costs and an uncertain outcome. It was a terrible weight dragging me down. However, I did wind up selling my business at a profit large enough to cover the legal fees. You could therefore say my lawyers functioned as brokers. Without their working on the case, I might not have received such a large price for the business. The offer from the competition set the price for sale to my partner.

The biggest lesson I learned from the case was that I can make a good business deal just like the big players. The episode therefore gave me the confidence and optimism necessary to make other deals. I know what I want to achieve, and I now know how to do it.

Comeback Scenario 32: Al Neuharth, Newspaper Mogul

Al Neuharth, the newspaper executive who launched *USA Today,* provides a clear example of how focusing on a major goal can fuel the optimistic spirit needed to overcome a career adversity. Thirty years before Neuharth launched *USA Today,* he started a small sports weekly printed on peach-colored paper. The paper was sold on a few hundred newsstands in South Dakota.

Neuharth had just resigned a steady $75-per-week job with the Associated Press. Too impatient with what he perceived as a career of slow progression at AP, Neuharth decided to embark on a risky venture. He planned to start his own newspaper, *SoDak Sports,* in partnership with a reporter friend, Bob Porter. The paper started operation in 1952.

Neuharth was highly optimistic about *SoDak Sports'*s chances for success. He and Porter saw the paper as one subgoal along the way to building a publishing empire. Their game plan was to be a publishing success in South Dakota, launch a similar sports newspaper in Minnesota, and then go national. Others around them were skeptical of their chances for success.

The first issue of *SoDak Sports* was published on November 21, 1952, with Neuharth as editor and Porter as business manager. Its newsstand price was ten cents and it was printed on peach-colored newsprint. Its promotional slogan was "Reach for the peach." To raise the $50,000 needed to launch *SoDak Sports,* Neuharth and Porter traveled around South Dakota selling $100 blocks of stock to sports enthusiasts. No one invested more than $400.

SoDak Sports printed many promotional claims about itself, including the idea that it was a complete sports newspaper. It contained every sports result in South Dakota, made its own rankings, elected its own all-star teams, and designated its own coaches of the year. Neuharth wrote that one of the goals of the newspaper was to "bridge the gap between east and west, north and south, and make South Dakota one big sports family."

As the months went by circulation remained steady but unspectacular. Things went well on the editorial side, but the business side was beset with problems. *SoDak Sports* was not making money because it could not attract enough advertisers. In the summer of 1954, Neuharth and Porter realized they lacked the money to stay in business. The two partners announced that their newspaper was going to take a break. Neuharth pledged that *SoDak Sports* would come back stronger than ever.

While the paper was on hold, Neuharth and Porter scrambled around to find more investors. A few were found, but the money was never collected. As a last resort, the partners held a bankruptcy sale. Neuharth has this recollection of the event:

> It was pretty sad. The thing that surprised us both was that a lot of our stockholders were in Sioux Falls, and a lot of them came by when we were selling off equipment, not to buy, but to thank us for all the fun. Hell of a surprise, because we thought we'd be run out of town on a rail.

In the winter of 1954, the aspiring publishing titans had to decide what to do next. Porter had a law degree, so he decided to stay in South Dakota and join a law firm. Today he is a successful lawyer. Neuharth decided to pursue another path to reaching his major goal of becoming a publishing mogul.[7] His first attempt at launching a newspaper failed, but he regarded it as a temporary setback on the way to achieving his definition of success. Neuharth's optimistic spirit has helped him become one of the major players in the history of newspaper publishing. The Gannett Company owns and operates *USA Today* as well as over 100 newspapers, television stations, and radio stations. The same optimistic spirit can work for you in overcoming adversity.

Bouncing Back Characteristic 49: Be Determined and Persistent

A practical way of expressing positive thinking is to be persistent, as reflected in the age-old adage, "If at first you don't succeed, try, try again." The positive thinker believes that if you keep trying, you are bound to achieve your goal. Persistence usually brings about the results necessary to overcame adversity. Being persistent also makes other people think you are achieving good results. An experiment was conducted on the reactions of individuals to certain types of administrative actions. A total of 222 people (including practicing managers and students) were asked to study one of eight case descriptions of an administrator's behavior.

Among other findings, it was observed that administrators were rated the highest when they followed a consistent course of action rather than experimenting with new approaches to the problem. In essence, if an administrator persisted, he or she was judged to be competent.[8] Be careful not to take these results too literally in attempting to overcome adversity. Persistence should be translated into an unswerving commitment to make a comeback, but not to tenaciously pursuing a path that does not bring results. Neuharth, for example, gave up on *SoDak Sports,* but persisted in his desire to build a newspaper publishing empire. It does not pay to beat one's head against a wall.

Comeback Scenario 33: Anthony Punzo, Amusement Park Manager

Punzo's story illustrates the sensible application of persistence and optimism to rebounding from adversity. He was concerned that when Elmira, New York, is mentioned in conversation, it is usually in reference to the city's notorious prison. His goal is to change that perception and promote the historical features of Elmira. Punzo's reasoning is that Mark Twain wrote several of his books in his Elmira home and the city is the soaring (a derivative of hang gliding) capital of the world.

Punzo is the manager of Eldridge Park, a 126-year-old amusement park that once attracted visitors from all over New York State and Pennsylvania. Eldridge Park is also home to one of the region's oldest carousels. In 1981 it was necessary to borrow $150,000 at 21 percent interest to renovate the park. Within seven years the park was in the black. However, in the interim the state ordered the roller coaster closed because drainage problems weakened the ground beneath its structure. Loss of income from the roller coaster has made it difficult to keep Eldridge Park in the black.

The loss of roller coaster revenue, combined with a dramatic increase in liability insurance premiums, made foreclosure an imminent possibility for Eldridge Park. Determined to keep the park open, Punzo traveled all over New York State in an attempt to obtain funding. Impressed with Punzo's efforts, the Elmira Preservation Society suggested that he attempt to register the park as an historic landmark with the Mark Twain theme. As a landmark, Eldridge Park would be eligible to receive various grants from the state.

Due to Punzo's optimistic attitude and persistence, Eldridge Park has remained open. His application for historic landmark status for the park triggered the community's interest in its preservation. Local businesses sponsored fund-raising events, and residents donated money to help the park pay the $30,000 insurance premium. Punzo says, "We haven't licked all the problems yet, but I'm hopeful. I've pulled off keeping the park operating through its toughest times, and I know I can do it again if necessary."

Anthony Punzo combined his optimism with creative problem solving. Optimism is important because it leads you to believe that your creative problem solving will yield good results.

Bouncing Back Characteristic 50: Visualize a Happy Outcome

Through visualization we imagine the outcome we want to achieve in order to facilitate making it happen. Visualization is widely used to improve sports performance. In playing tennis, for example, you select a spot on the opponent's court and then visualize the ball you hit landing precisely on that spot. In playing basketball, you similarly visualize the ball going through the hoop or a pass getting to the right teammate. The process is also referred to as *feedforward* because the person creates powerful images of a future reality he or she desires, before actually trying to achieve that reality.[9] The following descriptions of athletes in action will help you better visualize the process of visualization:

> Before each competition, 320-pound Mario Martinez, America's best super-heavyweight lifter, sits down in his bed, closes his eyes, breathes deeply for several minutes to calm himself and relax, and then begins to imagine himself pulling 500 pounds up off the floor and hoisting it over his head in a perfectly executed lift. So vivid is this imagined lift that Martinez can actually "feel" the bar in his hands. He can even hear the roar of the appreciative crowd cheering him on.
>
> "The thought of holding 500 pounds over your head can be frightening," Martinez says. "You might be strong enough to make the lift, but if you don't *believe* you can, the fear will make you fail. I use visualization to help make me believe."
>
> Likewise, 105-pound Doe Yamashiro, one of the United States' top woman gymnasts, pauses before each routine, breathes deeply, then pictures herself performing flawlessly. She even imagines the butterflies she'll feel, and then sees herself overcoming that nervousness on her way to victory. "If I can't see a routine clearly in my mind before I do it, then I have trouble," she says.[10]

Visualization also has application as a method of overcoming career adversity, and moving yourself toward peak performance. The process is uncomplicated. You imagine yourself having a successful outcome to the adverse circumstances you face. Carefully imagine the minute details of your comeback victory, such as a judge reading a verdict that you the defendant are not at fault and that the plaintiff must pay you damages. Imagine yourself sitting in a vice presidential office, while in the interim you are scrambling around searching for a new position in the company because the project you headed has accomplished its mission. Think of yourself delivering a flawless presentation to the budget committee, justifying the budget you need to continue operating.

Although visualization is uncomplicated, do not confuse it with idle daydreaming. Visualization projects you into such a specific set of actions, that it serves as a pinpointed goal toward which to direct your mental and physical energy. The process also works because it elevates your self-confidence by giving you a taste of the victory you seek.

Bouncing Back Characteristic 51: Have Faith

Several years ago I was discussing the topic of overcoming adversity on a radio call-in show. After five minutes of general discussion on the topic, the host accepted the first caller. The caller said bluntly, "I have something to tell your guest. He's got it all wrong. There is only one way to overcome setbacks in your life and that is to have faith in God. If you believe in God, He will take care of you."

The caller had a good point. Faith in a divine force can help most people through adversity. Nevertheless, you also need some emotional support from others and intelligent planning—a point that I have corroborated with several members of the clergy. The following case history is one of the many I have encountered that illustrates how managers overcome adversity by combining good planning with faith.

Comeback Scenario 34: Dave Spaulding, Food Company Manager

Dave left a promising career with a nationwide produce company to work for a small produce distributor (Nelson and Son) as vice president of sales and personnel. A few years after Dave joined the company, the owner, Don, had a major heart attack. At that point Don changed the business from a privately held to a closely held company owned by himself, his wife, and two vice presidents. Dave then owned 20 percent of the stock, with Don and his wife still owning 51 percent.

When Dave started with Nelson and Son, the company was near

bankruptcy. The company returned to profitability after Dave made such sweeping changes as providing employees with sickness and life insurance, uniforms, and conducting monthly employee meetings to discuss work and personnel problems. Sales and profits, along with morale were up, and employee turnover was lower than ever. In addition, Dave conceived, developed, and ran an entire seafood distributing operation.

Don had always run the company his way which included some personnel practices that violated state wage and hour laws. Dave and Don disagreed in many areas of management but particularly with respect to the most appropriate management style. Don practiced autocratic management, and Dave chose the participative style. Eventually this difference in style led to disagreements, culminating in Don firing Dave by voting him off the board of directors and terminating his employment. Dave was fired shortly after his fifty-sixth birthday.

The day following his firing Dave attended church and prayed for a successful resolution of his problems. Later in the morning he called his seafood customers and told them he was no longer with Nelson and Sons, and that he was establishing his own seafood company. The customers had always done business with Dave and had been satisfied with his service. Virtually all of them said they would be happy to do business with him again. Dave then called his suppliers with whom he had good business relations. Consequently they were willing to extend him credit. Next, he called his bank and obtained a short-term loan. The telephone calls, a rented truck, and some ice chests put Dave in business as the owner of Neptune Seafood Company. He also hired a driver who quit Nelson to work for Dave.

Dave and his brother Bill had formed a partnership to invest in real estate. Their most recent acquisition a few months prior to Dave's being fired was a small supermarket. This gave Dave an office for his business and freezer space for fish storage. The brothers agreed to add freezer space to give Dave the storage space he required without taking space needed by the supermarket.

After five weeks, Neptune Seafood was breaking even, and one month later was showing a profit. Dave bought a truck and found it necessary to hire a part-time driver using the family station wagon to fill all the orders.

Several months later Dave was approached by Joe, a former Nelson sales representative who had now founded Specialty Foods, Inc. Joe had observed the changes Dave had brought to Nelson's and the deterioration of the firm after he left. Joe was also aware of the exceptional success of Neptune Seafood. Joe wanted to hire Dave as a consultant to improve Specialty Foods. Dave agreed to take on the assignment, providing he would do more than write a report describing the changes needed. Instead, he wanted to help implement the changes and follow them until they were absorbed into the company as a standard procedure. Joe agreed, and thus became the first client of Caledonia Consulting Company.

After six months of the consulting relationship, Joe bought Neptune Seafood from Dave and hired him as an employee. Both men were aware that there was a time limit to this position. Dave improved customer relations and was responsible for implementing a computerized inventory system while he was there. After two and one-half years they agreed that Dave's mission was completed. Joe told Dave that he would keep him on until Dave found another job. When Dave started looking, to his amazement, he was offered three positions. He accepted a position as a regional sales manager for Alleghany Foods, a one-and-one-half-year assignment leading to the position of general sales manager at company headquarters. Dave believes that he has found a niche that fits his long-term interests.

In reflecting on his experiences, Dave said, "Religion has always been a strong force in my life. Without my religion I doubt I could have been so successful after being fired. The pressure was really on me. I had two daughters in college and one in high school when Don fired me. God gave me the strength to continue. My advice to anyone else going through a similar experience is to use your contacts. Let everyone know that you are looking for a job. Even if they don't have a job to offer you, they can often get you an interview through their contacts."

Dave Spaulding's faith made a major contribution to his comeback. However, he did not passively sit by and wait for a divine force to overcome his adversity. He also used his best problem-solving skills.

Action Tips

Positive thinking can help energize your comeback. To develop positive-thinking attitudes and skills, do or think the following:

1. Remember that optimism has healing power.
2. Develop the habit of hoping.
3. Make an optimistic interpretation of events.
4. Develop the Iacocca spirit.
5. Focus on your major goal.
6. Be determined and persistent.
7. Visualize a happy outcome.
8. Have faith.

6
Planning Your Comeback

After the inner turmoil associated with a crisis is under adequate control, it is time to focus on the rational, analytical side of your comeback. A constructive, detached perspective is to regard career adversity as but another major business problem to be solved. If you apply the same planned approach to overcoming your setback as you would to a vexing job problem, a workable solution will emerge. Planning in this context involves setting comeback goals and selecting methods to achieve them. As most managers and professionals recognize, planning is the most important method of accomplishing anything.

One of Theodore Roosevelt's campaigns provides a cogent example of how a calm, rational, and planned approach can turn disadvantage to advantage. The printing presses were set to run three million copies of Roosevelt's 1912 campaign speech. At the last moment the publisher discovered that permission had not been obtained to reproduce photos of Roosevelt and his running mate, Governor Hiram Johnson of California. According to copyright law, the fine imposed for such violations was one dollar per copy.

The campaign director calmly searched for a way to overcome this burdensome problem. He sent a telegram to the Chicago studio that had taken the photographs:

> Planning to issue three million copies of Roosevelt speech with pictures of Roosevelt and Johnson on cover. Great publicity opportunity for photographers. What will you pay us to use your photographs? An hour later the reply came back: "Appreciate opportunity, but can pay only $250."[1]

The tactics and strategies described next are arranged in approximately the sequence that should be followed in order to plan a successful comeback. However, individual circumstances may dictate a different order of tactics chosen. For example, the final tactic described, "Be Open to Unplanned Comeback Opportunities," with luck might be implemented on the first day of your comeback.

Bouncing Back Characteristic 52: Analyze the Reasons Behind Your Setback

A carefully planned comeback begins with an analysis of why the career reversal took place. Discovering the facts behind your setback is also the logical way to learn from your past mistakes. Usually, you have to calm down sufficiently to assume this objective, problem-solving posture. Getting an accurate answer may not always be easy, but the facts could help you avoid a similar setback at a later date.

Despite all that has been preached in recent years about the importance of honesty and openness in management, you may still have to probe to get an authentic answer as to why you were thrust backward. Most managers feel awkward and embarrassed when they have to confront a subordinate.

Comeback Scenario 35: Gary Muldoon, Middle Manager

Passed over for a promotion, Gary probed for the information he needed to make his comeback.

"How can I tell my wife," he thought to himself. "It's the third time that I have been passed over for a regional managership. Each time, the company told me that I would be warmly considered for the next promotion." Gary's reflection was followed by sullenness and then finally by action. He demanded a conference with his boss, Ed, to discuss why he was passed over again. With some hesitation, Ed did agree to review the reasons why Gary was not selected for the position of regional manager.

ED: Your work performance has been fine. It's just a few little things that made us decide to give somebody else a chance this time around. It's not too much to worry about.

GARY: Ed, that is precisely why I came to see you. It *is* something to worry about. Is there something holding me back in this company? I

must know. Maybe it's something I can correct. What are these little
things you refer to?

ED: Gary, this may hurt, but you asked for it. My boss and I think you
are rude to top management. It's this rudeness that is keeping you
back.

GARY: I don't recall being rude to anybody. Could you give me a couple
of examples?

ED: The best example I can think of is when Marv Finney, the executive vice president joined us for lunch. When we were returning
from lunch, you barged through the revolving door ahead of him.
During his presentation you clipped your nails. Just like you do in
other meetings, you interrupted him before he had a chance to finish what he was saying. Do you get the point? We think you need
more polish. In fact, you're gross.

Gary thought the company was being needlessly picayune, but now he
had a clear understanding of what aspects of his behavior were holding
him back. Gary saw these alternatives facing him:

- He could quit in a huff.
- He could continue along with his self-defeating behavior.
- He could conform to what the company thought constituted good
  manners in dealing with higher management.

By taking the third course of action, Gary's hopes of becoming a regional manager were reignited. At no sacrifice to his sense of morality,
Gary did become more deferent toward higher-ranking executives.
Fourteen months later, a new region was formed and Gary was selected
to manage it. Should you be set back in your career, your chances of
making a strong comeback will be enhanced by digging for the contributing reasons.

Comeback Scenario 36: Bill Cotter, Retail Store Owner

Gary had to make an analysis of the personal factors behind his setback.
Discovering the facts behind a major reversal applies equally well to analyzing what went wrong with one's business. The turnaround accomplished by proprietor Bill Cotter illustrates this point well. Cotter owned
and operated a small sporting goods store in a residential neighborhood
outside Pittsburgh, Pennsylvania. He chose the location because of its

low rent and proximity to his home, rather than conducting a thorough investigation of where such a store might be needed.

The entire Cotter family helped set up the store, distribute flyers, and put up posters. Bill also advertised in local papers and the Penny Saver. Sales the first month were low, but Bill was confident they would pick up the following month. The second and third month were just as low. Bill's profits did not even cover advertising costs incurred prior to opening the store. He worked 70 hours per week at the store, and his family also contributed a large amount of time. After much deliberation and agonizing over the problem, Bill decided to close the store to stem the tide of his losses, which had already mounted enormously.

Discouraged but not defeated, the following year Bill opened another sporting goods store. However, before he did this he researched why his first venture failed. The primary reason for his failure was a poor choice of location. Choosing a location because of its low rent and proximity to home was a bad idea because these were superficial business reasons.

Another factor behind the business flop was that Bill ignored "niche marketing." He neglected finding a uniqueness to differentiate himself from competitors. His store was simply a smaller version of larger stores with considerably more inventory. His new store took care of both these problems. It was located in a plaza with heavy traffic, and he specialized in iron-on T-shirt emblems. He also offered substantial discounts to sports teams in the area. Because he now specialized, he did not have to carry as large an inventory as did his first store.

Bill now spends about 50 hours per week at the new store and earns a satisfactory profit. He observes that he benefited greatly from having been burned the first time. Bill knew that his dream of owning a sporting goods store was right. He is convinced that his problem was that he just didn't get his facts straight on his first attempt.

Cotter succeeded in his comeback to a large extent because he conducted research about the reasons for his setback. Again, analytical thinking can facilitate bouncing back.

Bouncing Back Characteristic 53: Analyze Who You Are and What You Want

The early stages of a comeback represent an excellent opportunity for taking a candid look at who you really are and what you want out of your career. As career counselor Leslie Rose suggests, "Redefine yourself by what you *want* to do."[2] Many people who have been fired or laid off, for example, take the opportunity to switch careers.

Comeback Scenario 37: Lola Parsons, Administrative Assistant

Lola, an administrative assistant to a top executive, faced an emotional crisis when her boss was forced into early retirement after a takeover. She identified more with him than the company and was so angry with the organization that she quit. While pounding the pavement two days after she resigned, Lola realized that she never wanted to be somebody else's assistant again. Being an assistant didn't provide her the amount of self-esteem she craved. It was time for Lola to occupy center stage. Her solution was to sell interior designs for offices. Being an interior designer raised her self-esteem beyond the level she could achieve as somebody's assistant.

Lola's adversity of being unemployed was self-imposed. However, she made the most of the situation by assessing what she really wanted from her career. Her decision was that she needed more autonomy than she had experienced in her recent position. Selling office designs promised her more independence.

Comeback Scenario 38: John Kelly, Realtor

Lola seems to have quickly merged the steps of finding out who she is and specifying her goals. For many others, taking an inventory of their assets and liabilities (part of finding out who you are) is more deliberate and painstaking. A successful application of this technique was accomplished by John Kelly, a realtor. John worked for a real estate company for seven years, and then bought it from his employer. Despite his success at running the business, he was forced to file for bankruptcy after three years. John explains what happened and his method of recovery:

> I have always believed in honesty. I was brought up in a strict Catholic family where honesty, morality, and love of God were demanded. A few years after graduating from college, I joined IBM where I worked for three years. During that time I married, and my wife and I had three children. I felt stifled by the slow rise up the ladder at IBM. I yearned to do something where I could be more creative and move faster in my career.
>
> I left IBM to sell real estate for a small company. Soon I was doing so well that I was lured away to a larger more prestigious company,

Walker Real Estate. The owner was Don Halloway. I started out with a bang and kept up the heavy pace. Don kept praising me and telling me how I was going to enable him to retire early.

One day Don asked me if I would be interested in purchasing the company. I told him that I was interested but had limited funds. However, he convinced me that he would hold part of the mortgage plus give me a personal loan. Don assured me that he and I could work out the details.

Against the advice of my friends, I bought the business. Most of the agreements between Don and myself were verbal. The business was going very well for three years. I was beginning to see blue skies when the bottom fell out. Don had encountered some hard times and wanted the business back. I was devastated! Don unscrupulously took everything I had. When I fought him in court, I only had spoken agreements to offer as proof.

I lost all my savings, my house, and was forced to file for bankruptcy. I had reached what I thought was the darkest and most humiliating point in my life. I was filled with a sense of worthlessness and despair. I wondered what I could have done to deserve this.

After several aimless months of soul searching and feeling sorry for myself, I visited a career counselor and got his recommendations about making a new start. His first recommendation was to take a long, hard look at myself and make a list of my strengths and weaknesses. The counselor's next suggestion was to ask myself what I really liked to do. He also suggested that I should make a list of goals that I wanted to attain and begin with a prioritized plan of how I hoped to accomplish them. Because I had recently suffered an emotional crisis, I was urged to keep my immediate goals small.

I was advised to begin to make positive steps and improve both my morale and self-image through the sense of achievement that comes from accomplishing these goals. With the help of my wife and the counselor, I began getting back on track. My early accomplishments included such positive steps as losing five pounds and updating my resume.

I was now able to identify both negative and positive points about myself. First, I accepted the fact that it was not disgraceful to be a poor money manager. I admitted that I mishandled the family finances in the past. My wife and I agreed that she was the more logical person to handle the family finances because she was a better money manager.

John also realized that he was too honest and trusting in his business dealings. It didn't make sense to conduct business transactions on spoken agreements alone, as he had done with Don. John emphasized that spoken agreements are an unusual arrangement in real estate. Insisting on written agreements would make him appear to be a more formidable businessperson.

John made the observation that he had gained considerable expertise in real estate, and that he wanted to remain in the field. Although he felt he was not ready to jump back into house sales, he did need a job.

> While discussing employment possibilities at various real estate firms [said John], I was fortunate to find a company which did a great deal of commercial as well as noncommercial business, and was part of a national chain. The company had expanded so much that they needed an assistant manager. The president of the agency told me I was a more qualified candidate than they had hoped to find, and that I would be perfect for the position. Here was an opportunity to remain in real estate, yet get away from the pressures of selling.
>
> He informed me that the current manager had requested the first available transfer to a West Coast office. Therefore, if I worked out well, I would have a good chance of being promoted to the manager of the office.
>
> After I was hired, I felt a sense of vitality. I liked the diversity of the new company, and I felt that I could be successful. I was now dealing with honest people which meant that the cards were not stacked against me. The firm was pleased with my performance. Whatever administrative tasks they handed me, such as getting ads placed in the newspapers, I carried out dutifully. I also took the initiative to make improvements in the firm. A good example was an information system I bought for the firm. The system efficiently matched prospective home buyers with houses that fit their preferences.
>
> Based on my good performance, I was promoted when the existing manager did get her transfer. Although the job is a busy one, I now have time to spend with my family—something I had no time to do when I had my own business. My life has taken on new meaning and provided me with greater rewards than ever before.

Self-analysis helped move John from business ownership to becoming an employee. He came to realize that the pressures of self-employment were no longer well-suited to his psychological makeup. Self-analysis could also help you achieve a more rewarding career, should you be faded with the necessity of a job switch.

Comeback Scenario 39: Paul Piccotto, Computer Consultant

Analyzing himself moved Paul Piccotto in the direction of self-employment. Paul was a regional sales manager in the computer hardware division of a large business corporation. With the competition getting heavier all the time, Paul's company decided to divest itself of the computer hardware business. The company that bought the hardware business decided to eliminate the position of regional manager.

Paul was therefore without a job at age 45. He found this difficult to accept because he had worked so hard to become a regional manager.

He was also upset by the thought that the acquiring company thought so little of his potential contribution that they collapsed his position. Up to this point Paul had achieved a long series of successes. After graduating from Syracuse University, he joined his company as a sales representative and received four promotions during his 24 years of employment. Paul believed he had found his niche as a regional sales manager in the computer industry.

Having only looked for one job since graduating from college, Paul was confused and apprehensive. He knew he needed to conduct a a job search, but could not gear himself mentally to begin. Paul was temporarily immobilized by the ego-tearing insult of being laid off.

One day Paul was lamenting over his problem with his wife. In response, she confronted him in these terms: "What have you done for yourself lately other than wallow in your own misery?" Paul saw vividly his self-defeating behavior pattern. He now began by taking an inventory of what he had to offer the business world. His self-analysis, assisted by his wife, pinpointed these assets:

- He had good sales skills.
- He had substantial experience in the computer industry.
- His computer programming skills were well developed.
- He preferred working independently.

Paul concluded from his self-analysis that he should start a computer consulting business, specializing in installing turnkey systems, and in providing the supporting software packages.

Paul's wife supported his decision. The couple decided that the business could be funded through personal savings, a second mortgage, and his vested retirement funds. Paul rented a one-room office downtown, hired an answering service, and began calling on clients. Business was lean the first year, the second year was better, and by the third year he began adding to his staff and increasing his office facilities. After five years in business his client load was so heavy that he hired one professional and two support people. Today he owns and operates a prosperous and secure consulting business.

Piccotto's self-analysis thus moved him in the opposite direction chosen by John Kelly. However, the process is the same. A cold hard look at what you really want from your career can help ward off the future adversity of discontent.

Assess Your Priorities.   Another vital aspect of analyzing who you are and what you want is to reassess your priorities. Among the priorities (or values) of career people are:

High pay

High status

Job security

Exciting work

Working independently

Doing creative work

Achieving recognition and attention

Acquiring power

Having harmonious relationships with work associates

Avoidance of high pressure and stress

Achieving peace of mind

Sorting out what is most important can reveal some surprises. You might find, for example, that peace of mind is more important to you than high status.

Comeback Scenario 40: Jeff Carson, Technical Manager

Jeff Carson, a chemistry Ph.D., reached such a conclusion after experiencing the adversity of hurt pride. Carson had 30 years of managerial and professional experience with the research and development division of GEMA Corporation. His high level of job performance over the years included substantial innovation. Among his accomplishments were achieving a dozen patents for the company. Carson explains what happened to him and how he handled it:

> After 35 years of working with GEMA, I found myself reporting to someone of lower rank in the organizational structure than I did previously. My department was moved one step down in the company hierarchy after a reshuffling of managers and the departments reporting to them. The reshuffling stemmed from a corporate attempt to squeeze more profits out of the company.
> I had nothing against my new manager. To the contrary, I admired his technical capabilities and personal characteristics. But having a boss with a lower rank hurt my pride and personal vanity. My first impression was that the company lowered my reporting relationship to speed up my retirement, something that I had been looking at with fear and uncertainty.

After Jeff and his wife analyzed the situation intensively, he arrived at the following conclusions:

- The lower reporting relationship did not affect his financial status.
- The issue was not worth his struggling against organizational politics.
- He had to be realistic that retirement is a natural and inevitable process that is a function of time. He was not exempt from aging.
- Somehow he had to work smoothly with his new boss since he is a very talented individual whom Jeff personally appreciates.

The approach Jeff took to overcome this conflict was to conduct a self-esteem reevaluation. He placed vanity and pride at the bottom of the scale after this reevaluation. Concurrently, he placed a higher value on professional fulfillment he moved closer to retirement. Jeff decided to accept his downgraded organizational level and focus his energies on professional fulfillment for the balance of his career.

Bouncing Back Characteristic 54: Change the Behavior that Created the Crisis

Career setbacks, at their best, can be a valuable learning experience. Developing a plan to overcome the problem that led to the setback can often help prevent a similar setback in the future. The underlying problem to some career setbacks is a counterproductive mode of behavior. Counterproductive behaviors include:

- Insensitivity and abrasiveness toward others
- Being too passive and laid back
- Political naivete, such as criticizing your boss in a meeting
- Substance abuse on the job
- Sexually harassing company employees
- A clumsily conducted office romance
- Fighting battles you can't win (such as trying to depose your company president)
- Expense account chiseling

Comeback Scenario 41: Ray Hennessey, Trade Association Manager

Ray, a manager within a national trade association, was overlooked for a vice presidency he wanted. After recovering from the initial shock, he arranged to meet with the director of human resources. The human resources director candidly told Ray the vice president's position needed a person who would push through a program, even if some people were opposed. Ray had been perceived as "too nice, too easygoing, too willing to please." His gentleness and cordiality had worked against him. Other executives in the association believed that a vice president in their organization needed to be assertive and positive in most business dealings. Someone was needed who would tenaciously pursue programs even when faced with opposition.

The conversation with the human resources director paid off because it helped Hennessey realize his career was on hold. He began looking for another job with the mental set of projecting a different image. During interviews he emphasized the assertive and demanding aspects of his personality. He realized that an association executive who appeared too laid back ran the danger of being perceived as a wimp.

Good fortune came Hennessey's way when he landed an association vice president's position at a substantial salary increase. By projecting a more positive image, he convinced the interviewer that he could handle the job in question. Hennessey realized that his level of professional experience and his job knowledge were factors in his favor. However, his being passed over for promotion made him realize that some behavior change was in order.[3]

If Hennessey can incorporate the behavior he exhibited in the interview into his ongoing managerial activities, he will not be passed over again for being too agreeable. The message is that overcoming counterproductive behavior can make a comeback possible.

Comeback Scenario 42: Maurice Hendrix, Engineering Supervisor

Ray Hennessey experienced a major career disappointment because he was not sufficiently assertive. Maurice Hendrix was set back because of the opposite type of behavior. Hendrix explains what happened:

> I obtained my doctorate in physics and engineering from Carnegie Mellon at age 27 and I knew I had it made. I was a black man who graduated in the top 1 percent of my class and offers were still pouring in one year after I graduated. I chose the company that I did because the pay and benefits were outstanding, and Rochester was paradise in comparison to the Philadelphia ghetto I was raised in.
>
> I began with my present employer as an electrical engineer in research and development. I figured I would prove myself in two years, and be promoted to supervisor, and from there into upper management. I expected to head an entire division before age 40.
>
> I was promoted to supervisor by age 32 but subsequent promo-

tions never materialized. I was puzzled after being passed over the first time. I assumed that the decision makers weren't sure I was ready for additional responsibilities. Perhaps they didn't want me to move too fast and fall flat. The second passing over had me enraged and confused. I felt I was being jerked around as the company's token black whiz kid. In a way I was.

Hendrix spent two wasted years after his first promotion resting on his laurels and not publicizing his accomplishments. One of his managers confided in him that he was a terrible communicator whose arrogance created a barrier with others. Thinking through his problems with a senior executive, Hendrix came to realize that his real problem was insecurity. He knew he was one of the best at what he did. He just didn't feel totally accepted so he covered his insecurity by trying to coming across as Superman. Hendrix would point out peoples' mistakes in front of others. Often he would take over subordinates' jobs to get them done faster instead of giving them suggestions on how to perform more efficiently. Hendrix admits that he alienated quite a few people who haven't gotten over it yet.

According to Hendrix's analysis, one of his problems was that Carnegie Mellon did not adequately instruct its graduates on the importance of communicating job aspirations to key people in the organization. Students were given the impression that performance would guarantee promotions. Working relationships and office politics were not emphasized. Carnegie Mellon didn't offer a course in which students were taught to plan and manipulate their career choices.

> After that second promotion got by me [said Hendrix], I approached my supervisor and we had a long talk about my career development and the lack thereof. He took time to sit me down and explain where my personality conflicted with my job and the steps I could take to improve my approach. To bolster my communication skills I took an evening course and worked on ironing out my brashness. I picked up a technique called *conversation simulation* that explains in detail how to empathize with other people. I was certainly short on empathy. The technique forced me to put myself in the other person's shoes and imagine what my reaction would be to a person who approached me as I did others. I can tell you that technique went a long way in straightening me out. I suddenly realized that I was quite insensitive to the impact I was making on others.
>
> I practiced on the people in my area for four months. I subtly gave people suggestions instead of telling them what to do. My approach was to offer help if the person was really in a bind. Otherwise I generally stayed out of people's hair. After everyone decided that I was really serious about improving my work relationship with them, the response was much better than I expected or hoped for.

I also took to keeping a log of what I was going to accomplish, what actually got finished, and the overall status of my engineering group. My efforts paid off in getting projects completed more quickly. The team spirit I emphasized was exactly what the group needed. In order to keep from slipping back into my old arrogant ways I have implemented a group session to get feedback on how I am coming across.

I'm most proud of my efforts in the areas of minority recruitment and training to help women, blacks, and Asians understand exactly what kind of environment they are entering. At the age of 41, one year late [smile], I was promoted to operational manager of the research and development engineering department. That's a lot of words to say I learned how to get along with the right people eventually.

In a nutshell, Hendrix took the pains to overcome his counterproductive arrogance and insensitivity. Consequently he received the promotion he so desperately wanted.

Bouncing Back Characteristic 55: Engage in Creative Problem Solving

An inescapable part of planning a comeback is to solve your problem. Typically an off-the-shelf-solution is not available. Instead you need to search for creative alternatives. In review, a widely used problem-solving method follows these steps:

1. *Diagnose and clarify the problem.* What is the real problem created by your adversity? Are you suffering losses in income, self-esteem, job satisfaction, personal relationships, and well-being (or any combination of the preceding)?

2. *Search for creative alternatives.* What options are open? Many of the resilient managers we have described so far identified a creative alternative solution to their problem. Paul Piccotto, for example, started a business for which he was uniquely qualified.

3. *Make a choice.* If your personal crisis is to be resolved, you must make a tough decision at some point.

4. *Develop an action plan and implement.* What steps must be taken to get out of this mess? You will recall that Don Lennox at International Harvester (now Navistar) took a series of urgent steps to deal with the crisis facing him and his company.

5. *Evaluate outcomes.* Did your recovery plan work or will you have to try another alternative?

Comeback Scenario 43: Jack E. Pfohl, Sporting Goods Store Proprietor

Pfohl, the owner and operator of Valley Sports Center, engaged in the type of creative problem solving that can be repeated by many others. Jack's establishment is a bowling lane and accompanying restaurant. According to industry data, the bowling industry peaked in 1980. Jack notes that HBO, video games, and fitness centers started luring customers away from his lanes in the early 1980s. He also noticed that housewives' leagues were declining because so many women had joined the work force. To intensify his problems, his town was on an economic decline with many former manufacturing employees being forced to switch to low-paying retail and service jobs.

On top of all these unfavorable developments, the strict enforcement of driving while intoxicated (DWI) laws prompted many people to either bowl without drinking or not bowl at all.

Overall, Jack suffered a 30 percent decline in revenues during a three-year period. His establishment was barely breaking even; and the future looked bleaker. Jack estimated that if customer receipts declined another 10 percent, he would be forced to cease operation. One morning Jack took a sheet of paper from a bowling score pad, and began jotting down different methods of increasing the amount of money flowing into his bowling lanes. Of the sensible alternatives that came to mind, one stood out. Why not make an appeal to senior citizens?

Jack took immediate action to initiate senior leagues in the morning, afternoon, and evening. As cash receipts climbed from the senior leagues, Jack implemented more alternatives for improving business. Next, he offered a few family leagues. As the amount of money taken in increased still further, Jack became bolder. He installed a computerized scoring system that automatically recorded the number of pins knocked down on a viewing screen above each lane.

The innovations Jack introduced, along with a streamlining of the restaurant business, have increased income 20 percent over previous highs. Other bowling lanes in his area have been much less successful. Jack analyzes his successes quite simply: "I had to do something different than what I was doing. Implementing one good idea gave me the courage to try others. The biggest risk I took was investing in automatic scoring, and it proved worthwhile as it gave me a competitive edge."

Jack deserves more credit than he gives himself. By engaging in "brainwriting" (jotting down all the alternative solutions to a problem you can conjure up), Jack identified a course of action that brought him the profits he needed for his business to survive.

Bouncing Back Characteristic 56: Become Your Own Crisis Manager

Crisis managers specialize in getting a company through a crisis such as poisoned product reaching the public, a bankruptcy, or a nuclear accident. Several of the techniques crisis managers use to salvage a company can be applied successfully to overcoming a career crisis. The important first step is to gain immediate control of the crisis surrounding you. If laid off, quickly find out the magnitude of your severance settlement. Obtaining a written statement of what is coming to you is important. In some instances it may be necessary to get legal representation to make sure the company has fulfilled its obligations to you. Your lawyer may help you quickly obtain any money you are owed. Haste is important because many companies laying off valuable people are in deep financial trouble. Top management may be purposely delaying payment of all accounts payable, and money owed you is considered an account payable.

An important principle of crisis management is to *explain the problem to the public and employees*. In some types of career crises it may be necessary to make a public statement of your side of the story. For instance, a manager might be forced to leave a company because of alleged financial misconduct or sexual harassment. It is important for that manager to tell friends, family, and perhaps the local newspaper what *really* happened from his or her viewpoint. Such openness is likely to win more supporters than stonewalling the incident. An admission of guilt can also drive away your detractors and gain sympathy from others.

Adept crisis managers *avoid the quick fix*. Instead, they attempt to correct the underlying problem rather than grabbing an immediate solution—such as borrowing money at exorbitant interest rates when faced with a cash crisis.[4] A sounder financial approach would be to cut costs under such circumstances. For the individual, this technique may mean reducing living expenses to meet the current crisis circumstances. Cost cutting may be important because so many career crises include a sudden drop in income.

Many managers and professionals faced with a period of unemployment have had to reduce expenses by such means as cancelling club memberships, taking vacations at home, cutting entertainment expenses to virtually zero, and drastically reducing more expensive foods from the diet.

Comeback Scenario 44: Michelle DeCastro, Account Executive

Michelle, an advertising account executive laid off by a large agency, explains how she survived the five months before landing a suitable new position:

> I was laid off during the advertising agency crunch several years ago. Most of our clients had cut back on media advertising and switched into direct mail advertising or consumer promotions. Two of my biggest accounts went over to competitive agencies. My net expenses were $4,500 per month for my two children and myself. I was still receiving $800 per month in child support, and I had about $6,000 in the bank. Friends suggested I take a temporary job as an advertising assistant to help pay some of the bills while I was looking for a new position. I avoided that approach because working full-time would make it very difficult to find a new position. Even worse, I was afraid it would be difficult to obtain an account executive position again if I let the world know I was willing to work as an assistant. My career began as an assistant, and I thought it would be wise not to return to a lower-ranking position. I therefore opted to collect unemployment insurance, which paid about one third as much as an assistant's job.
>
> My solution was to cut expenses the best I could until I was once again earning a paycheck. The steps I took weren't pretty, but they were effective. My children, Karen and Steve, agreed to pack lunches for school, and to baby-sit, and collect bottles and cans for their own spending money. I made minimum payments on my two credit cards and line-of-credit executive loan. We made no toll telephone calls, and ate all our meals at home. I even asked a man I was dating to take the three of us out to a low-priced restaurant instead of taking me out to a high-priced restaurant.
>
> We walked instead of taking public transportation, and I sublet the car I had been leasing to a business associate who needed a car temporarily. We saved about $40 per month by keeping the apartment dimly lit and cool. I made food in bulk, and we bought no new clothing.
>
> I finally landed an account executive position in a highly creative ad agency that was doing fine despite the downturn in the industry. I still had $750 in savings left. Two happy outcomes can be found to my story. The first is that I learned how to survive a financial crisis; and the second is that I have permanently trimmed some of the fat out of my budget.

Michelle took the drastic measures necessary to cut costs while she searched for suitable employment. Because it is not easy for many people to dramatically trim costs, develop a subsistence budget as a contingency plan.

Stop the Financial Bleeding. When a crisis manager takes over a large company, one of the first things the manager does is to *stop any financial bleeding*. A "bleeder" might be a money-losing unit of the organization. The same technique applies equally well to smaller-scale crises with financial consequences. For example, a store owner might liquidate the inventory in a department that has never been profitable. Or the small business owner might be forced to lay off any sales representative who is not pulling his or her weight.

The individual might apply a compress to financial bleeding by such means as getting rid of income property that is creating a monthly cash drain. Another would be to plug holes in the windows that are consuming fuel used for heating or cooling. It may also be necessary to cancel further contracts for snow-clearing services when you can get by with a few as-needed driveway plowings.

Comeback Scenario 45: Pete Chan, Engineering Manager

An innovative approach to crisis management was applied by a manager whose organizational unit was tapped for relocation by upper management. About ten years ago, General Electric decided to move its semiconductor division from Syracuse, New York, to North Carolina, thereby creating layoffs and some unwanted relocations. Pete, the head of the reliability engineering section, did not want to relocate for personal reasons. He and his family were happily ensconced in their community.

Pete's survival plan was to attempt to merge his group with the electronics laboratory in Syracuse. The lab was conducting exciting research in radar, lasers, infrared cameras, and high speed, semiconductor devices. Pete wrote a report to division management explaining how his group would be more effective working with the electronic laboratory rather than relocating.

Much to Pete's delight, division management listened to his suggestions and incorporated his group into the lab operations. Several members of his group who wanted to relocate to North Carolina were disappointed, but others felt relieved about not having to struggle with relocation. Pete's group is now a very important part of lab operations, and other departments within the lab depend on his support.

Pete was able to keep his work and personal life intact by developing a sensible survival plan and selling it to management. His suggestion of merging his group into the electronics laboratory was especially good because it saved money for General Electric. Creative thinking should be part of your survival plan.

Divest Yourself of Comeback Impediments. Yet another lesson from crisis management is to divest yourself of activities that might impede a comeback. The crisis manager will focus on survival issues, and set aside until the crisis passes such activities as community involvement and new product development. As one manager facing the loss of his business put it, "You need tunnel vision to work your way out of a crisis."

If your company, your financial well-being, or your reputation is at stake, concentrate all your efforts on getting through the crisis. Cut family and social life down to the minimum necessary to maintain your relationships. Devote just enough time to relaxation, exercise, and entertainment to keep your stress level within manageable limits. Cut back on community activities unless they might serve as a source of contacts for helping you fashion your comeback.

Bouncing Back Characteristic 57: Redirect Your Career to Meet a Family Crisis

Deft planning may be required to adjust one's career plans to cope with a family crisis. At times the adversity faced by the family is a continuing financial need. In these circumstances, cost cutting alone will not take care of the problem. A new career direction may be necessary. For example, having triplets may be a joy, but caring for three new family members simultaneously would create financial adversity for most couples.

Comeback Scenario 46: Preston Carter, College Dean

Preston, the dean of the liberal arts college within a small university, faced a family crisis that required him to redirect his career. His third child, a daughter, was born with spina bifida, a protrusion of the vertebrae that requires repeated surgical procedures and other extensive medical care. Although the dean had medical insurance, the uncovered portions of his medical expenses were still extensive. He enjoyed his deanship, but it became apparent that he could no longer support himself and his family on a dean's salary.

In order to elevate his income to meet his expenses, the dean took several major steps. As a licensed psychologist, he had a small counseling practice. He began to increase his client load by letting potential sources of referral know that he had more hours available for consultation. He telephoned or arranged luncheon' meetings with six physicians, five clergy persons, three social workers, and four lawyers. The dean explained to each person that he was hoping to expand his private counseling practice in order to meet the substantial medical expenses he was incurring for his daughter. The dean also carefully explained the type of referrals he thought he was best qualified to handle, such as depressed adults, marital conflicts, relationship problems, and sexual dysfunctions.

He also intensified an interest in managing real estate by purchasing a four-family house to use as rental property. During the next year his medical expenses mounted, but his private practice increased, and he was able to purchase a two-family house with a modest down payment. Next he purchased a small suburban office building from an owner who was facing bankruptcy. The dean offered to purchase the building for no money down except to pay for the former owner's closing costs. The down payment would be met in the form of a second mortgage paid over a six-year period. The former owner would then become the holder of both the first and second mortgages.

Soon his private practice and his real estate dealings began to interfere with the proper conduct of his deanship. He therefore resigned from his position as dean, but retained a faculty position. As a professor he was paid about 10 percent less than the deanship, but he had more time to pursue other activities. His combined income from his faculty position, the practice of psychotherapy, and real estate management was soon high enough to cover all of his family expenses.

Rather than being disgruntled about what has happened to him, this man is thankful that he was able to readjust his career to take care of his family obligations.

Nonfinancial Adjustment. Responding to a family crisis can sometimes require a career adjustment other than increasing income. Such is the story of a woman who had worked her way up the human resources ladder from personnel assistant, through personnel supervisor, to assistant director of wage and salary administration at her company.

Comeback Scenario 47: Sue Hastler, Child Care Center Operator

While Sue was a personnel supervisor she gave birth to her first daughter, Katie. After Katie was a year old, the doctors discovered that she had hearing and learning disabilities stemming from a birth defect. Despite these problems, Sue reasoned that she could continue holding down her job and care for Katie. During the day, the child would attend a special day care facility.

As assistant director, Sue had heavy responsibilities and worked longer hours than in her previous position. When her second daughter, Megan, was born, Sue entertained the idea of shifting to a less demanding job. Her thoughts along these lines intensified after Megan was tested for hearing and possible learning disabilities. The diagnosis came back that Megan suffered from the same genetic disorder as her sister.

Sue and her husband agreed that she should find a less demanding position in order to give her more time for parenting. She resigned as assistant director of personnel to stay home with her daughters and conduct a job search for a position that gave her more flexibility.

Several months after Sue resigned, a former coworker, Pat, asked Sue if she would be interested in opening a day care center. Pat and Sue would be partners, and Sue's children would be able to be with her and the other children at the same time. Sue looked upon running a day-care center as a good opportunity to make use of her business experience and education (MBA), yet be available to help her daughters during the day.

After researching the market, Pat and Sue decided to open a child care center. They rented space inside a private school and advertised for both employees and customers. Pat and Sue hired one experienced child care worker and one trainee, and opened their doors for business. After four months, the center actually broke even. After one year, the profits from the center were still thin but Sue felt that she had made the right adjustment to a difficult family situation. Sue shifted from corporate employment to self-employment in order to accommodate her children's need for more contact with her.

Part of the reason for Sue's success in coping with adversity is that she sorted out her priorities. It was apparent to Sue that her children's welfare was more important to her than corporate success. Consequently

Sue developed a plan for earning a living that would allow her to give her children the care they needed.

Bouncing Back Characteristic 58: Reestablish the Rhythm in Your Life

People become more dependent than they realize on the natural rhythm of their lives—the daily routines they establish for themselves.[5] Commuting, answering mail, logging in on the computer, attending staff meetings, drinking coffee, telephoning friends, reading the news-paper, watching current events on television, showering, having sex, and jogging are but among the many activities managers and profes-sionals need to feel healthy and alert.

People have different activities in their routine, but most accom-plished people have a consistent pattern to their daily pattern of living. Break those routines for a considerable period of time, and the individ-ual is liable to suffer depression.

One of the most disconcerting aspects of career adversity is that the person's life loses the rhythm it has acquired. I first experienced this phenomenon about five years into my career. The most uplifting part of my job those days was working with a major client that I had at-tracted to the firm. For over one year I spent almost every Thursday on this client's premises. Suddenly the president of the client's company questioned the value of my services. His vice president of personnel in-formed me that from that time on the company would use my services on a "spot basis." I knew that meant I would never hear from the com-pany again.

Feeling discouraged and dejected, I then spent my Thursdays at the New York City office of my firm, doing work much less glamorous than being on a client's premises. My exciting routine (surprisingly some rou-tines can be exciting) was disturbed. Full-time consulting had suddenly lost its appeal for me. Not until two years later when I took on the as-signment of opening a branch office for the firm, did I overcome the psychological loss of losing that client.

The lesson to be learned from the importance of rhythms in life is to do what is necessary to maintain your daily pattern of living when faced with adversity. For example, job counselors urge unemployed people to arise at a regular time everyday and get to work conducting their job campaign. We mentioned earlier that it may be necessary to trim ex-penses to meet the financial circumstances facing you in a crisis. Never-theless, do not neglect reading the newspaper, exercising, or watching the evening news—if these are an important part of your routine. Telephone calls (toll free) to business associates should also be conducted as regularly as in the past.

Faced with a career crisis, many people reach out more than ever for emotional closeness with friends and family. Such reaching out for human contact is doubly important. It provides the emotional support so urgently needed in times of adversity, and also retains the human contact that is part of many people's routine. Conversely, people who withdraw from others during a career setback face the dual problem of lack of emotional support and a major disruption to the rhythm in their lives.

Bouncing Back Characteristic 59: Be Open to Unplanned Comeback Opportunities

Despite the virtues of any type of planning, it does have important limitations. Above all, if planning is followed too rigidly it can inhibit your spontaneity and prevent you from pursuing goals that were not incorporated into your planning. Keep in mind that a comeback opportunity may arise from an unexpected source. A real estate developer had built a group of luxury homes on small lots. Although beautifully constructed and appointed, they sold quite slowly. The developer needed to sell one more house to stave off bankruptcy. Returning from a business trip to raise some funds, the developer initiated a conversation with a passenger seated next to her on the airplane. The traveler was an executive moving to the developer's city. Interested in settling into town as quickly as possible, he proved to be the purchaser of the one more home the developer needed to stave off bankruptcy.

Comeback Scenario 48: Tony Falco, Shop Proprietor

The story of Tony Falco, the owner and operator of a ceramics shop, is a more complicated example of how serendipity can power a comeback. Tony had noticed that sales were decreasing while the number of ceramics hobbyists had increased. His shop was larger than most in the suburban area he served, and the quality and selection of his merchandise was also notably good. Tony was perplexed as to why his sales had declined and decided to analyze the source of his difficulties.

Tony's first step was to visit his competitors to uncover the reason he was losing market share. He noticed that these other stores were selling only a limited selection of molds, but the ones they did stock were in high demand. This marketing technique kept their overhead low and their prices down. Tony observed that these molds were standard items, and could readily be ordered from the manufacturers in Atlantic City. If Tony ordered the same molds as his competitors, he still would have to sell them at a higher price because of the large inventory of molds he maintained. Tony was hesitant to divest his full line of molds, fearing that he would lose the uniqueness of his store.

Tony knew he had to operate differently in order to stay in business, but he couldn't think of the right solution to his dilemma. One afternoon the solution came to him quite unexpectedly. A shipment of molds arrived from Atlantic City, with a freight cost of $300. Annoyed at the high shipping price, Tony muttered to himself that it would be cheaper to drive to Atlantic City and bring back the molds himself. When Tony ordered molds again, he did make the trip himself.

While visiting the manufacturers in Atlantic City, Tony discovered that there were many new molds that came out after the catalogs were printed. He had found the special edge he was looking for. He now could offer for sale new molds that his competitors did not stock. Because most ceramic hobbyists do comparative shopping, Tony quickly increased his customer base to the point that the survival of his business was no longer at stake.

Although the comeback of Tony and his ceramics shop did not capture the attention of reporters from *Business Week,* it has an important message. Just keeping in mind that you need something special to trigger your comeback may make you receptive to an unplanned opportunity that does the job.

Action Tips

To sum things up, effective comebacks usually require a game plan or roadmap. The planning that you need to plot your comeback is best accomplished after you have worked through the emotional turmoil surrounding your adversity. You are then ready to take such constructive action steps as analyzing the reasons behind your setback, analyzing who you are and what you want, and engaging in creative problem solving. Incorporate the following suggestions into your game plan:

1. Analyze the reasons behind your setback.

2. Analyze who you are and what you want.

3. Change the behavior that created the crisis.

4. Engage in creative problem solving.
5. Become your own crisis manager.
6. Redirect your career to meet a family crisis (if needed).
7. Reestablish the rhythm in your life.
8. Be open to unplanned comeback opportunities.

7
Capitalizing on Adversity

Despite its downside, adversity has much to offer. The vast majority of managers and professionals we spoke to learned a lot from both the adversity they faced and the adjustments they had to make in response to adversity. Most breakthroughs in business have taken place when a courageous individual searched for an innovative solution to a major problem. For example, many entrepreneurs conceived of their businesses when they faced the adversity of being squeezed out of their corporate job.

You can improve your chances of making a comeback, now or in the future, by squeezing something out of every adverse situation. The something you squeeze out could range from sharpening your problem-solving skills, to making a career out of helping others overcome the adversity you faced. In this chapter we describe some of the positive aspects of adversity.

Bouncing Back Characteristic 60: Personal Growth Possibilities in Adversity

Adversity helps people develop their intellect and personality. The intellect includes such things as mental alertness, creativity, and decision making. Personality refers to such things as self-confidence, compassion, risk taking, and a feeling of power. A securities sales representative whose client activity plummeted to 20 percent of its typical activity after the crash of 1987, made this comment:

> Before the crash, I guess I was just hard-working and lucky. After the crash I really learned how to hustle, and how to take good care of my clients. I gradually brought my volume back up by showing clients how I could help them make investments whose value was not so dependent upon the whims of the stock market.

Dealing with adversity is a learning experience. Above all, people learn from dealing with adversity. When their livelihood and prestige are at stake, people learn to call on inner resources they never thought they had. The opposite is also true—when things are running too smoothly, people may not feel impelled to learn new ways of tackling problems. Rich Levin, a Century 21 real estate broker, makes this point.

> The best motivator in our business is for an agent to be faced with a major financial problem. If an agent purchases a car he or she can't afford, the agent will hustle like crazy to earn enough to make those payments.
> One of our agents lost a bundle in the stock market by purchasing penny stocks with borrowed money. When there was no market for selling some of the stock to meet payments on the loan, he faced possible bankruptcy. Instead of panicking he scrambled to get some new listings and to consummate a few pending sales. You could see the gleam in his eyes as he came to work.

We develop improved problem-solving skills. Faced with adversity, people often become more innovative than in a tranquil situation. A good illustration of this phenomenon is found under the system of zero-based budgeting, used in both government and business. Its basic premise is that no unit of the organization is guaranteed a permanent life. At the end of each year, the manager of the unit must explain why his or her group should be funded for another year. If the manager's reasoning is rejected, the unit is abolished. Faced with this type of potential disaster, the manager will usually provide a well-reasoned explanation of how the unit contributes to the good of the total organization.

Our self-confidence increases. Surviving a career crisis is a great confidence builder. Hyatt and Gottlieb contend that having failures early in life is an important contributor to career success. They think failure is so important that children should be given their parent's permission to fail: "Learning early that you can survive defeat makes you tougher and more resilient for the rest of your life."[1]

We learn compassion and humility. Having experienced a significant career setback is a humbling experience. Typically the survivor becomes more sensitive to the problems of other people who have suffered reversals and also more tolerant of their mistakes.

Comeback Scenario 49: Joseph Biden, U.S. Senator

Senator Joseph Biden of Delaware is an excellent case study of a person who learned compassion and humility from adversity. In 1987, Biden withdrew from the presidential race amid a storm of controversy about his exaggeration of his academic record and his alleged plagiarism of a speech from a British politician. After withdrawing from the race, Biden returned with renewed vigor to his responsibilities in the Senate, including a key role in hearings about the Intermediate-Range Nuclear Forces (INF). He is now Chairman of the Judiciary Committee.

Biden openly accepted responsibility for most of the mistakes and misjudgments that led to his withdrawal from the race. He described himself as "cocky," "immature," and "naive," about the demands of a presidential campaign. The path Biden chose to overcome this adversity was working to gain respect for achieving outstanding performance in his present job.[2]

We develop a new perspective on risk-taking. After having experienced an overpowering setback, many people become averse to risk taking.

Comeback Scenario 50: Brian Strauss, Attempted Entrepreneur

Several years ago a manager left the Hewlett-Packard Company to establish his own electronics firm specializing in the development and manufacture of laser printers. His would-be company never became operational. He was unable to obtain sufficient funding, he could not hire the right talents, and he could not sell any products without even a prototype available. Heavily in debt, he put his tail between his legs and asked to be hired back at Hewlett-Packard in whatever position they had available. Based on his nine years of outstanding performance in the company, HP rehired him (but in a nonmanagerial role).

Asked to evaluate his experience, the engineer said, "I've learned my lesson. I thought I could leave the nest and soar like an eagle. Instead,

I got into the air but then quickly dropped to the ground and landed on my belly. I appreciate my job at HP more than ever now. I have no intention of ever again risking my life savings and my house on a new business venture. Job security has become very important to me."

Setbacks Are Emboldening. In contrast to the above engineer, many people are emboldened by a significant setback. The person who survives a catastrophe may develop a positive attitude toward risk taking. "If I could start out from scratch before and survive, why not try it again?" Also, if your failure is big enough, people still admire your ability to manage something big. For example, many executives who were in charge of a major business loss readily find new employment at the same level.

Taking an example from the seedy side of enterprise, many operators of "boiler room" scams who are put out of business by the authorities, simply move to another town and start again. We refer in particular to companies that offer too-good-to-be-true travel or merchandise bargains over the phone.

We have the chance to sort out our values. Experiencing a career crisis helps many people realize what is *really* important in life. In some instances a politician who lost a landslide election may return home and appreciate more than ever the emotional support received from the family. The career reversal still stings, but it becomes vividly clear that the family is more important than a career. Perhaps in the future, working 90 hours per week on a political campaign at the risk of becoming emotionally detached from the family is not sensible.

Adversity and the struggle to overcome it can sometimes make people more religious and spiritual. Because they have relied on religion to get through the tough times, they upgrade the value of religion and downgrade the value of external success. Worldly success may still be important but it becomes outranked by religious values. Upgrading the importance of religion in one's life is part of the process of reexamining one's life in the midst of significant setback. An executive who survived an airplane crash in Los Angeles said, "My career as well as my entire life was almost snuffed out in ten seconds. I survived while many others didn't. My faith in God is now one of the driving forces in my life."

We become more introspective. Another way in which coping with adversity strengthens our intellect is that we often become more introspective. We learn to examine what our role was in the crisis we encountered. The introspective manager might ask, "What was it about my presentation that led top management to withdraw funding for my department? Did they smell a rat? Was I deceptive? Have I overstated the contribution that my department is really making to the organization?"

Another way of being introspective is to reflect upon how well we handled the adverse situation. Looking backward the person might conclude, "I handled the situation well. I was cool under pressure and did what had to be done to prevent the total collapse of my career." Or introspection might bring forth a negative diagnosis: "I handled things poorly. I panicked. I didn't ask the right people for help. I ignored all the little signs that a crisis was on its way. If I had acted sooner, I would have emerged from the crisis in much better shape."

Bouncing Back Characteristic 61: Welcoming that Rock Bottom Feeling

A convoluted, yet effective, way of capitalizing on adversity is to be happy when you hit rock bottom. Once you accept the fact that things cannot get worse, you are mentally prepared for a comeback. Oddly enough, the stress of things being so bad that they can only improve sometimes brings on a temporary euphoria. One explanation is that people laugh at how bad things are as a way of relieving tension.

When you are truly convinced that your problems have bottomed out, you are preparing yourself emotionally for a recovery. That nothing-else-can-go-wrong feeling helps mobilize your energy to begin your counterattack.

Comeback Scenario 51: Warren Kirwin, Company President

Warren, the president of a small company, has used this technique on more than one occasion. The spirit of optimism that underlies his rock-bottom technique has pulled the company through hard times on more than one occasion. To illustrate, one day Warren turned to his administrative assistant and said,

> Cheer up, Mary. It looks like we have finally hit the bottom of the barrel. From now on, things are going to get better. We have laid off half of our work force, our business has shrunk 45 percent this year, and our new computerized order system has caused us endless problems.
> The future looks better. Business conditions are improving, and

the people in the company are mostly our better employees. It's a good feeling to know that things won't get any worse.

Stock market speculators have intuitively used this rock bottom strategy for many years. An experienced investor attempts to purchase stock at its lowest point. To that investor, something hitting bottom is a signal of good news—assuming the prediction about bottoming out is correct.

Positive Mental Attitude. The rock bottom feeling technique is indirectly related to developing a positive mental attitude. Once you are convinced that things cannot get worse, you are prepared to begin thinking positively about the future. Today many managers welcome the news that their companies have completed restructuring. It could mean that bad times have finally bottomed out, and worries about job security lessen.

Bouncing Back Characteristic 62: Acquiring Business Savvy from Mistakes

"We learn from our mistakes," said your teachers, parents, athletic coaches, and other people who tried to console you. Many of the managers and business owners we spoke to applied this principle in order to capitalize on job adversity. These people had learned specific lessons that enhanced their business acumen, and that will help them prevent repeating their mistakes. Although some of these mistakes could have been avoided if the managers had paid careful attention to accepted principles of management, they needed a painful lesson to personalize the information.

Comeback Scenario 52: Dave Perlman, Engineer

Dave was a bright engineer employed by a large firm. While working with two other engineers in a development laboratory, the three began to experiment with ultrasonic detection. Soon they realized the potential for the application of ultrasound technology to the manufacture of burglar alarms. All three resigned from their employer to go into business for themselves. During its first two years of operation, the fledgling company was beset with many problems. The most overwhelming of these were the lack of appropriate financial backing and limited knowledge of how to market their product. The company folded and the trio went back to work for their employer.

Toward the end of two years of reemployment, the three engineers decided to give the burglar alarm business another try. Although polite about the matter, their employer assured the engineers that they would never be hired back again. As things worked out, the engineers did not have to worry about burning their bridges. The ultrasound company made it the second time around.

Perlman explains what he learned from his company failing the first time around:

> When we first set out on our own in the burglar alarm business, there was unequal say in the decisions due to unequal financial commitments. We had no capital other than our individual savings and numerous personal loans. So we had no margin for mistakes. However, we were very confident of the design of our product and our business abilities.
>
> The business went fine in the first year, but in the second year we ran into a production problem that we could not afford to solve. Consequently the company folded and the three of us were out quite a bit of money. However, we learned some very valuable lessons from these disastrous mistakes.
>
> Our second venture was launched only after a number of conditions were met. First, everyone had an equal vote because everyone's future and reputation were involved. Second, a financial expert was hired as a consultant. He made an important contribution by locating a venture capitalist to invest in our company. Third, and most important, we devised a plan to set up and run the company. By adhering to this plan, the company finally became successful.
>
> I spent many 80-hour weeks on engineering problems. After approximately one year, the fruits of our hard work finally began to materialize and we started to show a profit. I believe strongly that having a formal plan the second time around made the difference. I cannot emphasize enough the fact that you should always have plans if you want to succeed. In a little over seven years, my associates and I have turned our small business into a $15 million company.

Dave Perlman and his associates capitalized on adversity by learning about the importance of formulating and following a business plan. A setback also teaches other lessons about running a business.

Comeback Scenario 53: Bill Doan, Computer Store Franchisee

Bill learned valuable lessons in human resource management from his business setback. Several years ago, four of the top sales representatives at his Computerland store left to form a franchise within the same city for Entre Computer company. As a result, sales at Bill's store plunged severely.

Bill got to the root of the problem immediately. Two exit interviews revealed that the sales representatives who left were disturbed over management's failure to recognize their needs for job growth and high compensation. To their thinking, operating their own franchise outlet offered more opportunity for satisfaction.

Bill's recognition of the problem was too late to stop the loss of market share to the newly formed Entre store for the moment. However, he thought he could control the future. He developed a job progression ladder for sales representatives, and a compensation plan that offered higher commissions for more senior sales representatives. The job satisfaction of the newly hired sales reps appears satisfactory, and Bill Doan's Computerland store narrowly escaped extinction. Over a two-year period, sales have gradually crept back up to the level they were before the four sales representatives jumped ship.

The adversity created by the turnover of key personnel reminded Doan to pay more careful attention to human resources management. His new compensation plan should prove valuable in reducing turnover and the havoc it can wreak on a small business.

Bouncing Back Characteristic 63: The Hidden Opportunities Within Adversity

A potent way of capitalizing on adversity is to look for its hidden opportunities. (In one way or another all of the bouncing back characteristics or tactics relate to this idea.) Don King, the flamboyant boxing promoter who has engineered comebacks for his fighters and himself, makes this comment about finding good opportunities when things have gone wrong: "I've eradicated 'failure' from my vocabulary. Sure, at times my faith in myself waivers. But I know my talents will grow if I have the courage to keep using them. I've found all my jewels in adversity."[3]

Managers who specialize in turning around crises are often adept at reaping financial gain from negative circumstances. Following the stock market crash of 1987, many chief financial officers (CFOs) directed their firms to capitalize on the sudden downturn in stock prices.

The Merits of a Fall in Stock Prices.   When stock prices fell, bonds rebounded creating opportunity in the midst of adversity for many firms.

Eastman Kodak Co., raised $300 million in four-year notes at an interest rate of 8.84 percent. The Kodak treasurer took the opportunity to replace some short-term adjustable-rate debt with fixed-rate debt (at 8.84 percent). Around the same time, Consolidated Natural Gas Co. sold $100 million in five-year debentures at 9⅛ percent—a rate they considered quite favorable.

A more widespread tactic for capitalizing on hidden opportunity was for corporate treasurers to buy back stock at bargain prices. Executives at IBM spent about $1 billion repurchasing its shares. Executives at Olin Corporation bought close to 300,000 shares of its own stock. The advantages of a company purchasing its own stocks include stabilizing prices for the stock and taking advantage of good values. For instance, when the stock market rebounds, the company can sell the repurchased stock at a sizable profit.

Although the financial transactions just described relate more to corporate than individual adversity, they are indirectly tied to the welfare of individual managers. Financial officers who cannot help their employers get through adverse times may suffer some adversity of their own.

Taking Ownership of an Unwanted Organizational Unit. Another application of finding hidden opportunities within adversity is when a manager moves an unwanted unit outside the organization. Following this technique, a manager whose new product group is dismantled by the company may decide to quit the firm and start a new company to make the new product.

Comeback Scenario 54: Ron Gindick, Used Computer Specialist

Ron, a middle school teacher, applied this gutsy technique within the context of his organization. Gindick's position required him to coordinate all the computer operations and classes taught within his district. He enjoyed his job and he performed well. His position, however, was jeopardized because of budget cuts. Local taxpayers decided that too much money was being invested in new computer equipment. (This situation occurred before computers became so entrenched in middle school education.) As a result of the budget cut, all facilities dealing exclusively with computers were abolished along with Ron's position. He was reassigned as a regular teacher who taught four math courses per day.

Recognizing that computers were not going to be used for the foreseeable future, Ron planned and reacted quickly. He applied for a low interest loan and purchased the computers and related equipment from the school district. Next, he refurbished a spare room in his basement to serve as headquarters for a used computer equipment business. Ron's business prospered enough for him to resign his faculty position, effective the next school year.

In addition to generating a living from the business, Ron was able to claim one-fifth of his housing expenses as a business deduction. He also was able to spend more time with his family than he had while working for the school system.

In commenting on what he accomplished, Ron said, "I'm not the risk-taking type. At least I wasn't until the computer budget was slashed. I am confident now that if in the future, something comes up that seems like misfortune, I would be able to turn it into something profitable."

Ron Gindick, similar to other people whose stories are told in this chapter, spotted an opportunity in the midst of adversity. You too can capitalize on adversity if you are aware of the fact that it may contain hidden opportunities.

Bouncing Back Characteristic 64: Salvaging Your Mistakes

A variation of finding the hidden opportunities within adversity is to salvage what you can from a mistake you committed personally. An amusing off-the-job application of this principle took place when a manufacturing supervisor constructed his own built-in swimming pool despite the admonitions of his wife and two close friends. His cement pool was esthetically sound, but structurally unstable. During its first winter it developed two massive cracks. Feeling temporarily defeated, and somewhat humiliated, his first thought was to remove the pool. His substitute course of action was to fill the pool with dirt and make a flower garden. His choice received the spirited cooperation of his wife. The enjoyment he and his wife now derive from the flower garden exceeds the enthusiasm they had for the pool during its brief period of functioning.

On-the-job mistakes are not as easily salvaged as an improperly constructed pool, but the underlying principle remains the same. Salvage what you can from a job reversal. At times an imaginative solution will be required to complete the salvage operation.

Comeback Scenario 55: Craig Oliver, Financial Analyst

Craig, an ambitious 29-year-old, worked as a financial analyst for a large company. Having heard much about the importance of being well rounded in order to become an executive, he pulled strings to obtain a transfer to the marketing research department. Both Craig and his new boss were quite pleased with the result. Craig was making a contribution to his new department and obtaining valuable experience in the process.

Then came the budget crunch after Craig's employer was bought by another company. Craig's boss told him that because he was the last hired into the department, he would have to be the first fired. Craig's old boss informed him that there was a freeze on adding any more people to the financial division. Craig then went back to his marketing boss asking if there was anything at all he could do to stay in the market research department or marketing division. His boss said, "The only thing I know of is a sales territory in the north country. They just lost their fourth sales rep this year. Go speak to the sales manager with my blessing."

Craig was told that he could have the sales territory but at a 20 percent reduction in pay. Craig reasoned that the job could give him good experience and that the income he received from the job would be better than no income. Craig endured in the job for two years, at which point he was offered a position as supervisor of financial analysis. The manager of the financial division of the company reasoned that Craig was more valuable than ever. His sales experience in a tough territory had made his financial judgment more astute.

Craig had truly salvaged his mistake of having transferred into a job that lasted only a few months. Many people would have quit in disgust rather than patiently working out a solution to the prospects of being laid off.

Inventory Remarketing.   The principle of salvaging your mistakes underlies *inventory remarketing,* whose purpose is to find a new use for a failed product. The failed product is a major adversity to the manager in charge of product development. The new use for the product represents the hidden opportunity. A classic example occurred when Crown Zellerbach, the forest products company, took some of the waste for its paper processing operations and shaped them into pellets. The pellets were bagged and then marketed as Discreet brand cat litter.

The cat litter met stiff resistance from its end users. Relatively little liquid was absorbed by the litter and most cats would not go near it. The cats that did picked up a fine black dust and tracked it all over their owner's dwelling. (A mistake was obviously made in not field testing the litter.) An inventory remarketing firm called Tradewell industries bought all 4.3 million pounds of the cat litter. To salvage the mistake of a failed product, the litter was sold to racetracks and horse farms as a sawdust substitute.[4]

Bouncing Back Characteristic 65:
Hanging on to the Good
Part of the Past

Adversity, setback, or failure always involves a loss. As described earlier, the losses can be separated into three categories: self-esteem, money, and status. The sting of adversity can sometimes be ameliorated if part of the loss can be regained. A germane example occurs when a distinguished professor retires. The loss in status and self-esteem may be substantial for a person who delighted in carrying the job title "professor." The most distinguished of these retiring professors are awarded the title, "professor emeritus," thus preventing a substantial loss in status and self-esteem. The professor emeritus thus capitalizes on the negative circumstances of retirement: He or she retains the status of a distinguished professor but now has more free time to pursue professional and personal interests.

Comeback Scenario 56: Marshall
Infantino, Wrestling Coach

The career decision of Marshall, a former high school wrestling coach, represents a feasible application of the principle of hanging on to the good part of the past. Marshall was a full-time coach but did not have a faculty appointment. After three years of good performance, including two undefeated seasons, he was dismissed because a faculty member at the school wanted his position. Marshall was hired under the condition that he would be replaced if a qualified coach who was also a teacher wanted his position. The school's budget for staff could not be expanded to create a job for Marshall.

Although not bitter, Marshall was hurting. Coaching young athletes brought him considerable personal satisfaction and pride.

> I knew about midway through the season that I was going to be fired. It was really hard to accept. I felt bad for myself but I also felt bad for the team because of the coach the school had hired. I knew the guy was a loser. My judgment was right. The guy was so terrible he was forced to resign at the end of his second season.
>
> I had to decide what I was going to do. I could have gotten the coaching job back, and I would have been able to keep it if I completed my bachelor's degree. I decided against that because of my age and the fact that I had a family to support.
>
> I was attending a wrestling tournament when a coach from another school asked me if I ever thought about selling insurance. I looked into it, and the potential for making good money was definitely there. My reasoning was that if I could convince someone to

lose 30 pounds to make weight for a wrestling tournament, I could probably convince people to buy insurance.

I accepted the challenge, and did quite well selling life insurance and related financial services. I became one of the highest producers in my region. I am making more money now in one year than I did in all my seasons of coaching. The only thing that bothered me about leaving the coaching was my love for the sport. That is why I became a referee for wrestling matches. I still get to see all my old friends, and I get to see good wrestling. I couldn't be happier.

Bouncing Back Characteristic 66: Becoming an Adversity Specialist

A growing number of people are capitalizing on their own adversity by helping others overcome the same adversity they faced. You overcome your own adversity by showing others how to conquer theirs. The phenomenon of capitalizing on adversity by making a career out of showing others how to do it, takes many different forms. Some former drug addicts become drug counselors, some former alcoholics become alcoholism-counselors, and a few former shoplifters conduct seminars on how to control shoplifting. A former bank robber from California now gives seminars to bank employees on how to foil robbers. He took up this occupation upon his release from prison.

Capitalizing on adversity by becoming an adversity specialist can also be done by managers, professionals, and business owners. A case in point is a woman who left hospital nursing because of dissatisfaction with pay and the extent of her decision-making authority in patient care. Burned out and disgruntled, she had to find another way to earn a living. Her solution was to conduct seminars for disgruntled nurses on how to make a career switch.

The underlying principle to the adversity specialist technique is the basis for a classified ad that offers a surefire technique of making money through classified ads. The kit costs only $25. When the kit arrives, it instructs you to place a classified ad that offers, "A surefire technique of making money through classified ads." You charge $25 for your kit!

Comeback Scenario 57: Joseph P. Genera, Van Modifier

An ethical and positive application of becoming an adversity specialist is the accomplishments of Joseph P. Genera of New Haven, Connecticut.

In November 1982, a car being serviced in his father's garage fell off a lift and struck Genera, breaking his spinal cord. "It broke me in half, literally," he said. Genera is now in the business of modifying vans and cars for the physically challenged. Established in 1986, his company is called Independence Van, Inc. "As much as I hate being in a wheelchair, it gave me insight as to what disabled people go through and what people need," said Genera.

About two years after the accident, Genera was hired by Trans Vans, a Danbury, Connecticut, a company that also modifies vans for the physically disabled. Genera's size-up of the market indicated that another such company in New Haven would fill a geographical gap in the market. By means of personal financing, bank loans, and help from the New Haven Community Investment Corp., Genera raised $60,000, and set up shop in a 6,000-square-foot garage.

The company has four full-time employees plus part-time help. The basic work of Independence Van is to modify vans and cars for physically challenged people who want to drive them or travel as passengers. Another service is to install luxury items in vans for both able-bodied and disabled people. The specialized equipment includes a lift that gets the wheelchair user in and out of the vehicle. Another is a floor section in the driving area that can be elevated or lowered to give the driver in a wheelchair a good line of vision.

Other specialty equipment includes hand or arm controls for the brakes and accelerator, as well as a steering gear that can be operated with one hand. Some of the controls are for people who are physically challenged by arm or leg injuries but are not wheelchair users. Genera said, "The biggest thing that people need to know is what avenues are open to them. There are lots of people out there who can drive even though they don't."

One of Genera's projects was to outfit a van with a lift for wheelchair. "The man I modified the van for hadn't been out of the house for seven years. His wife couldn't handle getting him and his chair in and out of a car anymore," said Genera. "He has a whole new sense of freedom. It gave him back a sense of normalcy."

Potential customers are advised by Genera to check first with the Department of Motor Vehicles. The bureau will help physically challenged people determine whether they can drive, provide driving lessons, and give them an operator's license. A modified van can cost up to double the price of a standard one, which could restrict the number of people Genera can help. He points out, however, that the state education department's Division of Rehabilitation Services will pay for the modification if the van or car is used for work-related transportation.

Genera is so intent on helping people that he will drive to a potential customer's house if that person has difficulty leaving the home. "About half the time I will talk to them about the vans. The other half is a lot of interrelating. For one thing, we see eye to eye," he said.

A senior counselor with the state rehabilitation services is very pleased with the quality of services provided by Genera's firm. She said, "Joe Genera is very prompt. He has been wonderful working with my clients. He has just really gone out of his way to make equipment recommendations that are very appropriate."

Genera believes that his business will be profitable. His attitude, however, is expressed this way: "This isn't a business where I can become a millionaire and that's not the reason I went into it."[5]

Joe Genera is achieving an important type of success—doing well by doing good. He is helping people with the same type of physical challenge he experiences. Genera also exhibits characteristics and traits of other resilient people, such as an indomitable spirit.

Helping People with Similar Setbacks. A variation of becoming an adversity specialist is to donate time to helping other people who have encountered setbacks similar to yours. However, you do not switch occupations.

Comeback Scenario 58: Bill Bush, Ethical Resistor

One such person is Bill Bush of Huntsville, Alabama. Bush is accurately classified as a whistleblower or "ethical resistor." He lost his position at the National Aeronautics and Space Administration (NASA) for reasons he thought were related to his age, not his job performance. After successfully challenging age discrimination in the human resource policies of NASA, Bush was reinstated. Nevertheless, he was given a position that included fewer tasks and resulted in an increasing sense of alienation. Instead of resigning, he has become heavily involved with what he terms "his family of whistleblowers."

Bush is now the hub of a complex national *network of former whistleblowers*. He maintains a computer file on hundreds of workers who have challenged ethical and legal violations by their employers. Bush receives frequent calls from dissenters for information, advice, and emotional support. He capitalizes on every opportunity to inform Congress, the media, watchdog agencies, and scholars about people in trouble for being dissenters.

Despite his suffering during years of isolation within NASA, he feels he has vastly improved the ethical quality of his life: "In spite of the avalanche of hatred I brought upon myself, I learned for the first time the pleasures of assisting others in trouble. My associates began to confide in me about their concerns, personal and public. Helping others and participating in nonviolent activism are personally more rewarding than selfishness and passivism."[6]

Bill Bush thus capitalized on adversity by helping others who have experienced the setback he experienced. Bill feels better about himself because he is doing something socially responsible. Perhaps you might find a creative application for this technique should you experience career adversity.

Bouncing Back Characteristic 67: Stay Productive in the Midst of Confusion

Mergers and acquisitions usually create problems for the combined company. The confusion begins as rumors fly prior to consummating the deal. After the combination is completed, the real trouble begins. An American Management Association survey of 54 merged companies found widespread evidence of:

- Loss in worker productivity
- Loss of market share
- Lesser profitability
- High employee turnover.[7]

You can capitalize on this organization-imposed adversity by remaining calm during all the turmoil. Others around you will be fawning over key decision makers, finding ways to back-stab people they don't like, and looking for new employment on company time. You will need to engage in some self-protective behavior also (as described in Chapter 2). However, a good way of capitalizing on the adversity is to stay calm and productive. If you are calm and productive, you do not have to use servile flattery to impress higher-ups. Of course, neither should you become politically insensitive.

Demonstrate to top management that you can help the corporate ship weather the storm created by the takeover. While the place seems to be falling apart, devote as much time as necessary to help patch things together. But make customers or clients your number one priority. The people in power who are sincerely trying to make the merger work will be impressed by your tenacity and coolness under fire. Consequently, the self-imposed corporate adversity will boost your career.

Action Tips

In quick review, stay alert to opportunities to capitalize on adversity. With adversity swirling around you, have you:

1. Searched for the personal growth possibilities in adversity?
2. Welcomed the rock bottom feeling?
3. Acquired business savvy from your mistakes?
4. Found the hidden opportunities within adversity?
5. Salvaged your mistakes?
6. Hung on the good part of the past?
7. Become an adversity specialist?
8. Stayed productive in the midst of confusion?

8

Getting Some Quick Results

In addition to making short- and long-range plans to rebound from adversity, it is usually necessary to grab some quick results to stop the downhill slide. Being your own crisis manager could be considered a short-range strategy. Many other ways of treating the symptoms of career adversity also exist. "Treating symptoms" means that you take immediate actions to overcome adversity without necessarily conquering the underlying problem. One person who did this is a resort comedian who was getting fewer and fewer bookings. He looked upon his loss of popularity as a career crisis. The comedian's agent told him that it was difficult to book him because so much of his material was sexist, racist, and generally out of tune with the times.

After several discussions on the topic, the comedian decided he would gradually change his image. The immediate action the comedian took was to work for half his former fee. Because he was working, his self-esteem was patched a little. During his many hours of spare time the comedian worked up some new routines that were less stale and discriminatory. He thus was treating the cause of his problem. Soon he got a few more bookings at his regular rate, and his career was back on track.

Bouncing Back Characteristic 68:
Take Direct Action to
Handle Problems

The all-purpose principle of managing adversity is to take direct and constructive action toward resolving the problem facing you. Taking direct action is particularly applicable to obtaining immediate results to help you weather a crisis. A company that does mass mailings for magazines and advertisers committed a large blooper in handling one of its largest accounts: It sent out hundreds of pieces of mail with a mismatch between the addresses on the envelopes and letters. For instance, an envelope addressed Ms. Dolores Wing might contain a letter addressed to Ms. Evelyn Wingate. The error was caused by an unintentional human mistake of mixing up the order of a large batch of envelopes, but the client was irate. The president of the letter company was concerned about both losing his major account and tarnishing the reputation of the quality of his services.

The president took immediate action to rectify the situation. At no expense to the client, he ran a corrected mailing of the envelopes and letters. The following insert was enclosed in each envelope:

> Recently you received a letter which is the same as the letter enclosed. You may have noticed that your name and the address on the letter and envelope did not match. This was due to an inadvertent (the letter company forgot to use an electronic spell check) mistake by one of the employees when matching and inserting the letter. We regret any inconvenience this may have caused and we apologize for the mistake.
>
> Sincerely,
>
> Apex Letter Company

The client was happy with the patchwork done by the letter company, and not one addressee lodged a complaint about the mix-up. Aside from being a good adversity-management tactic, sending out the apology letters was morally correct. Admitting one's mistake and then rectifying it is thus an effective way of getting quick results to combat adversity.

Comeback Scenario 59: N. Douglas Mazza, Automotive Executive

Another example of dealing with a crisis head-on rather than waiting for it to blow over took place at American Suzuki Motor Corp. *Consumer Reports* magazine had published information that Suzuki's hot-selling Samurai rolled over during quick maneuvering. The results of this test were broadcast on most television news shows in the United States and Canada. *Consumer Reports* wanted Suzuki to stop selling the Samurai and to buy back the 160,000 of the vehicles on the road. News about the alleged rollover problem spread so rapidly that it became the butt of a bumper sticker joke. A number of Samurais were observed with bumper stickers attached upside down, stating, "If you can read this turn me back over."

More bad news piled up fast. Samurai owners filed several class action suits. One sought full refunds or compensation for the decreased value of the vehicles caused by negative publicity. Another suit alleged that American Suzuki and its advertising and public relations agencies marketed the vehicle fraudulently by masking its dangers. Filed under the Racketeer Influenced & Corrupt Organizations law (RICO), the suit could result in heavy punitive damages.

From the moment it heard about the *Consumer Reports* press conference about the rollovers, the Suzuki crisis team, headed by general manager N. Douglas Mazza, swung into action. The team set up an advertising and public relations blitz. Mazza made the decision to purchase advertising time on the next night's network news shows, reasoning that would most probably report the rollover story. Advertising specialists reissued an ad full of published praise of the Samurai.

The night before the *Consumer Reports* press conference, Suzuki executives publicly declared they would respond. A satellite hook-up was set up to beam Mazza's answers to TV stations. With the assistance of the company's public relations firm, Mazza was on the air four hours later. Although not all stations accepted the news-related ad, Suzuki ran it nightly at a cost of $1.5 million in ten days. Mazza explained, "It's expensive. But what choice is there?"

The next direct action Mazza took was to conduct a press conference showing vehicles made by other companies flipping over. The ad blitz continued for over one month after the *Consumer Reports* release. "We're not going to sit back and hope this crisis will go away," said Mazza.[1] Six months after the crisis, Samurais were still on the road and sales had crept back up. One dealer in upstate New York said, "I think all the publicity has actually helped sales. We get a number of curiosity seekers in our showroom who then become attracted to the sharp-looking Samurai."

We don't know if Mazza is correct that *Consumer Reports* made unjustified negative reports about the safety of the Samurai. Whichever side of the issue represents the truth, Mazza's direct action helped himself and his company weather severe adversity. Tackling an adverse circumstance head on is a winning tactic.

Bouncing Back Characteristic 69: Take the Punch and Get Back On Your Feet

"My motto is take the punch and get back on your feet," says Steven Shussler, a man who has experienced poverty, misery, and a great comeback in the nightclub business.[2] Shussler's attitude is a good way of getting some quick results, just as a prize fighter must do who wants to make a comeback within a fight. The mental attitude implicit in "taking the punch" is that you are willing to absorb some punishment in order to reach your goal. Because you accept punishment as an inevitable part of competing, you do not get discouraged when it occurs. Instead, you return immediately to pursuing your goals.

Comeback Scenario 60: Louis L'Amour, Novelist

L'Amour, the famous writer of westerns, has amassed incredible successes in his field. Approximately 170 million of his books are in print around the world. L'Amour achieved so much fame during his career that he was dubbed "Mr. Western." His books in domains other than westerns have also achieved considerable success. Nevertheless, L'Amour faced considerable rejection early in his career. His attitude and behavior were always the same—he would return immediately to his typewriter and try again. L'Amour didn't have the time and financial circumstances in those early years to stew over his reversals. "I got rejection slips like you wouldn't believe," L'Amour says. "I just couldn't quit. When you're knocked down, you get up. Lots of times, when you get up, you win."[3]

Bouncing Back Characteristic 70: Fight Fear by Facing It

"Fight fear by facing it" follows the same logic as "take the punch." Returning quickly to the situation that brought you adversity is a form of reconditioning or desensitization. You learn to overcome the fear associated with the adversity by placing yourself back in the fearful situation. When used as a form of psychotherapy, you return to the fearful situation in a very gradual manner. If you were involved in an auto accident and now feared driving, your first step might be to simply sit behind the wheel of a car for five minutes. You fight fear by facing it.

Comeback Scenario 61: Adele Barnes, Purchasing Agent

"Fight fear by facing it" can also be used to obtain quick results. Adele, a purchasing agent, dreaded speaking in front of a group. Because the group would be judging her performance, Adele regarded public speaking as a highly competitive situation. Realizing that her career might be blocked if she could not overcome this fear, Adele enrolled in an effective speaking class in an adult education program. The day finally arrived for Adele to give her presentation.

Catastrophe of all catastrophes, Adele stood speechless in front of the class. Her mind went blank with respect to all the things she had prepared to say. The instructor recognized her problem as stage fright and gave Adele the sage advice, "If you sit down and relax, your thoughts will return. If you prefer, you can wait until the next class to present your talk."

Adele sat down immediately and analyzed what was happening to her. She reasoned that if she left this class today without speaking, she could never face them again. Adele entertained thoughts of running to the registrar's office and dropping the course. Toward the end of the class session, Adele made her commitment to give the talk. Somehow her fright diminished enough for her to walk to the front of the class. This time her words flowed freely.

Adele's effort to overcome her fear of speaking proved successful. She finished the course as a reasonably adequate speaker. Today she is able to make a presentation as her job sometimes requires. Had Adele not remounted the horse that threw her, she might have developed a permanent inhibition about making presentations. Try directly facing a situation that is fearful to you.

Bouncing Back Characteristic 71: Take One Last Desperate Shot

Faced with a loss in the last seconds of a basketball game, a coach's attitude toward reckless behavior changes drastically. The coach will grant permission for one of the players to take a last desperate heave at the basket. If the shot doesn't make it, the team loses, as it would have without the shot. If the shot goes through the hoop, the player, team, and coach are all lauded for their great comeback. The same principle applies when you need some quick results to bounce back from a grim situation.

Comeback Scenario 62: Harold Johnson, Sewer Specialist

One man successfully applied the last desperate shot tactic to achieve economic salvation, and found gold in the gutter.

Too broke to enter a small-stakes poker game, Harold "Curly" Johnson sat down to watch because he didn't want to go home and face the family he could no longer support. The former commodities trader from Oklahoma City was down to selling space part time in the yellow pages. After a decade of struggle, he jumped at the chance to sell commodities. "I was good at B.S.," he says. "But I was too confident." When the market shifted, Johnson let his losses mount, and was fired. He became bitter. "I thought everyone was against me."

At the poker game, Johnson met a man whose sewer-maintenance franchise in Texas had gone bust. Fed up, he sold it to Johnson for all he had—a dollar. Now Johnson owned a worthless sewer company. His life had become a bad joke. Suddenly Johnson didn't see it that way. After months of negativity and despair, he had actually been presented with an opportunity. He saw salvation in the sewer.

Johnson rushed home and begged his wife and two daughters to leave Oklahoma City, go with him to San Antonio, and run a Mr. Rooter franchise. "My family took it in stride," he says. "And I stopped complaining and telling people my troubles." They scraped together $5,000 and left Oklahoma City. At last report Curly Johnson owns three plumbing and sewer-maintenance companies with net sales of $2.5 million.[4]

The last desperate shot Johnson took was to operate a sewer maintenance franchise. Becoming a Mr. Rooter franchisee (not affiliated with Roto-Rooter) was a desperate shot because Johnson had no experience in the field and gambled his last family money. However, becoming a franchisee is usually a much less desperate shot than starting a new business because of the advertising support and training provided by the franchiser. You too should have a last-ditch tactic in mind in case everything is going wrong.

Comeback Scenario 63: Al Copeland, Fast Food Chain Operator

A man who went into competition with a well-known franchiser provides another illustration of how taking a last desperate shot can be an effective comeback strategy. Al Copeland of Louisiana went into head-on competition with Kentucky Fried Chicken and was severely trounced. The episode began in 1962 when Copeland's brother, the owner of a chain of Tastee-Donut shops, gave him a franchise in Arabi, Louisiana, as a wedding gift. The young Copeland ran the store successfully for three years until a Kentucky Fried Chicken outlet opened across the street.

"I was working around the clock," said Copeland, "watching the chicken people work eight hours a day and earn twice as much as me."

He decided to compete with Colonel Sanders by creating a tastier chicken recipe. "For the next six years the deep cooker in the kitchen was always going. My wife was frying chicken at 3 A.M. And the kids got sick of eating that bird. Friends loved the spicy Cajun recipe I finally came up with, but they convinced me it wouldn't sell."

Consequently in 1972 when Copeland opened Chicken on the Run, he chose a milder recipe. The choice proved to be a mistake that forced him to close shop seven months later because of poor business. Copeland then rethought his dream of becoming a fast food mogul. "I was $12,000 in the hole and thought maybe I don't know a damn thing about the chicken business. But I wasn't about to deal doughnuts in my brother's shadow forever. Besides, I couldn't get chicken out of my mind."

Copeland then took down from the shelf his spicy recipe, and three days after closing Chicken on the Run, he reopened as Popeye's Fried Chicken. The last desperate shot proved to be a winner. Demand surged for his Cajun-style chicken in Arabi. Today Popeye's is a growing chain of close to 600 stores in 35 states.

"The first day I hung out that Popeye's sign, my wife said, 'That's a crazy name.' I told her I wasn't going to be like Colonel Sanders or anyone else. I told her she had to believe in me."[5]

Copeland's last desperate shot was his spicy chicken. All else had failed, so it made sense for him to try his last idea. Besides he already had the restaurant and equipment. Hopefully you won't have to use this tactic, but keep a last desperate shot in mind.

Be Willing to Accept Some Job Slippage. Despite the acute labor shortage facing the United States and Canada, many managers and professionals who face the adversity of job loss have difficulty finding a comparable position. A major underlying factor is that many of the jobs going begging are in low-paying jobs in retailing and the service sector. The Grand Union food chain may desperately need more employees — but they are short of cashiers, not regional managers. Hewlett-Packard may have a critical need for skilled machinists and tool and die makers, but the company is not in short supply of plant superintendents. Many unemployed managers and professionals who want to return to work quickly must therefore accept the possibility of some job slippage, another name for being underemployed.

Comeback Scenario 64: Jim Montimerano, Plant Manager

What happened to Jim, a 54-year-old former plant manager, is typical of the problem. As a result of his dedication to his job, Jim rose from a production worker to a manager responsible for the operation of all the plant's assembly lines. He was proud of the status he achieved as a manager. Jim was laid off after 38 years with the same company because of a corporate merger. Jim steadily searched for a job for five months, assisted by GROW, a support group for middle-aged job seekers. "After the fifth month I felt like I was just washed out," he said. "You wake up in the morning and you wonder why you bother to get up. You just don't feel like you're a whole person. Maybe it was just the way I was brought up, but sometimes I don't feel I deserve to eat at the table."

During the five-month search, Jim said he applied for 350 jobs from production management, his area of expertise, to private detective work. At one point he made 75 phone calls in two days of searching for a job. Jim finally found a position as a sales associate in a home improvement supply store at one-third his former pay. "The job was a killer. We were expected to help set up the entire store in addition to taking care of customers. After working there a few months, a buddy of mine who worked for a small manufacturing company helped me get hired as a production coordinator."

Four years later Jim was still with the same company and had been promoted to purchasing agent. His salary is now 60 percent of what it was before he was laid off. Jim sizes up his job in these terms, "It isn't perfect, but at least I'm working. A lot of people my age who were laid off never found anything."[6]

Jim suffered too long before finding employment. He was willing to accept job slippage, but it took a long time for him to make the proper connection. He believes strongly that his advanced age made it difficult for him to find employment.

In the economy of the 1990s many people will achieve quicker results than Jim did by accepting a lesser position now and worrying later about working back up the occupational ladder. The risk in accepting a lesser job, however, is that your new employer may perceive you as being content to work at the rank at which you were hired. Many managers who accept nonmanagerial positions find that it is difficult to be promoted back into management. Yet if you need quick results to stave off financial disaster, accepting job slippage may accomplish the job.

Comeback Scenario 65: David Fico, Appliance Stores Operator

David is the president and owner of a small chain of appliance stores in Orange County, California. At a crisis point in his career he took an entrepreneurial approach to job slippage that staved off a career disaster. He began his venture into home appliance sales in 1976. Business was going well for him until 1978 when his geographic area suffered devastating rains and flooding. His store was located at the base of a large hill. The rains washed away part of the hill, collapsing the back wall of the store and covering everything inside with three feet of mud.

Because his insurance policy did not fully cover this type of damage, Fico faced bankruptcy. Instead of accepting this fate, he went into quick action to save his business, his credit, and his reputation. By borrowing whatever funds he could from his family and friends, he was able to pay back his creditors and avoid bankruptcy.

Fico still did not have enough capital to start another store, so he did what he considered to be the next best alternative. Fico began repairing appliances out of his home, after preparing a list of leads from his previous customers. Business grew steadily enough to cover David's basic expenses, but he wanted to expand more rapidly. His creative idea was to place a classified ad in the Orange County edition of the *Los Angeles Times,* offering to buy an appliance repair business. By chance, a man who was about to give up his appliance repair business and move to Florida, saw the ad and responded. For $1,500, Fico was able to purchase the man's established business of over 200 customers and his business phone number.

The quick results David Fico obtained from job slippage (going from store owner to appliance repair technician) were parlayed into substantial long-term results. He was able to pay back the money he had borrowed from friends and family and had enough capital to start another appliance store. Through hard work and persistence, Fico now owns several appliance stores and operates the largest appliance repair service in Orange County. If necessary, be willing to accept job slippage in order to regain your career thrust.

Part-Time Self-Employment. A lesser version of entrepreneurial job slippage is for the resilient person to engage in part-time self-employment while working out a longer-range solution to career adversity.

Comeback Scenario 66: Marlene Fitzpatrick, Business Consultant

Marlene worked for a management consulting firm as a specialist in helping small firms establish financial controls. She traveled about 75 percent of the time in order to serve clients and drum up new business. Returning from a getaway weekend with her boyfriend, she was in a serious automobile accident. She suffered a broken leg and a fractured pelvis. Her boyfriend survived the accident with lacerations of the face and skull. Marlene's leg was not mending properly, so her surgeon decided that it had to be rebroken and reset. Marlene faced at least a six-month period of time in which she would be unable to engage in business travel. She also faced reduced-income, and perhaps a period of time in which she would no longer be covered by disability benefits.

After three months of frustration, Marlene took some job slippage both to improve her mental health and to stave off pending financial problems. She became a self-employed income tax preparer operating out of her apartment. Marlene generated her first clients by calling friends, acquaintances, and placing a classified ad in a suburban newspaper. She also invested in a tax preparation computer program. The clients she attracted were mostly people with uncomplicated tax returns. It took a year for Marlene to gain the physical strength and agility she needed for heavy travel, at which time she returned to her firm.

In reviewing her experiences, Marlene says: "I'll never forget my days as a public tax preparer. People seemed to enjoy coming to somebody else's apartment to have their taxes prepared. They appreciated the informality and the low rates. Everybody treated me so kindly when they saw that I was mobility impaired. If I stayed in the tax preparation field, I would want a more elegant set-up. The happy little business solved a lot of problems and I think I helped a lot of people. I'm proud of the fact that I never encouraged anybody to cheat the IRS and that I would challenge any deduction that appeared suspicious to me."

Marlene accepted job slippage temporarily in order to survive. In doing so she challenged the assumption that the only way she could generate income was through her regular occupation. Ask yourself, "If I were unable to work at my regular occupation for awhile, what else could I do to earn money?"

Bouncing Back Characteristic 72: Get the Team Pulling Together

Collective effort is often required to overcome a crisis faced by a manager. For example, David Fico needed swift assistance from his employees to deal with all the problems associated with the mudslide ruining his store. Another example is when a manager faces a crisis created by zero-based budgeting. It may be necessary to pull together key members of the department to brainstorm a proposal that will convince upper management of the department's contribution to the organization.

Unless the team is mobilized to experience a sense of urgency, obtaining quick results will not be possible.

Comeback Scenario 67: Robert Knapp, Computer Store Manager

A computer store manager effectively used collective effort to prevent financial disaster. In Wappingers Falls, New York, on a Saturday afternoon in early November 1983, fire broke out in the wicker furniture store adjacent to and in the same building as Computer Systems Specialists (CSS). The fire started in the back storage area and swept rapidly through the store partially because the wicker furniture is covered with lacquer and paint. A CSS sales associate was returning from lunch when she noticed the smoke billowing out of the adjacent store. She immediately alerted the store employees and customers.

After all customers were evacuated, the store employees made several trips back into the burning building to retrieve computers, software, and important store records. No other salvaging of inventory was possible. By the time the fire department trucks arrived, CSS was an oven of heat and black smoke.

Several weeks prior to the fire, the owner of CSS had rented a similar size store that was used exclusively as office space. Robert Knapp, Jr., the vice president and store manager, decided to bring over to the other store all the salvaged office records and computer equipment and software. Over the objections of the fire chief, one of the store employees retrieved the keys to the store that Knapp kept in his desk drawer.

After the keys were located, Bob rented the largest Ryder™ truck available to move the salvaged records and merchandise to the new store. Bob shouted out to the group, "We need all the help we can get from any member of the CSS team. Anyone who is willing to help estimate the damage and salvage equipment is welcome to stay the night."

In a few hours the entire store staff was on the scene helping to estimate the consequences of the damage. It was apparent that everything left behind was destroyed. The heat, smoke, and water damage melted the plastic wrapping around the software and covered the exposed computers with acidic smoke.

The next morning the CSS team met at the new location. Bob and the owner, Scott Quimby, informed the staff that it was their intention to reopen the store in the new location within one week. Bob told the staff, "With the total cooperation of everybody on the team, we can still get back in operation for the Christmas season. If we aren't open for the holiday season, we'll go out of business. So let's all get ready for a true fire sale."

The task appeared monumental, considering that the new store site was just vacant space without even carpeting or painted walls. Bob made arrangements Monday morning for the telephone and burglar alarm companies to install temporary systems in the new location. The insurance claims examiner estimated the damage to be around $175,000.

In one day the CSS staff rebuilt 2,000 square feet of office and sales space from scratch. With the help of employees and their friends and relatives, the new location was cleaned and painted in one day. Carpeting was installed the following day. During the day the carpeting was installed, and the employees cleaned the salvageable furniture and fixtures from the old store. The furniture and fixtures were transported and installed in the new store that night. By Friday a new sign was placed over the front of the store.

With 12-hour days the norm, the following Monday the store reopened in the new location with a limited selection of merchandise. Over the next few weeks stock shipments arrived but a settlement with the insurance company was not reached until the following March. A store employee who played a key role in the reopening of CSS made this analysis:

> Throughout this ordeal Robert Knapp had faith in his employees' ability to rise to any challenge. We rebuilt in one week, and I was not the only one to work 80 hours. Bob was there the entire time, giving us the direction and leadership we needed to avoid going out of business. We had the best Christmas season in the store's history. CSS weathered the storm and I was proud to be part of the team.

Robert Knapp overcame adversity by using one of the most important managerial techniques for achieving results through people—pulling the team together. Mobilizing collective effort in the form of teamwork is a winning strategy for overcoming adversity faced by a group.

Bouncing Back Characteristic 73: Make a Tough Business Decision

"Tough-minded management" endures as a popular buzzword in business. The term implies that a manager takes whatever actions are necessary to solve an important problem, even if the decision may be unpopular or even if it hurts some people. A tough-minded manager also has the courage to make a decision of any type that is necessary for the survival of an organizational unit or the entire enterprise. Tough business decisions are a powerful method of achieving quick results when faced with adversity. Tough business decisions must be made by managers of modest-size enterprises as well as larger ones.

Comeback Scenario 68: David B. Weatherup, Security Fencing Manufacturer

David Weatherup (who has an ideal name for an adversity manager) went heavily into debt when recession hit his twelve-year old builders supply company 20 years ago. The firm itself had a satisfactory level of sales but with the business downturn, many builders who owed it money went bankrupt.

Weatherup could have filed for bankruptcy, but surrendering clashed with his value system. Instead he looked around for a business in a stable market to pursue. Based on his intuition, he decided on security fencing and almost immediately started Central Fence. Weatherup paid his debt off in three years and gradually built his new company into a $2-million-a-year enterprise with 50 full-time and seasonal employees. Central Fence is in the top 5 percent of a field dominated by small businesses.

Central Fence is now "more than just a fence company," as one of the slogans on its stationery states. It sells electronically controlled gates, alarms, television monitors, and all the other components of a total security system.

Weatherup was accustomed to dealing with adversity from an early age. His father, a farmer who supplemented his depression era income as a district manager for Maytag, died in an accident. David's mother became the family provider for him and his two siblings. Trained as a social worker before her marriage, she obtained a caseworker position with the county welfare department. She supplemented her income by selling Maytag washing machines evenings and weekends.

Weatherup remembers his family would take the back seat out of the sedan to make room for washing machines to be delivered. His mother would do such innovative things to make them happy as trading a washing machine for a pony.

Weatherup's work in the lumber business, including an assignment as a sales manager, assured him that he was ready for self-employment. He convinced a large manufacturing company that its interests would be served well by allowing his prospective company to be the central

New York outlet for its cedar building materials. With some capital of his own and credit from the manufacturer, Weatherup launched Central Builder's Supply in 1957.

Asked how he coped with the recession that indirectly led to the demise of his business, Weatherup said he was reminded of one of his favorite sayings: "Success is spelled W-O-R-K, and the only place where success comes before work is in the dictionary." Hard times in the industry simply meant that, "I went back to work and found a new direction."

Security fencing seemed to be the logical choice. Stepped up highway construction created an additional demand for fencing by highway contractors. Weatherup's informal research also discovered that no local fence company was in the area—only the Cyclone Division of United States Steel (now part of USX). Weatherup had thought to himself, "If you're going into this, you might as well challenge the biggest one."

He also made the tough business decision of taking on work no other company wanted. "We always look for the most difficult jobs—for example, special cages that may be 30 or 40 feet in the air and that somebody else will say cannot be built. We do not know any better so we build them." Weatherup's style of tackling adversity has influenced the thinking of his employees. He says his employees just don't understand the words, "You can't do it."[7]

If you are facing adversity, keep in mind the tough idea of taking on business no one else wants to work on. The undesirable work could be a difficult assignment or a whining customer.

Comeback Scenario 69: Rich Moet and Tom Johnson, Service Station Owners

Tough business decisions made to stave off disaster are sometimes legally questionable. Before implementing such a decision, it should therefore be scrutinized by a lawyer familiar with the appropriate legislation. One such quasilegal business decision involved two service station owners. Rich Moet owned and operated a Mobil station on the opposite corner from Tom Johnson's Gulf station. Every time Rich lowered his price, Tom would lower his by another two cents. What started out as price competition became a price war.

Rich was concerned about what to do next. He was already rapidly heading down toward his break-even point. If he lowered his prices any more he would be selling gas at a loss. On the other hand, if he did not lower his prices he would lose a major share of his business to his competitor across the street.

Rich figured that Tom was probably facing a similar dilemma about profits and potential lost business. Although they had become virtual enemies, Rich phoned Tom and asked him if he would like to meet and discuss the problem of price competition and squeezed-out profits. The two met late one night at a nearby diner. Shortly into the conversation, it became apparent to Rich that Tom also was close to not earning profits from gasoline sales.

Rich and Tom reached a tough business decision that brought then quick results. One would call the other every Monday to set the price that both were going to charge for gas that week. The two also agreed to set a price that would give them a reasonable profit margin. Customers who now wanted to choose between the Mobil and Gulf stations would have to base their decision on some factor other than a price differential. Rich and Tom continue to fix prices to their mutual satisfaction, and both have avoided a business collapse due to selling below cost. (Price fixing, as referred to here, is an agreement among two or more competitors to set the same price for their goods or services. In this way, neither competitor has a price advantage over the other.)

We are not recommending price fixing as a solution to business adversity. But we are recommending that you be strong enough to make the difficult decision needed to spark your comeback.

Bouncing-Back Characteristic 74: Pull Off a Dramatic Achievement

When the organization is about to create adversity for you, one way to ward off disaster is to make a dramatic achievement quickly. Your show of quick results may trigger a change of heart among the decision makers about to strip you of power or remove you from the organization. An illustration of this principle took place in a large bank. Top management was about to downsize the human resources department and move its reporting relationship down one level. The director of human resources was indignant and angered. She quickly tied up loose ends on one of her department's most important activities—minority recruitment. In one week her department pinned down letters of acceptance into its management training program from four hispanic, three black, and two Asian college graduates. Top management then decided it had "reevaluated the importance of the human resources function" and would only reduce the department by attrition. And the department wad not moved down an organization level.

152

Chapter Eight

Comeback Scenario 70: Darryl Carpenter, School CFO

A more complex example of pulling a dramatic achievement to combat adversity took place in a developmental center for mentally disabled children. Darryl, the chief fiscal officer of the school, had gotten into trouble with the head of the school and the board of supervisors. The problem was that the school operated with a deficit rather than the promised surplus. The board of supervisors was furious because they needed funds from the school to cover a deficit of their own, thus ensuring reelection for another two years.

Motivated partly by an interest in diverting attention away from their own deficit, the board of supervisors publicly announced the school's deficit. They also called for Darryl's resignation, pointing to his inaccurate budget projections and his poor work habits. (Darryl admitted he had a procrastination problem that resulted in delays of key projects.)

As the weeks passed, the public pressure to force Darryl to resign grew. Feeling both pressured and frightened, Darryl formulated a short-term financial plan that eliminated the budget deficit. It included such maneuvers as not heating the swimming pool, investing funds in high-yield commercial paper, repairing and refinishing rather than replacing school furniture, and consolidating some resources with another school. The board of supervisors then softened their demands for Darryl's resignation. Instead, they took the position that they would carefully evaluate Darryl's long-range financial plan before recommending further action.

Darryl thus earned himself a stay of execution by pulling together a short-range financial plan that satisfied his boss and the board of supervisors. He was then able to work on the underlying problem of his poor work habits that contributed to his inaccurate budget projections. His dramatic achievement to achieve some quick results was his short-range financial plan. If you need some quick results to overcome a setback, look for something quick and dramatic, such as a big sale or a cost-saving idea.

Bouncing Back Characteristic 75: Cash in on Your Good Reputation

A career person's reputation is a major asset that can determine how readily adversity is overcome. A reputation based on years of good service will bring you the support of others when faced with a reversal. A city manager awarded a contract to a construction firm that had built her summer home for an unusually low price. The local newspaper demanded an investigation, implying that an ethical violation had been committed. At first it seemed as if the manager's career was at stake. In reviewing the case, the city council decided that the woman had used poor judgment but had really done nothing unethical or illegal. A major factor swaying their judgment was the clean record the city manager had established during her past ten years of service.

Comeback Scenario 71: Harry Malek, Bakery Owner

A good reputation is also an important asset to the self-employed person who faces career adversity. Harry operated a successful neighborhood bakery on the south side of Boston. His business was doing well, and he was supporting a wife and three children despite "crazy hours and a lot of time on my feet." After a difficult start, he was confident he had established a stable business.

In the cold predawn hours of a day in January, disaster struck. Harry's bakery went up in flames. "What wasn't burned beyond recognition was ruined by smoke and water. Everything was gone—my supplies, my equipment, my store."

The day after the fire Harry analyzed his predicament. His casualty insurance did not fully cover his loss, but he knew that he still wanted to run his own bakery. As he tells it, "I really had no choice. I had to find a way to start over in the bakery business."

Upon analyzing what he had left after the fire, Harry concluded that one of his most important assets was his zeal for paying bills on time. His analysis proved correct. Harry located a sensibly priced, vacant building two blocks from his old location. It was larger than the old store, and it needed work, much of which Harry believed he could do himself.

Harry negotiated a 20-year mortgage with his bank, with an option to prepay, using part of his insurance settlement for a down payment on the building. Harry then approached his suppliers, one by one, and offered small down payments on orders for new ovens, baking equipment, store fixtures, and baking supplies. He also requested that his payments begin six months after the bakery reopened. Harry reasoned that six months would give him time to regain his former customers and enough cash flow to live on and make debt payments. Within two months Harry was back in the bakery business at his new location. He recollects, "I was exhausted, more in debt than at any time in my life, but still an independent businessman. It made me feel good that being so fanatical about paying debts in the past helped me get back up on my feet when I needed it."

Harry's bakery actually fared better after the fire. With a larger building he was able to install additional ovens and hire a second baker. With his enlarged facility, he began to think of ways of expanding his business. In talking over his expansion plans with customers, he realized there was an untapped market for specialty cakes in his neighborhood. With a baker working for him, Harry now had time to experiment with creative baking. His bakery quickly developed a reputation for making beautiful wedding cakes.

As Harry sums up his experience of rebuilding his bakery, "I wouldn't want to go through it all again. But you never know what you can do until you have to. I was amazed at how soon after the fire I was back in business."

Harry had really begun his comeback long before he faced adversity. The good credit record he had established over the years enabled him to obtain favorable terms from the bank and suppliers after the fire. Similarly, the reputation you are establishing now will help you enlist the support of others to help you overcome any future adversity.

Bouncing Back Characteristic 76: Take Collective Action

Individual action typically brings quicker results than collective action — the time required to make a decision multiplies rapidly as additional people are consulted. Exceptions do exist. Used appropriately, collective action can lead to quick results in overcoming a threat of disaster.

Comeback Scenario 72: William Steinrotter, Ski Area Operator

Steinrotter, the chief executive officer and owner of Brantling Ski Slopes, Inc., in Webster, New York, chose collective action to overcome his business adversity. A few years ago Steinrotter faced a catastrophic season because the snow fall was way below average, and the temperature was usually too high for making snow. Business was so poor that Steinrotter was running out of money. Facing one warm day after another, the ski resort owner knew he had to act quickly to ward off bankruptcy. Steinrotter contacted other ski resort owners in New York State who were also suffering from limited snow. He and the other owners petitioned the state legislature for low-interest loans to tide them over their rough season.

The legislators were sympathetic to the group of independent ski owners because the ski resorts owned by New York State faced a similar problem. Legislation was quickly passed enabling the owners to obtain low-cost loans. The loans were processed quickly enabling Steinrotter to stay solvent for the year. Next, he attacked the underlying problem—snowmaking equipment that could not be used to make snow at temperatures above freezing. Steinrotter contacted a company that was experimenting with snowmaking equipment capable of creating snow at above-freezing temperatures. The company sent out the new equipment for Brantling to try out at no charge. The new process created enough snow to salvage the last part of the ski season, and Steinrotter minimized his losses for the year. He purchased the new equipment for the next season and has kept it permanently.

Steinrotter's handling of adversity is significant because it communicates an important lesson. He first took constructive (and collective) action to achieve quick results, and then resolved the underlying problem once the wolf was away from the door.

Bouncing Back Characteristic 77:
Show How You Fit into
the New Culture

One of the major stumbling blocks in making a takeover work is melding the cultures of the two firms. For example, the acquiring company might value risk taking, innovation, and flexible policies and procedures. In contrast, the acquired company might be much more traditional and slow moving. Its key players—without admitting it publicly—might prefer to take low risks, stick with the familiar, and rigidly adhere to rules and regulations. Dress is another way in which the two cultures might differ. Managers in one of the combined companies might dress in the traditional, conservative mode. Managers in the other company might dress more flamboyantly.

Whatever major cultural differences you find, it is to your advantage to show that you can fit in with the culture of the takeover (not *taken* over) firm. If you are perceived as a misfit, you might be quickly added to the expendable list.

Comeback Scenario 73: Saul
Silverman, Company Controller

Saul was the controller of an electronics company bought by Honeywell. He explains how he dealt with the situation:

> I didn't fit the stereotype of a typical controller. Our company believed strongly in spending money to make money. Rather than

looking for ingenious ways to not spend money, I helped our product development people find money to fund new ventures. We were a free swinging crew, who knew how to spend money and live well.

When it became apparent that Honeywell would be our new parent, I quickly sized up their culture. They are a very conventionally run outfit with tight financial controls. Somehow their conservatism has contributed to their success. When the Honeywell people came around, I changed my tune. I explained how important innovation was to our company. Yet I also pointed out that I thought we could still be innovative with a more disciplined approach to spending money.

Don't think I was duping Honeywell. I can live with different corporate philosophies, so long as I don't have to engage in any dishonest business practices. My adapting to the Honeywell style paid dividends. Within one year, I was appointed as controller of my old company and another company that was folded into ours.

Saul's political astuteness helped him prosper in the takeover. He sized up the new corporate climate, and then changed the emphasis of his operating style to fit the new culture. Saul thus survived without substantially sacrificing his values.

Action Tips

Faced with severe adversity you often need to obtain some quick results in order to jump start your comeback. Choose among tactics to get off to a fast start:

1. Take direct action to handle problems.
2. Take the punch and get back up on your feet.
3. Take one last desperate shot.
4. Be willing to accept some job slippage.
5. Get the team pulling together.
6. Make a tough business decision.
7. Pull off a dramatic achievement.
8. Cash in on your good reputation.
9. Take collective action.
10. Show how you fit into the new culture.

9
Climbing Back Into Power

Power is highly valued in the workplace. Consequently, losing power badly affects one's self-esteem. To lose power, in the eyes of many, is to be less worthy than previously. Losing power also creates adversity because executives crave power, and effective executives are the most power-hungry of all. Losing power for many people therefore leads to humiliation and frustration. An important aspect of rebounding from adversity is climbing back into power.

The tactics and strategies described next can help a person regain the power lost through such means as a demotion, being ignored by upper management, or being assigned a drastically reduced budget.

Bouncing Back Characteristic 78: Earn Back Your Reputation

One way to understand how to climb back into power is to look into a worst-case scenario—earning back one's reputation after being stripped of power because of illegal or quasilegal activities. President Richard M. Nixon is perhaps the best-known example. After resigning from office to ward off the threat of impeachment proceedings, Nixon slowly regained his reputation as a world leader. We can also learn from lesser-known people who have earned back their reputations.

Comeback Scenario 74: Robert Shall, Small Business Owner

Shall owned and operated a company that sold cleaning supplies and calcium chloride to combat ice and snow on roads. To maintain sales,

Shall instituted a practice of making cash payments to company and local government officials. Although he preferred not to make these bribes, he wrote them off as business expenses. An audit by the Internal Revenue service led to his eventual conviction for tax evasion. He was sentenced to five years in prison for white collar criminals, and was released after 18 months. While serving time, Shall left the running of his business to two of his managers.

> The first thing I did when I returned to work was to call a company meeting [said Shall]. I explained to them that I had made a mistake and paid for it. I said that by being sent to prison, I wasn't going to have a scarlet letter tattooed on my chest. During the 18 months I was in prison our sales had slipped badly. Our company had lost much of its market share, and I was feeling pretty powerless. Showing the team that I was eager to rebuild the business was the first step in earning back my respect.
>
> Rebuilding the business was no picnic. About one-third of my former customers never talked to me again. I showed my other customers that I had a product or products that they needed to conduct their business, and that I was willing to deal generously with them within the bounds of proper business ethics.
>
> It was as if I was restarting the business. In those early days when I was trying to establish the reputation of my company, I gave cuts in prices. I threw in extra favors such as free delivery.
>
> It was no easy task, but I was motivated to do my best because I had to sell myself all over again. I had to prove to our customers that I wanted to rebuild our reputation by winning their business in an entirely above-board manner. My attitude rubbed off on everybody in the company. We began to get our original buyers back and developed new customers also. Within two years after I returned from prison, our sales had reached an all-time high.

Bob Shall's comeback was facilitated by the fact that he admitted his mistakes and humbly rebuilt his reputation. Preferably, you will not be in a position whereby your reputation has to be rebuilt. But should it be necessary, a winning strategy is the admission of wrongdoing combined with patiently showing others that your behavior is exemplary.

Bouncing Back Characteristic 79: Take One Step Backwards to Achieve Two Steps Forward

The power lost through demotion can sometimes be regained if the person has the patience to step backwards in order to achieve larger gains eventually. Such was the case with Vince Delmonte.

Comeback Scenario 75: Vince Delmonte, Project Head

Employed as a project head, Vince was demoted to a design engineer with no prospects in the near future of being reappointed to his former position. His company had decided to excise one layer of management in order to trim costs. The slight loss of power was important to Vince because he aspired to engineering management.

Instead of being overwhelmed by the demotion, Vince quietly searched for a new position outside the firm. He landed a job with a new and rapidly growing electronics firm which had just introduced several new products. Because the new firm was investing so much money in new equipment, they were temporarily quite rigid about starting job grades and pay. Vince was forced to enter the firm as a technician, one full step below the job level of design engineer. Owing to his vast knowledge in electronic design, Vince was soon promoted to senior design engineer and project planning manager. Within 18 months after leaving the firm that demoted him, Vince had more than made up for his temporary setback.

Vince's tough decision to take a temporary demotion in order to achieve long-range gain proved to be a winner. In an economy where promotional opportunities are not so plentiful, the stepping backwards tactic is sensible. However, it does require patience.

Comeback Scenario 76: Pete Anderson, Market Forecaster

A more convoluted approach to taking a step backwards to achieve two steps forward was implemented by Pete. He took a job as a market forecaster in the research and development division of a large, multiproduct company. Pete's assignment was to decide whether a new product was worth developing in terms of anticipated sales and profits. Pete found the position challenging and rewarding. Nevertheless, he couldn't resist an offer to become the vice president of marketing for a plastics recycling business the company was starting. The new position was a big gamble, but the payoff would be large cash bonuses and the opportunity to retire early.

Pete worked diligently in his new position, but soon learned that the "purse stringers" from the parent company had a different philosophy of marketing. Although Pete's division was classified as a separate company, the parent company exerted much influence on the new venture. The parent company had poured several million dollars in the new venture and was eager to receive a good return on its investment.

Pete believed strongly that implementing the parent company's marketing strategy would eventually result in a business failure, thus making him look bad. He took the bold step of going to top management in an attempt to convince them that his marketing approach was the most fruitful. The key people gave Pete the green light but let him know that they wanted quick results. With his head on the block, Pete returned to his division with a mixture of enthusiasm and apprehension. He knew that top management was looking to jump on any fault or mistake in his program.

Pete did land some good accounts, but things weren't progressing fast enough for the parent company. Top management wanted to revise his entire strategy. Pete, however, clung to the belief that his strategy would be more effective in the long run. Sensing that he was soon to be stripped of his position, Pete announced that he was stepping down as vice president for marketing and was available for reassignment within the company.

Knowing of Pete's talents, the head of R&D offered him a position as the marketing manager for a chemical division that was developing a new process for making useful products from recycled tires. Using Pete as the negotiator, the company set up a joint business venture with the pharmaceutical division to market the process. The division then bought the rights to the process, and a wholly owned subsidiary was formed. Pete was appointed as president of the subsidiary.

Through hard work, talent, guts, boldness, and deft maneuvering, Pete bounced back from almost being placed on the corporate chopping block to rise to new heights.

Using a Low-Status Position as a Path to Power.   A variation of taking one step backwards is to stay in a low-status position because it appears to be a good path to achieving more power. Tess Carpels pulled such a maneuver.

Comeback Scenario 77: Tess Carpels, English Teacher

After 11 years of experience as an English teacher, Tess married and relocated to a small town in New England. Rather than look for another teaching position, Tess used her credentials to obtain a position as an associate manager of training in the branch office of an insurance company.

Tess made many innovative training suggestions for the branch employees. Phil, her immediate supervisor, used Tess's ideas in training sessions across the country without giving her credit. Tess recalls in anger, "Phil dumped most of his responsibilities on me and gave me little recognition for what was accomplished. In addition, I spent three years

taking courses and earning my CLU (chartered life underwriter) certif-
icate. I was earning far less than the people I was training."

Several years ago the company underwent a budget cut and reorganization. The training department was entirely wiped out except for
Tess, largely because she was the lowest paid professional member of
the training staff. Because the assistant vice president and two directors
were terminated, Tess now reported directly to the branch vice president. She worked closely with him over the next year, convincing him of
the value of the program by demonstrating that sales agents who were
trained became higher producers.

At the end of the year, Tess was promoted to manager of agent training and traveled across the country to various branch offices conducting
seminars and developing her training skills. Thirteen months later,
Tess was promoted to director of agent and management development
and made an officer of the company.

Tess credits her success to her perseverance and determination to
succeed in spite of the obstacles she had to overcome. As she analyzed
the situation, "Many of the males in the organization were not used to
having a woman suggest how things should be done. I showed them
that I could combine professionalism and womanliness. To me, obstacles are what you see when you take your eyes off your goals." Tough-
ing it out in a lower-status position than you prefer can be a winning
comeback tactic, but it takes patience. To help you over the rough spots,
keep thinking of your long-range goal.

Bouncing Back Characteristic 80:
Perform Well in Your
Demoted Position

An even more basic strategy than "one step backwards" is to regain your
former position by turning in excellent job performance as a demoted
employee. Although this strategy may appear obvious, the bitterness often experienced after a demotion can interfere with performance. Demoted people often drag their heels, sometimes without realizing it.
Next, we describe a situation of a man who was wise enough not to fall
into such a trap.

Comeback Scenario 78: Conrad
Ellis

Conrad faced a big surprise upon returning from a business trip to
Mexico for his company. Another man was seated in his office, per-

forming his job. Conrad had no warning before his trip that he would be replaced.

Conrad had been corporate standards manager for several years and had received above-average performance evaluations. Prior to this position he held the post of manager of information systems, and his work was well received by management. When Conrad checked out what had happened, he discovered that his boss had been replaced with a new vice president and the latter had brought in his own people. All the changes had taken place during Conrad's two-week business trip.

Conrad was told that he had six months to find another job within the company. Having been on the corporate staff for ten years, Conrad decided to switch fields within the organization. He sought a position in the company's education department, and was finally able to secure a position as a trainer in the information systems field. Although he was not forced to take a pay cut, Conrad's new position was a three-step demotion and his pay would be frozen for three years.

Conrad dug into his new job with the enthusiasm of a person who has been given a new lease on life. Within 18 months, due to his hard work and diligence, he was promoted to manager of the education department and his job was upgraded one level. He observes, "I'm happier today as a manager of a small, effective department than I ever was as a member of the corporate staff. There is less pressure on me, and I think I'm actually making a bigger contribution. If I had left the company in a huff, I might not be in such good shape today."

Conrad overcame a potential bottoming out to his career by performing admirably in his demoted position. To do otherwise would have been self-defeating.

Cross-Cultural Application.   Performing well as a demoted employee can work well in many different cultures. A case we have in mind is from Africa.

Comeback Scenario 79: Kris Meister, Weaving Department Manager

Kris was the manager of the weaving department at Western Textile Mills, Ltd., in Lagos, Nigeria. "I remember clearly the time I first received the bad news from my general manager," says Kris. "I was told that a new manager would be replacing me. Yet the firm would be glad to keep me on as a supervisor in the same department.

"I felt hurt, annoyed, frustrated and totally bewildered. I wondered if the company was trying to humiliate me, or if I had done something drastically wrong. I had many sleepless nights thinking about how I would face my colleagues when they learned of my demotion."

A few days after receiving the news, Kris decided to take action. He recalls, "I was convinced that the reason I had been demoted was that the firm wanted to place a woman in a high position, and the general manager had replaced me with her. I thought the best way to get my old job back was to prove to the firm that I was an excellent worker, and that I was overqualified as a supervisor.

"I did all I could to prove myself to management. I worked very late hours, and volunteered for as much work as I could. I made myself known to almost everyone in the firm, and I worked hard to motivate my employees. I exerted tight control over my department, knowing at all times how we stood in relation to reaching production quotas. I helped the new manager as much as I could by doing several of her tasks, and sharing my knowledge with her about running the department."

Kris earned the praises of the manager who had replaced him. She told the company that she agreed with Kris that he was overqualified as a supervisor. The general manager reasoned that Kris deserved his old position back but the company could not justify demoting his replacement. The compromise reached was to appoint Kris to the next available department manager position for which he was qualified. Four months later, the manager of the finishing and dying department resigned and Kris was named as his replacement.

Kris was now in better shape from a career standpoint than he was before his demotion. By managing another department he was receiving the broadening he needed to someday qualify for a general manager position. His outstanding performance as a supervisor led the company to promote him back to his former level.

Bouncing Back Characteristic 81: Adapt to the New Management Style

After a firm has undergone a leveraged buyout, the management style in vogue often changes. The change in style is driven by the post-LBO financial condition of the company. Now saddled with extraordinary debt, managers—and their employees—are expected to push all the harder for productivity. As James P. Bere, the CEO of Borg Warner puts it, "The pressure to pay down debt in an LBO eliminates a sense of complacency."[1]

Placed in a company that is being operated under a leveraged buyout or drenched in debt for other reasons, the message is clear. If your management style is not characterized by a sense of urgency, begin hustling. Become a swashbuckling cost cutter, and spur your people to keep customer needs paramount. In this way you will be able to climb back into power more quickly, should you have been deposed in the LBO or other shakeup.

Bouncing Back Characteristic 82: Attend a Survivor Program

The negative side effects of takeovers and LBOs are so well known that survivor programs are gaining popularity. The purpose of these programs is to help the survivors adjust to the new corporate realities and to understand how their careers will be affected. In addition, individual and group counseling sessions are conducted to help the survivors cope with their tension and guilt. The guilt stems from having a job, while many productive co-workers have been terminated.

Political advantage can be gained from survivor programs. Should you be fortunate enough to be a survivor—although demoted—avoid bitterness. Instead, attend the survivor program with elan. Eloquently express your appreciation for having been one of the elite chosen to help move the company forward. During the group sessions, encourage others to close ranks and begin battling the competition instead of ruminating over the past. The survival program consultant might pass on a kind word about you to top management; that will help you inch your way back up the corporate ladder.

Bouncing Back Characteristic 83: Move Out of the Graveyard as Soon as Possible

Kris Meister's strategy of staying put in his new assignment and performing well obviously worked. In other situations, the best strategy is to find a quick way out of a *graveyard* assignment. There is a nuance of difference between an undesirable assignment and a graveyard. Many positions may be undesirable but a graveyard position is clearly a deadend job. A sound strategy is to try to be transferred away from a deadend assignment after you have made a sincere effort for a reasonable time to improve the situation.

Comeback Scenario 80: Judd Parsons, Middle Manager

A large corporation established a salvaging department staffed mainly by employees with disciplinary problems or by those whose illnesses made them unsuited for stressful jobs (such as people with cardiac problems who had been medically advised to minimize job pressures). From the outset, the department became known throughout the corporation as The Graveyard. Managers in the department were generally considered unpromotable.

Fifty-five-year-old Judd was appointed against his wishes to a middle manager position in The Graveyard. A friend in the human resources department gave Judd her honest opinion about the situation: "Judd, you've just about been put out to pasture. The only way you will ever get out of this department is through retirement. But if you like that kind of work, your future is assured with the company. Besides, the people working there are stable and appreciative. You might feel like you're doing good for them."

A vigorous man, Judd did not wish to see himself placed in a terminal position. Yet he did enjoy the challenge of a salvage operation. He decided that he would stay in his graveyard position until he acquired enough knowledge about salvage operations to enter business for himself. Two years later, Judd, his brother-in-law, and a close friend established a small metal recycling business. His career was anew with excitement. Judd had bounced back from The Graveyard. He took the risk of self-employment in order to overcome career adversity.

Bouncing Back Characteristic 84:
Form a Coalition

One of the most basic political tactics is to join forces with another party in order to enhance your power. The other party can be another department in the company, a labor group, a business competitor, or a person in a related business.

Comeback Scenario 81: John P.
Rynne, Real Estate Appraiser

Rynne formed a coalition with a related business in order to climb his way back into the power associated with having a successful business. Four years after receiving an MBA, John launched his own appraisal business. He specialized in corporate appraisals and advising companies on real estate purchases.

Business was excellent for the first two years. Sales grew constantly and John established good working relations with area banks, his largest customers. However, competition began to increase steadily. Banks hired more appraisers of their own, and John's business dropped off precipitously. The future looked uncertain for John's firm and he entertained thoughts of joining the appraisal staff of a bank. However, he regarded such a position as a major step backward in his career because in his perception, self-employment held high status.

John found a solution to his dilemma before being forced to close the business. He became friendly with Larry Murphy, the owner of a well-established real estate appraisal firm that specialized in residential work. John and Larry agreed to consolidate their firms, with John offering a concentration of commercial appraisals, and Larry offering strength on the residential side. The two reasoned that their combined contacts with banks would be synergistic. A new firm, Real Estate Appraisals, Inc. was established in a small downtown office. The coalition has worked well, with gross revenues much higher than anticipated. To help cope with the large flow of business, they have subcontracted some of their residential appraisals and concentrated on the more profitable corporate appraisals.

John Rynne overcame adversity by doing what many large business organizations do. He combined forces with a complementary firm in order to enhance the customer base and reduce costs. Keep coalition formation in mind as a possible way out of adversity you might face.

Aligning Oneself with a Mentor.   Another way of forming a coalition is to align oneself with a powerful mentor. Finding a mentor is a standard technique of career advancement. The support of a mentor can also be helpful in climbing back to power, as was the case with an eminent neurologist.

Comeback Scenario 82: Walter E. Dandy, Neurosurgeon

The late Walter E. Dandy. M.D., was Professor Emeritus and Chairman of the Department of Neurological Surgery at Johns Hopkins Hospital. Dandy was reared on a farm in Missouri, and showed exceptional scholastic ability in elementary and high school. Young Dandy wanted to continue his education but his parents could not afford to send him to college. The town's general merchant, who was a close friend of the family, paid the entire bill for Walter Dandy's college and medical school education.

Dandy graduated from Johns Hopkins Medical School in 1910. After his internship, Dr. Dandy worked for the world-famous surgeon, Professor Harvey Cushing. During their year together, Dandy and Cushing had many personal clashes. In 1912, Cushing was appointed Professor and Chairman of the Department of Surgery at Massachusetts General

Hospital. He left for Boston with his entire professional staff except for Dandy.

The young Dr. Dandy was rendered jobless, powerless, and financially troubled. Not knowing where to turn, Dandy explained his plight to Dr. Winford Smith, the Director of the Johns Hopkins Hospital. In an act of kindness, Smith provided Dandy with free room and board for six months. During this period Dandy worked feverishly on a project dealing with the origin, circulation, and absorption of cerebrospinal fluid. Within a year, under some guidance from Smith, Dandy published his findings which provided the first scientific understanding of hydrocephalus.

Dr. Dandy was subsequently reappointed as surgical resident to continue his training in neurosurgery. In 1914, Dandy developed two important techniques for diagnosing blockages in the blood vessels and lungs. His discoveries were great breakthroughs, because they enabled physicians to accurately locate the position of a brain tumor. Dandy's brilliant career qualified him for a place in the Neurological Hall of Fame.[2]

The fact that Dr. Dandy was able to quickly find a new mentor after being dropped by his original one made it possible for him to achieve such fame and power. Working closely with a mentor can also help many others regain power.

Bouncing Back Characteristic 85: Sell Your Qualifications to the Predator Firm

A recurring challenge today is how to regain power after the company firm who has acquired your employer demotes you. The problem often arises because the predator firm needs to find ways to reduce expenses to help pay for the takeover. One method of reducing expenses is to decrease the number of managers and professionals. Another potential threat to your power is that the new firm may want to bring in its own staff of managers. Selling your qualifications to the predator firm can sometimes help you regain power lost in the shuffle or prevent a further erosion of your power.

Comeback Scenario 83: Barbara Harris, Assistant Store Manager

Barbara faced a potential erosion of power when the fashion store she worked for was bought by a nationwide firm and converted into a subsidiary. The new owner's initial move was to replace existing management with their own people. Because of this, Barbara was on the verge of losing her job as assistant manager. Harris explains what happened:

> One week after I graduated with a degree in fashion merchandising, I obtained a job as a sales associate in a local retail outlet. Within a year I was promoted to assistant manager, and business was quite good. Three months after I was promoted, we were informed that a new company was buying the store. We were told not to worry about our jobs being disturbed.
>
> What we didn't know was that our job security was not guaranteed by the terms of the sales agreement between the companies. Upon acquiring our store, the new owners decided to move its own people into key positions. You can imagine the chaos that hit when we were told our jobs had been virtually eliminated with the stroke of a pen!
>
> The day the new company representative came to give us exit interviews we were told that the sales associates would be let go but that Julie (the store manager) and I would be able to work as sales associates. We were told that if we worked up to their standards, we might be reappointed as assistant managers in the future. Julie considered the offer to be a slap in the face after seven years in the business and submitted her resignation that day. Who could blame her?
>
> I told them I'd like the weekend to consider my options and would give them my decision the following Monday morning. I spent Friday and Saturday fuming about the callous way we were all treated. By Sunday I got down to the serious business trying to understand what these changes meant to my career. I came to the conclusion that because it was still early in my career, I had nothing to lose by accepting the company's offer. My one stipulation was that I be hired as a management trainee with the same pay and benefits as before.
>
> As I explained to the representative that Monday, I had a degree and nearly two years of merchandising experience, including supervisory duties over sales associates. I felt I was overqualified for an associate's position and knew I had much information to offer regarding local customer attitudes, behavior, likes and dislikes, and preferred lifestyles.

Barbara smiled as she remembered:

> I can't believe how bold I was. I told that man that I had no qualms about learning another style of management and that working for his company could only add to my career development. I wanted the chance to broaden my experience base, and I could think of no reason why the company and I couldn't enjoy a mutually beneficial association.
>
> I couldn't believe my nerve, and I guess he couldn't either. I was

hired that day as a manager trainee. I have to confess I never thought my pitch would work, but you never know until you try. It's five years later and I am now the assistant regional manager for this chain. My boss is that same manager who was sent to reorganize the outlet I originally worked in.

We endorse the tactic chose by Barbara Harris. She sold herself as a marketable product. She stuck her neck out and had enough confidence to take a chance. By presenting your qualifications as an asset to an organization, it will be easier to get the position you really want. or at least the one which will get you where you want to go.

Justify Your Retention of Control.   Another way of selling your qualifications to the predator firm is to justify to management why you should be allowed to retain control over a piece of the organization.

By this method you either retain or perhaps gain power. A street-wise middle manager at IBM implemented this tactic adroitly.

Comeback Scenario 84: Charlie Dugan, Software Manager

Charlie began his career as a manager in the purchasing department of IBM Poughkeepsie. IBM maintained that its managers should be able to supervise the operations of various types of processes based on their general problem-solving ability. Charlie was therefore transferred to the product safety department when the need for an experienced manager existed. Shortly after his arrival, a proposal for reorganization of the department threatened to strip the power from his new position. The reorganization plan called for the creation of a new industrial hygiene department that would substantially reduce the number of people Charlie supervised. Rather than accept the situation, he was determined to find a way to restore his lost empire.

Charlie turned to contacts he had in the information systems group within manufacturing. They notified him of a large software support project which was in the analysis phase. The project would eventually service five different departments and would require a full-time systems analyst/designer, a staff programmer, and many junior level programmers and assistants. He developed a report for upper management explaining the advantages of basing the project in product safety under his charge.

Charlie argued that the most experienced of the five department managers encompassed by the project reported to him. Also, almost all of the necessary information flows were already directed through product safety (his department). Charlie's department was therefore the natural choice for the center of the project.

Charlie's persuasive arguments and persistence paid off. He was awarded control of the computer software system. The acquisition brought him substantial prestige and power, and his department became the hub of the site's safety information network. He overcame adversity by providing a convincing rationale as to why he should control a segment of the organization.

Bouncing Back Characteristic 86: Show Others You Can Help Yourself

An eminently ethical tactic for climbing back into power is to demonstrate to influential people that you are capable of helping yourself. At that point you may receive the help you need because most business people prefer to put their money behind a winner.

Comeback Scenario 85: Chuck Frye, Human Resources Vice President

Chuck Frye, the vice president of human resources for Warner Amex Cable Communications of Cincinnati, illustrates this principle well. Frye did not aspire to become a vice president when he left Central State University with a football injury in his second year. He wanted to be a drafting technician and a professional football player. But he was too small to play professional football, and "that was prior to the 1964 Civil Rights Act and they weren't hiring black draftsmen then."

Consequently Frye held a series of jobs assisting others beginning with supervision of 24 incarcerated boys at a state institution. "I thought I wanted to be a social worker." He then held positions with the Job Corps, the county welfare department, and the federally funded Manpower Training. Frye looked for answers to the problems of blacks through the training programs he headed. At that point, however, "Some consultants convinced me the way to equality for blacks was not through training or through the job market, but through black capitalism. So I began to investigate the possibility of setting up black business."

Next came what Frye thought was a triumph. He raised about $440,000 to establish a company with the help of a poverty agency in

Columbus, Ohio, the Chamber of Commerce, and a Small Business Agency grant. "I started a company manufacturing wood pallets. We were running two shifts with strictly black employees. We thought that was going to be our piece of the pie. But being new to the business world we ran into a number of operating problems. We had more money running out than coming in, and ended up closing down the facility and liquidating the assets after one year of production.

"I hit rock bottom. No job. Nowhere to go. I was out of a job for four months and finally ended up going to work at night for a janitorial service."

Frye felt a dramatic change in his lifestyle. "I had been in the limelight when I had that manufacturing company. I was in the newspaper, on the radio, giving speeches all over the city, even around the country. People were coming to me. Then all of a sudden it was like I didn't exist anymore. I cleaned buildings and emptied waste cans from 5 till 11 at night and worked for a personnel placement agency in the daytime."

Frye then obtained a third position with Xerox Corporation, as a midnight shift supervisor in their printing press operation. "For a year and a half I worked those three jobs to make ends meet."

Frye experienced an attitude change while working as a janitor. "In my earlier days when I was with the poverty agency, I was an aggressive individual. I would go out and do anything and say anything. I was one of those individuals who was likely to help burn down cities.

"But all those lonely nights when I was running buffing machines and mopping floors, I had time to think. 'Where did I go wrong?' I began to examine the way I behaved, the way I acted, and said, 'Let's make a change. Let's make people see you in a different light.'"

Soon Frye was promoted to a position in personnel and public affairs at Xerox in Columbus. After successes in running community political and issue campaigns, he was promoted to the personnel director of the former Xerox publishing group. In 1981 he left Xerox to work at Warner Amex. By 1983 he was on top again as a vice president.

Frye believes he has learned from his setbacks. "I learned a lot of the discipline you need in the world of work. That's one reason I worked three jobs. I learned that if you want to do some things you have to help yourself first.

"You have to demonstrate to others that you're going to take responsibility for yourself, for your own career, and for whatever success you want out of life. And I think you do that by demonstrating that you're willing to make some sacrifices."[3]

Frye's comeback tactic then was to demonstrate to others that he was a worthy cause. His behavior indicated that given a fair chance he would make an important contribution to an organization. Frye also showed others that he was not too humble to take a step back in his career in order to be self-sufficient.

Bouncing Back Characteristic 87: Develop New Expertise

A time-consuming, but fundamentally solid approach to regaining power is to develop new expertise valued by the organization. Because you possess this rarified knowledge, you are in a position to regain some or all of your eroded power. For example, a manager in a stock broker-age firm might be demoted to a financial analyst in a political battle. She accepts her loss temporarily, but in the meantime develops esoteric knowledge about several industries. Her recommendations about buy-ing and selling securities in her industries are so profitable that she is invited to become a partner in the firm.

Comeback Scenario 86: Jack Bobry, Design Engineer

Jack, a highly respected design engineer at an electronics company, made good use of the "new expertise" strategy. He was appointed as lead engineer on the development of a consumer product—one that was forecasted to sell 500,000 units per year and yield a handsome profit margin. Four engineers and eight designers reported to Jack on this project. The project moved along smoothly through its develop-ment and prototypes stages. Millions of dollars were budgeted to get the product ready for actual production.

While the new product was progressing through its quality assurance checks, a recurring problem arose. The engineers reporting to Jack as-sured him this problem could be solved. Jack had faith in the technical acumen of his team members and looked forward to overcoming this temporary glitch.

In the meantime, quality assurance engineers working separately from Jack analyzed the product, discovered the unresolved problem, and sent their findings to higher management. Jack was called into a meeting with divisional management and asked to respond to the qual-ity assurance report. At this point Jack's optimism faded and he con-cluded that the technical problem could not be solved without compro-mising the competitive edge of the product. Top management made the decision to halt production and scrap all materials and the completed products. Jack's group was dispersed, and he was given a routine assignment as a design engineer.

Jack went through several months of soul searching, and concluded that he needed to restore his image. He decided to become an expert in three subfields critical to electronic product design. Jack also decided to work independently in order to restore his confidence in his own engineering skills. As knowledge of Jack's new expertise spread throughout the engineering division of the company, he was called upon to consult with numerous design groups. Two years after his group had been dismantled, Jack was appointed as project leader on another promising product. According to his analysis, "By biting the bullet and taking the time to dig out some new technology, I reestablished my reputation. My loser image has completely faded."

Jack's winning comeback tactic can help many people overcome adversity. Learning an important new technology can also help prevent adversity by increasing your value to the organization.

Bouncing Back Characteristic 88: Overcome a Personal Disqualifier

Working on the weakness that created your loss of power is another time-consuming but potentially effective tactic for regaining power. Unfortunately, too many people become defensive when confronted about a weakness or shortcoming that has set them back. Instead of overcoming the personal disqualifier, they aggravate the condition. You will recall that John (the abrasive manager who was helped by a human resources professional) began his climb back to power after self-improvement. A similar situation occurred with a manager of special services at a telephone company.

Comeback Scenario 87: Ed McCullough, Special Services Manager

Ed worked for a telephone company in Tennessee. He supervised 90 skilled and clerical workers, most of whom were union members who were accustomed to the policies, procedure, and accepted social behavior of the phone company. Ed used an authoritarian, task-oriented approach to manager. "Let's do it" was the first part of Ed's motto, and "It's done" was the second part. When a project was done, it was a signal to Ed to take on another challenge.

If a craft worker had a problem testing a phone circuit, Ed would sit right down at his or her computer terminal and arrive at a solution. Sometimes this effort was appreciated, but often the worker was left with no more ability to solve a problem than when the worker started.

What made matters worse in the eyes of others, Ed exuded an unusual bravado regarding technical accomplishments in the SSC. He would often try to impose innovative approaches to problems on other service centers. He openly challenged policies set up by staff personnel. While Ed was occupying himself taking on the burdens of his people, he neglected many of his managerial duties. Ultimately he alienated his work force, his peers in other SSCs, and the staff personnel. In retaliation, these people passed the message about Ed up the line.

Ed was asked to resign from his position, and termination procedures were pending. Fortunately for Ed he had impressed a staff manager enough that the manager took the opportunity to rescue Ed and assign him to a rigorous technical project. Ed would be responsible for implementing a new computer system but would have no subordinates. In order to complete the project, Ed had to work with many other units of the telephone company. He saw this as an opportunity to capitalize on his technical ability and simultaneously show the company he really knew how to handle people.

Ed was intent on mellowing his approach to people. He worked diligently on the new project and spent extra time working closely with the SSC craft workers in another region where he could make a fresh start. Ed's main concern in implementing the new computer system was the users—ensuring that the system would do what they needed in a simple yet powerful way. Ed became sensitive to the craft worker's point of view by working with them and trying to understand their viewpoint.

Ed paid careful respect to the organization's policies and procedures—something he was aware he neglected in previous assignments. He tried his best to cope with the bureaucratic procedures of the phone company rather than trying to ram things through. To do that, he had to communicate carefully with people so they could move the paperwork along, install the new system, and cooperate in evaluating its effectiveness. He sought the approval of each group by finding out what they needed to get their part done, and then worked within company guidelines to help them.

The 60-hour work weeks paid off; the project was a success from the standpoints of both technical effectiveness and worker acceptance. Ed recently requested a promotion to manage staff people. Word came down from top management that he was maturing so rapidly as a manager that his request would be given warm consideration. Specifically, Ed demonstrated to management that he had overcome his heavy-handed, authoritarian approach to people that was creating morale problems.

Political Insensitivity.   An important personal disqualifier can also be political insensitivity. The individual who ignores the realities of office politics is liable to be removed from a position of power. Unless the person becomes more politically astute, he or she will not be able to hold onto a powerful position again.

Comeback Scenario 88: Martin Freund, Vice President of Management Information Systems

Thirty-eight-year-old Martin is one person who needed to hone his political savvy in order to regain power. Martin was the vice president of management information systems for a manufacturer of automotive springs and shock absorbers. While playing golf one Memorial Day weekend he was called off the course to answer a telephone call from his boss of six years. The message was that Martin was fired and that he would be given six months' severance pay. Martin's golfing buddies noted the dramatic change in his demeanor after the call, and tried to comfort him and find out what happened. Martin downplayed the incident, preferring to suffer in silence for the moment.

Several days later Martin did tell his wife and a few close friends what happened. Much to his surprise, he received their sympathy and support. Martin spent the next few days reflecting on the real reason he might have been fired. After considerable introspection and a talk with his brother, an organizational psychologist, Martin concluded that he was not properly tuned into the political climate in his company. He said, "My disdain for playing politics was the true reason they got rid of me. I was outspoken and never went out of my way to get people in my corner. I realized at that point that I needed to curb my temper, be more flexible, and act nice to other executives even if I didn't like them."

Martin did get another chance; he was hired by an advertising agency to direct their computer operations. Shortly after joining the firm he began his campaign to form cordial working relationships with key people. He purposely let others win a few arguments, even over factual matters, just to show his conciliatory nature. Two years after joining the firm, Martin was promoted to vice president and accepted the invitation to join the firm as a partner.

In summarizing the changes in behavior he initiated, Martin Freund said, "I became more sociable and less rigid. I raised my antennae to receive signals of political undercurrents. The process worked. I'm where I want to be today." He was at least sensitive enough to realize that his political insensitivity was damaging his career. His campaign to build alliances in his new firm paid handsome dividends.

Bouncing Back Characteristic 89: Conduct a Thorough Job Campaign

An obvious tactic for regaining power is to search thoroughly for a new position with as much or greater power than you held previously. What is not so obvious, however, is that a job search can often be conducted within your own organization. You pound carpet or vinyl floors instead of pavement to regain power. A major plus for your career is that an internal job switch is looked upon more favorably than an external one: You appear well rounded rather than disloyal or unwanted.

Comeback Scenario 89: Gail Kamin, Engineering Manager

Gail, a first-level manager of industrial engineers, faced a reorganization in the corporation. Two industrial engineering units were merged into one to eliminate a few support positions and one managerial slot. Gail lost her supervisory position and was reassigned as a senior industrial engineer. The reshuffling upset Gail because she was intent on moving up into manufacturing management. Losing a managerial position therefore represented a serious career setback.

> I didn't let myself slip into a passive mode [said Gail]. I realized the merger was necessary to keep my division cost effective. I realized someone had to be demoted, I just wished it weren't me. The minimum benefit for me from the reshuffle was that I could resharpen my professional skills by working as a full-time engineer.
>
> Within two months, I launched my plan to get back into management. I sat down with my manager and developed a career path, specifying the jobs I needed to reach my long-range goal of becoming a manufacturing vice president. My manager took my path seriously, and gave me permission to interview in other divisions of the corporation for a manager's job. After four months, I secured a new

position as the manager of industrial engineering in the aerospace division of our company. The division had just landed a large government contract and were actually short of talent.

The lesson to be learned from Gail's climb back to a modest amount of power is that she used a sophisticated approach to finding a new position within her organization. Instead of simply circulating her resume around the company, she explained her career plans to her immediate superior who then became her ally in her job search.

Bouncing Back Characteristic 90: Make a Career Switch

A more radical approach than switching jobs to regain lost power is to switch careers. The typical problem, however, is that most career switches result in a power loss rather than a power gain. Becoming an entrepreneur can result in a power gain if the business is very successful. (More will be said about this in the next chapter.) Switching fields in corporate employment usually requires accepting a position of less income, rank, and power than your last employment—at least temporarily. A career switch in corporate employment can help you regain power if you are willing to invest the time.

Comeback Scenario 90: Geri Mitchell, Clothing Buyer

Geri is an example of making a career switch early in life in order to ultimately increase your power. She was a clothing buyer for a medium-size department store. Geri was demoted to floor supervisor when the owner's son graduated from the Fashion Institute of Technology and wanted her job. Unhappy with the situation, Geri pondered what to do next. She had enjoyed the excitement and glamour of being a buyer, but her demotion sparked her into thinking of some of the disadvantages of retailing. She realized that there would always be holidays spent away from family and friends, long hours, few weekends off, and relatively low pay.

With encouragement and financial backing from her mother, Geri visited a career counselor in private practice. The results of self-analysis, interviews, vocational testing, and computer-assisted career guidance indicated that packaging engineering looked like a promising field for Geri. Designing packages for consumer products would give Geri a chance to use her flair for style, and place her into an occupation with growth potential *and* standard working hours.

Geri enrolled in a program of packaging engineering, and was able to cash in enough transfer credits to obtain a degree in two years. Three years after graduation she is happily employed as a packaging engineer and is in line for a supervisory position. Because she has advancement potential, Geri says, "I've got more oomph to my career than I did when I was a buyer in a local store."

Geri switched careers on the basis of considerable introspection and professional assistance. Because her career switch proved to be an improvement over her previous career, Geri overcame adversity. An impulsive career switch is less likely to help a person bounce back.

Bouncing Back Characteristic 91: Sue for Your Rights

If you are patient, have a lot of money to gamble with, and don't mind taking the risk of being bad-listed for the rest of your career, suing for your rights can get you back into power.

Comeback Scenario 91: Lawrence Cranberg, Physicist

Cranberg is one person for whom the legal route was a spectacular success. Several years ago, Cranberg wad hired by the University of Virginia as the Director of the Van De Graaf Accelerator Laboratory. One reason for hiring Cranberg was that his prominence would be helpful in obtaining a government grant to construct the Van de Graaf accelerator and to conduct research after its completion.

Soon after the grant was successfully obtained by the university, Lawrence Cranberg was fired and replaced with a new director, Roger Ritter. Cranberg had received no forewarning of his firing, and had received good appraisals of his work. In retaliation, Cranberg began legal proceedings against the university on the grounds of an unjust firing. His lawyer filed a lawsuit for $500,000. The university could document no tangible reason for firing Dr. Cranberg, and lost the case. Cranberg received a $250,000 settlement and was given back his position as Director of the accelerator laboratory. Despite his favorable settlement, Dr. Cranberg moved on to a high-paying job elsewhere shortly thereafter.

Lawrence Cranberg used the legal route to compensate him for the temporary adversity of having been fired. Because he had a good case and a good lawyer, he won a generous settlement. Dr. Cranberg is unusual in that he was able to find a better job despite having sued a former employer. We still recommend caution against suing because it could taint your image among prospective new employers.

Bouncing Back Characteristic 92: Wait for Your Enemy to Leave or Self-Destruct

A strategy for climbing back into power when one person is responsible for deposing you is to take no offensive action at all. Simply perform well in your demoted position and wait for somebody else to depose your deposer, or for him or her to self-destruct. If sending you to Corporate Siberia was unjust, arbitrary, and politically motivated, your deposer may commit many other similar acts. Eventually your antagonist will begin to falter and others will help him or her plummet from power. His or her abrasive, intimidating, or manipulative tactics will backfire when tried against the wrong person. Under these circumstances you may be able to regain power providing you have told your side of the story to the right people.

Let key people know that you neither welcomed nor deserved your demotion. Tell them you were involuntarily stripped of the power you cherished. Explain that you want more responsibility so that you can continue to make all the important contributions you were making before you were moved out of the mainstream. If your record shows you are indeed Mr. or Ms. Clean, the replacement for your deposer may give you a second chance.

Waiting for your enemy to leave is an effective strategy for another reason. In many mergers, 50 percent of the senior managers leave within one year, and 75 percent are gone within three years. So typically, the merged organization needs to make some additional personnel cuts after the initial downsizing. Senior managers are a good target because of their high pay. Also, the stress-filled working environment of the post-takeover firm propels many managers to find a more tranquil work environment. Competitors fill many top-management openings with executives who have been forced to manage in a frenzied postmerger organization.[4]

Action Tips

Should career adversity make it imperative that you climb back into power, keep in mind that others have made the journey back. Take one or more of the following action steps, as relevant to your circumstances, to facilitate your comeback:

1. Earn back your reputation.
2. Take one step backwards to achieve two steps forward.
3. Perform well in your demoted position. (Don't let your motive for retribution be self-defeating.)
4. Adapt to the new management style (after a takeover).
5. Attend a survivor program.
6. Move out of the graveyard as soon as possible.
7. Form a coalition.
8. Sell your qualifications to the predator firm.
9. Show others you can help yourself.
10. Develop new expertise.
11. Overcome a personal disqualifier.
12. Conduct a thorough job campaign.
13. Make a career switch.
14. Sue for your rights.
15. Wait for your enemy to self-destruct.

10

Entrepreneurship as a Solution

For a growing number of people, the preferred response to career adversity is self-employment. Entrepreneurship thrives on adversity. Sometimes a drastic problem in one part of an urban area's economy—a major plant or office shutdown, or a shakeout in a dominant industry—can stimulate the start of new enterprise. The human motives behind this phenomenon are easy to comprehend. What do people do when they have been laid off by their company or forced into early retirement, and every other similar company is also cutting back? The alternatives include taking a lesser job outside of one's field or starting their own company.

Seattle, Washington, was an example of the entrepreneurial solution to career adversity. When Boeing laid off approximately 50,000 production workers, engineers, and managers in the early 1970s, many of those laid off were reluctant to move. A surge in small-business startups created a diversified economy that led to a much-improved economic climate in the present.

A similar phenomenon took place in Boston when cutbacks in defense expenditures and contracts pushed the unemployment rate close to 11 percent in 1975. The recent economic prosperity in Massachusetts was rooted in the several thousand companies formed during 1975 and the few bleak years thereafter. One of the great strengths of the United States economy is the emergence of entrepreneurship as a safety net that lays the groundwork for a rapid and lasting recovery.[1]

Bouncing Back Characteristic 93: Evaluate Whether You Are Entrepreneurial Material

Despite all these accolades for starting your own business to conquer a career setback, entrepreneurship is not for everybody. Risks are involved because one-half of new businesses fail within the first five years. When the Dun & Bradstreet Corporation attempted to analyze why so many small businesses fail, they uncovered these reasons: incompetence, 44%; lack of management experience, 17%; unbalanced experience, 16%; inexperience in line management, 15%; neglect, 1%; fraud or disaster, 1%; and unknown, 6%.[2]

Looking beneath these figures, many small business failures can be attributed to the owners' not having the right stuff. For example, many instances of incompetence can be attributed to not having the attitudes and personality suited for entrepreneurship. Professor Jeff Bracker supports this view. Reflecting on his experiences at the University of Arizona in training people for entrepreneurship, Bracker noted: "We found that a lot of the training was a waste of time. It is difficult to teach entrepreneurship to the people who don't have the right stuff. If you lack the guts and the imagination you'll never hack it as an entrepreneur."

Because the types of businesses started by entrepreneurs differ so widely, we cannot pin down a highly accurate stereotype of the ideal entrepreneur. However, there is enough consistency among core attributes of entrepreneurs to help you appreciate whether you fit approximately the entrepreneurial style.

- A heavy motivation to get work accomplished, combined with a direct approach to giving instructions to employees.

- An intense sense of urgency that motivates many people and discourages some. Many entrepreneurs have such an intense sense of urgency themselves that they expect others to feel the same way about work.

- Impatience and brusqueness toward employees because entrepreneurs are always in a hurry. They often wear loafers to avoid spending time tying their shoes, and they frequently eat while on the run. Many entrepreneurs operate more on hunches than careful planning; they therefore become discouraged with employees who insist on studying problems for a prolonged period.

- A charismatic personality that inspires others to want to do business with the entrepreneur despite his or her impatience.

- A strong dislike for bureaucratic rules and regulations, which makes the entrepreneur impatient during meetings. A typical example is the entrepreneur who sells his or her business to a larger firm, thus becoming a division president. Within two years, the entrepreneur leaves the firm because of frustration with rules and regulations imposed from above.

- A much stronger interest in dealing with customers than employees.

- A strong achievement drive which translates into being a self-starter fueled by the need to succeed and accomplish something. Entrepreneurs are constantly keeping score.

- A willingness to assume personal responsibility for the success or failure of a given activity or event.

- An ability to spot problems and opportunities that other people overlook. For example, it took an entrepreneurial mind to observe that the United States and Canada needed a chain of budget-priced motels such as Day's Inn.

- A belief that one's accomplishments and failures are under one's personal control and influence, and that luck is not such an important factor in contributing to success or failure.

- An ability and willingness to live with a certain amount of uncertainty in life. This uncertainty can relate to job security, business deals, and personal life.

- A willingness to take calculated and sensible risks. A *calculated risk* means that the chances of winning are neither small enough to represent a big gamble nor so large as to be almost certain.

- A willingness to accept setback, and then to recover and keep going. The entrepreneur embodies the spirit of the resilient manager.

The more of the above traits, characteristics, and behaviors you possess, the greater the chances that the entrepreneurial solution will help you rebound from adversity. Many small business failures can be attributed to people setting up shop who are unsuited to such activity. One failed small business owner told me:

> After being giving an offer of early retirement I couldn't refuse, I opened an office supply store. I enjoyed planning the store, stocking the inventory, and negotiating the deals. What I couldn't handle was standing in the store waiting for customers. During the first week we only made two sales, both of them very small. I knew then I couldn't tolerate so much uncertainty in my life. I was finally able to sell my new store and find another corporate job.

Bouncing Back Characteristic 94: Overcome Adversities through Entrepreneurship

Establishing and operating your own business resolves several types of adversities. Some people become entrepreneurs after losing a corporate job because no other comparable position is available. Others start a business when faced with a financial crisis because they could not live on any job they might be able to find. Still others try self-employment because they have committed acts or engaged in behavior that makes them unemployable.

Comeback Scenario 92: Matthew Tubinis, Company Founder

Matthew Tubinis chose entrepreneurship as a way of handling adversity primarily because no other job at his level seemed available at the time. Early in his career, Tubinis was hired as an electrical engineer at the Cunningham Corporation, a manufacturer of switches. Over a period of 15 years, Tubinis moved up through the ranks to become vice president of engineering. One of the projects developed under his leadership was a cross bar switch that became a standard of excellence in its field.

Two years after Tubinis became vice president, the president of Cunningham decided to sell the company to a larger firm. Tubinis was apprehensive about the takeover. Nevertheless, if the acquiring firm was willing to support and continue the various product lines of his company, he would stay put because he enjoyed his position. It soon became apparent to Tubinis that the acquiring company wanted to restructure the smaller firm. Within six months the new parent firm began to bring in its own managers and abandon some of Cunningham's products.

Tubinis was called into the president's office one day and told, "Either you resign or we will lay you off in three months. We are eliminating the vice president of engineering position." Tubinis resigned reluctantly. He enjoyed working with electronic switching equipment, and realized that there were few opportunities open in his industry.

"The only sensible alternative for me at the time was to start my own company. I was far too young, and not wealthy enough, to retire. And I saw no possibilities of my finding a vice presidential position in the electronic switch industry. The primary purpose of my new firm was to sell an up-to-date version of the cross bar switch and replacement equipment for the Cunningham product line. The parent company had abandoned this important and potentially profitable market."

Tubinis took his small replacement cross bar business from a one-person shop to a small business that employs approximately 70 people and earns an average annual profit of several million dollars. His escape into entrepreneurship was sensible and well planned. Tubinis founded a company based on a product and a market he understood thoroughly.

Comeback Scenario 93: Verna Walker, Home Improvement Business Founder

Verna Walker is retired today, but 40 years ago she chose small business ownership as the only plausible means of supporting her three daughters and a 4-year-old son. After her husband died in 1950, she knew that she would need more money than she had been earning as a canvasser for a home improvement company. However, home improvement was the only field she knew. Verna therefore decided to go into the home improvement business for herself.

"They kind of laughed at me when I applied for my city license. They thought I was nuts. I wasn't sure they weren't right," said Walker. "I worked out in the country at first. I was sort of afraid to talk to the people in the city. I don't know why."

Walker recalls that her first customer must have known how nervous she was and even suspected it was her first sale as a proprietor. The customer sent her a Christmas card every year until she (the customer) died. In the early days, Walker would leave her house at 8:30 in the morning and often not return until 11:30 at night between selling and making inspections. Her oldest daughter watched her young son.

> When I first started out, I had just had my regular home phone. People said, "She can't be very much if she's not listed as a business phone." But I couldn't lie and let people think someone else was backing me.
>
> I had some bad experiences. You can tell right away if men aren't doing the work right but sometimes a worker won't show up or will steal. Most of my bad experiences have been with salesmen. They promise things that can never be delivered or they give dates you can't meet.
>
> I've met a lot of nice people, particularly a pair of blind ladies who became close friends of mine. I sold one of then storm windows and I didn't know she was blind until I delivered them, and she asked me to show her with my hands how to operate the window.

Walker says that if the clock were to turn back and she had to face the same challenge of supporting her family, she would unhesitatingly take the same path she took. Walker is also not overly critical of the mistakes she made because she believes that most of them were inevitable.

Walker, similar to Tubinis, chose a form of self-employment where her probability of success was the highest — a business already familiar to her. Jumping into a business you know very little about will often create more adversity than it overcomes.

Self-Employment for the Unemployable.   Self-employment can also be the route to survival when a person becomes virtually unemployable. Such was the case with the former administrator of a rural hospital.

Comeback Scenario 94: Jeff Minard, Health-Care Consultant

Jeff Minard, a hospital administrator, developed a drug abuse problem. It impaired his job performance and threatened to destroy his 11-year marriage. At age 46 he was both unemployed and dependent on cocaine. After several months of acute depression, Minard decided it was time to put his life back together. With encouragement from his wife, Minard entered group therapy for drug abusers. After several months of intensive therapy, Minard felt strong enough to cope with his unemployment problem. His first two job interviews resulted in stern rejections with the explanation offered that his medical problems made him unsuited for hospital employment in any capacity.

Minard then decided that his best hope of earning a suitable living would be to start his own consulting business. By so doing he would not have to explain his long periods of unemployment to anyone. Minard believed that he possessed excellent knowledge of hospital administration, and that he no longer had a drug abuse problem. He then opened a small office downtown, installed a phone and a computer system, hired a secretary, and began tracking down business.

Business was slow at first, as Minard predicted. Soon afterwards he secured several good-sized contracts in the health care industry. His client base expanded so rapidly that Minard hired an associate. Today his firm employs a professional staff of fifteen with much of their work still in the health care field. In addition to solving organizational problems, Minard Associates helps hospitals and nursing homes computerize their billing and insurance claims processing. The firm also runs seminars and workshops on managerial skills for physicians and their office managers.

Within five years of operation, Minard's firm has become well established and respected. His annual income has reached six figures — something he would not have been able to do if he had not been fired. Minard still periodically attends group therapy sessions to make sure he stays off drugs. In evaluating his present life, Jeff Minard boasts, "My business is prosperous, my self-esteem is high, and my marriage is good again. And I have achieved inner peace."

Minard's reputation made it difficult for him to be hired as a hospital administrator. Today refusing to hire him because of his past drug abuse would be in violation of the Americans with Disabilities Act of 1990. Minard, like many others who have used self-employment to overcome career adversity, chose a business directly in his field of expertise.

Bouncing Back Characteristic 95: Going into Competition with your Employer

A sensible path to entrepreneurial success is to enter into competition with your employer. This path works well because the entrepreneur enters a familiar field. In many situations competing with your former employer may represent poor ethics. Nevertheless, the company that created adversity for you may have treated you shabbily.

Comeback Scenario 95: Steven Jobs, Computer Company Entrepreneur

The story of Steven Jobs is a classic example of a mistreated executive going into competition with his employer. During the Spring of 1985, Apple Computer, Inc., hurriedly reorganized. Twenty percent of its work force was terminated, a first-ever quarterly loss was announced, and Steven P. Jobs, cofounder and chairman, was stripped of all his operating authority. John Sculley, Apple president and chief executive officer who was brought to the company by Jobs, was responsible for removing Jobs from line responsibility. Until June of 1985, Jobs was in charge of the development and marketing for the Macintosh computer. His other responsibility was that of chairman of Apple.

Apple's board of directors, along with outside investors, had been encouraging Sculley to assert himself against Jobs, who was perceived by some as being too autocratic and temperamental. When Jobs learned of plans to oust him from office, he attempted to persuade Sculley and the board of directors to let him retain his position. The board and executive staff, however, supported Sculley in his decision to remove Jobs. Two of Apple's key executives—the vice president for sales and chief executive officer—had been chosen personally by Sculley.

Sculley delayed removing Jobs for two reasons. First, he was concerned about a major reorganization of the company. Second, he was hesitant to hurt the feelings of Jobs, a close personal friend and the person who recruited him to Apple. Nevertheless, Sculley felt impelled to reorganize, thus neutralizing Jobs, when he learned that Jobs was plotting to have him removed from office. After the reorganization, Jobs and Sculley toured the company to explain Jobs' new role as "global visionary," an internal consulting assignment without a specific job description.

Disagreements between Jobs and Sculley began to surface as friction between the Macintosh and Apple II divisions increased. Managers and employees in the Mac division considered themselves to be the company's elite. The Apple II division was producing a higher proportion of the company's sales and profits, yet they believed that Mac personnel were getting most of the perks. At one time these perks included free fruit juice and a masseur on call.

Company insiders claimed that Jobs was concerned about the success of the company's oldest product, the Apple II. He badly wanted the Macintosh line to become more successful. Jobs once addressed the Apple II marketing personnel as "the dull and boring product division." In contrast, he was overprotective of Mac personnel and usually took their side in disputes between the divisions.

Shortly before Jobs was deposed, a board meeting was called in which plans were discussed to hire a new general manager for the Mac division. Jobs had mixed reaction about such a move. During the meeting, the directors urged Sculley to make it clear that he was the chief executive officer by taking a stand on reorganization. Sculley responded that it was difficult to act like a CEO when he had to supervise a manager of the Mac division who happened to be board chairman.

When Jobs was given final word of the reorganization, he was told that the chairman would now have absolutely no operating role. Jobs was hurt, crushed, humiliated, and disillusioned. He was also angry and resilient enough to rebuild, and had the financial wherewithal to do so. He had accumulated $90 million in Apple stock. Jobs also was confident of his powerful charisma; he knew he could charm and cajole employees into pushing toward the outer limits of their capabilities.

Jobs retaliated against Apple by building a new computer company, Next, Inc. The Next computer, designed for universities, is highly sophisticated. Although off to a slow start, it shows promise of excellent sales.

Andrea Cunningham, a former publicist for Next, Inc., analyzes the motives behind Jobs' comeback: "Part of Steve wanted to prove to others and to himself that Apple wasn't just luck. He wanted to prove that Sculley should never have let him go." Jobs believes that the Next computer should earn him the title he wanted most: "No. 1 innovator in the most innovative of all U.S. industries."[3]

Few people have the resources or talents of a Steven Jobs when they want to go into competition with a former employer. Yet resources alone cannot create a successful competitor to a large employer. Jobs was also strongly motivated by revenge against Sculley.

A More Modest Level of Competition with Your Employer.   Managers of more modest means than Steven Jobs have also rebounded from adversity by going into competition with their former employer. Among them are the vice president and general manager of a division of an aerospace firm.

Comeback Scenario 96: Jay Whitson, Founder of an Aerospace Company

When I first took charge of the Connecticut division of my company in 1975 [said Whitson], it had been operating at a loss for some time. By 1982 it was finally profitable, thus helping to balance the books for its parent company which was experiencing severe financial problems.

The company experienced two major problems the next year. The demand for the products made by the Connecticut division cooled down, and funds were mismanaged. It was therefore necessary to lay off a large percentage of the work force. The board decided to close the New Jersey facility and consolidate the entire operation in Connecticut.

To the outsider, closing the New Jersey division didn't make much sense. But you must realize that the corporation was originally based in Connecticut, and the board of directors and members of top management were located there. The New Jersey division was opened as an offshoot of the Connecticut division to handle a specific product line. When the overall company got into financial trouble, top management knew that a consolidation was necessary. They chose to close my division in order to minimize the personal inconvenience for them.

A lot of dislocation resulted from that decision. Several persons in essential technical positions were invited to join the Connecticut division to perform in the same capacity as before once the product line was reestablished. But people in managerial positions were not offered new jobs because most of them would be redundant with positions in Connecticut.

As division manager, there wasn't an equivalent opening for me in Connecticut. I might add that personality conflicts between myself and certain people in headquarters had not endeared me to them. I accepted a generous severance offer which bought me some time in finding a suitable job.

I felt I had several options to pursue. The first thing I did was to submit an offer to purchase my division from the corporation. I would borrow most of the money, using a leveraged buyout on a small scale. My offer was not only refused, but also served to generate a certain amount of hostility from top management.

I still felt I had the knowledge and capability to competently manage a manufacturing business in the aerospace field. Market research indicated there was very little competition in the product niche I had in mind. Another factor in my favor was that I had acquired a specialized technical knowledge of the product, as well as valuable connections in the field. During my years in the industry, I had developed an excellent reputation. The products I managed were of high quality, and my personal integrity was good.

Based on all these factors in my favor, I decided to launch my own corporation. I arranged an adequate bank line of credit, sold stock, and hired key personnel from the New Jersey division which had closed. I was even able to obtain some of my old equipment through an auction. We began manufacturing on a limited scale, with a modest-size labor force. To reduce managerial expenses, I functioned as vice president and general manager, as well as chief product manager, controller, and sales manager.

Today our company is fairly successful. We've won back most of our former customer base, and have received several large government contracts. During the past year, I have computerized most of our budgeting, payroll, and purchasing functions. Our sales have reached the point where we could use a few more good people.

Looking back, I have almost no regrets. The initial start-up costs were somewhat prohibitive. I still cannot afford to pay myself what I would expect to be earning in an established aerospace company. The job itself can be very demanding because there are no limits to my responsibility. I work until the job gets done, period. In the long run the risk and the opportunity costs will have been worthwhile. My career had taken a setback, and now I'm at a higher vantage point than ever. I also get a personal kick out of giving my old firm a run for its money.

Whitson capitalized on a very important business principle in founding a company to go into competition with his former employer. He identified a product niche he was qualified to handle.

Comeback Scenario 97: Stacey
Coddington, Pharmacy Operator

Both Steve Jobs and Jay Whitson overcame career adversity by establishing a manufacturing company to enter into competition with their
former employers. Stacey Coddington is an example of a person who
opened a retail outlet to compete successfully with a former employer.
She had worked as a pharmacist for an independently owned pharmacy
in a small town. The agreement was for Stacey to buy out the owner
when he retired in a few years. She would give the owner a down payment, and mortgage the balance of the purchase price.

One year before the business was to exchange hands, a major pharmacy chain made an offer to purchase the business. The owner was reluctant to sell because it would mean backing off on the agreement with
Stacey. However, the cash offer was twice the price Stacey had agreed to
pay. The owner accepted the offer, and Stacey felt devastated. She saw
her dreams of owning a profitable pharmacy disappear.

Stacey was made an offer to continue on in her position as a pharmacist in the store. Although she preferred not to work for a chain, Stacey
accepted the offer. The starting salary was higher than her current pay,
and she liked the store's clientele. After working for three months in
this position, Stacey realized that working for a corporation did not fit
her long-range plans. Her dislike for bureaucracy was intensified by her
simmering discontent over having been betrayed by the owner, however
justified he was from a financial perspective.

Stacey put her plans for owning a pharmacy back on track. She continued to save money toward someday investing in her own retail pharmacy, and investigated other possibilities for purchasing a pharmacy in
the surrounding area. Nothing attractive presented itself, so Stacey formulated another strategy. She began to look for store space on a good
location that was suitable for conversion to a pharmacy.

It became apparent that the best location would be in the same neighborhood where she was currently working. The only nearby pharmacy
(including general merchandise) was the one she worked for. In addition, the population could support another pharmacy, and Stacey had
developed a solid base of customers who valued her services.

With the assistance of a real-estate broker, Stacey searched for the
right location. Six months later Stacey found empty space in a small
plaza that seemed to fit her requirements. The plaza contained a supermarket, launderette, whiskey store, and adequate parking—all important back-up features for a pharmacy. Within four months Stacey was in
business. She made good use of the experience she gathered working
for the chain with respect to merchandising and handling employees.

Over the next four years, Stacey expanded the store twice and purchased the plaza. She now employs two full-time pharmacists, a store
manager, and approximately 30 part-time workers.

Asked if she intends to become a chain, Stacey replied, "No, I've accomplished what I wanted for now. I've got a nice little empire I can
wrap my arms around, and I'm competing with a chain in at least one
location." Coddington, similar to many successful business people, sticks
to her knitting and sets realistic goals. In this way she is not substituting
one adversity for another.

Bouncing Back Characteristic 96: Convert Your Hobby into a Business

One of the major challenges facing managers today is coping with the
job stress created by understaffing. As organizations trim down, managers are expected to not only get by with less staff support, but produce even more. A customer service manager in a printing company
with a national customer base, looks at the situation in these terms:

> October and November was our busiest season. Most of our employ-
> ees were working about 15 hours of overtime. At least they were re-
> ceiving overtime pay. The managers and supervisors were putting in
> 70- and 80-hour weeks with no extra compensation. The tension was
> unbelievable. Most of us knew that if we didn't get the orders out on
> time, our jobs would be in jeopardy. Our company treats production
> and clerical workers better than they treat managers. The reason is
> simple: there is a shortage of people for entry-level jobs, but there
> are a lot of managers looking for work.

The printing company manager's comments have an indirect link to
coping with adversity through entrepreneurship. Many managers who
cope with adversity through self-employment are leaving a super-
charged, stressful work environment. It is therefore sensible to attempt
to escape some of the high stress when one becomes an entrepreneur.
Yet for many would-be entrepreneurs, establishing and operating a
business can be even more stressful than the adverse environment left
behind. It is therefore sensible to start a business whose basic work is
inherently enjoyable. Converting a hobby or pastime into a business is
helpful because doing work one enjoys is less stressful than an equal
amount of time invested in distasteful work.

Comeback Scenario 98: Mike Gilbert, Franchise Operator

Mike was forced into early retirement at age 56 by his employer of 23 years. With six months' severance pay and a partial pension he was not destitute, but he needed to earn a moderate income to cover his family expenses. After several months of looking for new corporate employment, Ted became discouraged.

> I hadn't risen high enough on the ladder to qualify for an executive position [said Ted], and the world was hardly beating a path to the door of a middle manager my age. I therefore decided to join the ranks of franchise operators. The best financial deal I could find was operating a franchised rug cleaning business. The franchisers were true to their word. Rug cleaning is a good business. By putting in my 70 hours per week, I was making a living. I didn't have to clean rugs myself, but I still didn't care one iota for cleaning rugs. Clean carpets are aesthetically pleasing to me, but I just can't get excited about them. Trying to promote my business became a drag.
>
> My motivation for staying in the rug cleaning business was simply to make money, and it was a good deal. But the negative pressures were building up inside of me. Because the franchise was a success, I was able to sell out at a small profit. I then bought an instant car service franchise. Since I had always taken impeccable care of my own cars, I took an immediate love to the business. I was like a cat lover taking in stray kittens. Each car that came in for servicing meant something to me. The profit margins may be a little thinner than in carpet cleaning, but I feel some inner peace. I get a little charge every time I see a serviced car pull out of the place.

Mike Gilbert's success in his instant car service franchise was partly attributable to his inherent interest in maintaining automobiles. Unless you enjoy the nature of the work you have chosen to overcome a setback, your adversity may intensify.

Comeback Scenario 99: Ted Ehrenfried, Exercise Machine Entrepreneur

A former marketing executive, Ted Ehrenfried, took a riskier route to converting a hobby into a business in order to resolve a career crisis. About 13 years prior, Ehrenfried, who was the marketing director of his firm, made a bid to become company president. Instead of receiving the promotion, he was fired without explanation. Ehrenfried was crushed. "Letting others control my life totally deluded me," he says.

Ehrenfried was so depressed he could hardly get out of bed for a month.

Finally two of his sons challenged Ehrenfried to pull himself together and do something. When he asked his sons what he should do, Ehrenfried was told to start his own business. He was encouraged to market the thigh stretching machine he had built in his spare time for his younger son. Although skeptical that the machine would sell, Ehrenfried mobilized himself to begin a comeback. He spent months developing the machine in his garage in Newport News, Virginia.

In 1982 he began selling his machines by taking a couple of "Power-stretchers" to a karate tournament in Atlanta. During the first day of the tournament he wrote 36 orders for his machine. Encouraged by the good reception, Ehrenfried wrote a business plan and presented it to several banks. The bank officials were skeptical, noting that people can stretch themselves on the floor. They were also concerned that Ehrenfried had never run a business previously.

Ehrenfried decided to persist despite the lack of bank support. To raise cash, he sold his house, the car, and other personal belongings. "My two college age sons joined the Marines and saved me the expense of tuition," recalls Ehrenfried. "My old executive office at the company had been bigger than the shack I rented for the new business. All my friends thought I had gone off the deep end."

Fortunately for Ehrenfried, his friends misjudged the potential in his business. Within three years, sales for his new business, Treco Products Inc., exceeded $2 million. An unintended blessing from the business occurred after Brook, one of his sons, was injured in a terrorist bombing in Beirut. The Power-stretcher proved instrumental in Brook's physical rehabilitation.[4]

Ted Ehrenfried did take a big risk to overcome the adversity of being fired. However, the passion he had for his thigh stretching machine helped fuel a successful business.

Bouncing Back Characteristic 97: The Search for Creative Ventures

Searching for a creative venture is particularly important for the person who pursues the entrepreneurial escape route from adversity. To be creative, a venture must be unique and useful, both important qualities to avoid a business failure. Quite often the person who becomes an entrepreneur to escape adversity can ill afford another major setback in the present.

Comeback Scenario 100: Bud Ross, Communications Entrepreneur

Bud Ross is an example of a resilient manager who successfully searched for a creative venture to turn around his career. Bud rebounded from bankruptcy to start Birdview Satellite Communications, Inc., a decade ago. The Chanute, Kansas, firm manufactures an earth station system that allows customers in isolated areas to view television programs via satellite. Although satellite systems for television are commonplace today, Ross was a pioneer in seeing its possibilities for side distribution in the early 1980s.

Ross's entrepreneurial career began in his family's garage in Overland Park, Kansas. After several years of guitar playing experience for a rock and roll band, in 1963 he started Kustom Electronics, a manufacturer of guitar amplifiers. Ross ran the firm for eight years without losing money, then moved to larger space in Chanute. He broadened the product line to include many other electronic devices such as public address systems. As his success grew, Ross founded eight other companies making such diverse products as boats and high-speed printing presses.

"People started coming to me with ideas, and I started putting up the dollars," Ross explains. "Before long it had gotten totally out of hand. It was physically, mentally, and financially more than I could go through."

In 1973, Ross was forced to sell the business and liquidate his other assets to pay his creditors. He went bankrupt and was divorced the following year. He remarried a year later and moved with his new wife to Colorado. Ross became a full-time homemaker while his wife worked. By 1977, he wanted to work outside the home once again. After returning to Chanute, he dabbled in several businesses, until one day he spotted an idea for a product that stirred up his creative energy. The 1980 Neiman-Marcus Christmas catalog listed a private satellite receiving station for $12,500. Ross says, "I had me a new toy."[5]

Ross was convinced he could manufacture and sell a comparable system for much less money. Within six months, Birdview was turning out its product for under $3,000: a complete earth station system with a satellite receiving dish, the mount to hold the dish, a device for converting signals to the right frequency, and a station selector. (Ross's creative contribution was not in inventing the earth satellite system but in recognizing a good idea and then producing it at a much reduced price.)

The future of Ross's company awaits the outcome of pending legislation about the legality of a system that can be used to circumvent paying for cable TV programs. Even if the satellite dishes are ruled illegal, it is possible that the pay-TV firms will sell decoders to "dish" owners that will allow them to unscramble their signals.

Whatever the final outcome of the satellite dish industry, Ross had completed his comeback by 1983. He had become chairman of SPACE, a Washington-based earth station industry association. Ross told his wife, "If God ever prepared someone to do something, he prepared me to do this."[5]

Ross's words point to an important principle of job satisfaction. If you believe that the work you are doing is a calling, your motivation will be so high that you can ward off many potential forms of adversity.

Bouncing Back Characteristic 98: Purchase Part of Your Company

Another entrepreneurial escape route from a career crisis is to purchase part of your company. In this way the people who have created your adversity become partners in helping you overcome your problem.

Comeback Scenario 101: Art Chase, Distributor for His Former Employer

Art Chase successfully pulled off the caper of buying part of his former employer. His company manufactured expensive ballpoint pens and their refills. Chase, an abrasive and intimidating individual, was the manager of the refill division. Top management of the company decided to phase out the refill division because of its slim profit margins. A contributing problem was that lower-priced refills were readily available in the aftermarket.

Chase came up with a simple plan to save his job, preserve the division, and keep his employer happy. He proposed to top management, "Let me buy out the refill division and serve as the refill distributor for your pens. The advantage of my proposition is that it will allow us to maintain our old customers and develop new ones. I am willing to make a down payment, and pay the balance out of profits over a five-year period. Also, this will get me out of your hair on a daily basis."

Chase and top management agreed on a satisfactory purchase price, and he developed a successful pen refill distributorship for his firm's ballpoint pens and for other brands. Chase was particularly happy about the deal because he now had his own business and did not have to risk looking for a marketing position with his limited background.

Art Chase was in a unique situation, but his curious idea for self-employment has an important message. Search for creative alternatives when your livelihood is on the line.

Bouncing Back Characteristic 99:
Try a Part-Time
Self-Employment Solution

A modified entrepreneurial approach worthy of consideration is to be self-employed part time until full-time employment is again available. The part-time approach could include doing contract work for a company or running a small business on a part-time basis. Both maneuvers can help stave off financial collapse until a more permanent solution to a career crisis is found.

Comeback Scenario 102: Phil
Meadows, Part-Time Training
Director

Phil was the director of technical training for an electronics firm in Houston. Both he and his family enjoyed their life and intended to become permanent residents of their community. As part of a cost reduction program, the company substantially reduced its training budget and Phil was laid off. Phil tried for several months to find new employment close to home but was unsuccessful.

Working his personal contacts, Phil learned of a training director's opening in Cleveland. He telephoned the firm, sent his resume, and was invited for an interview. The director of human resources told Phil they were impressed with him but that the timing was poor—they could not yet afford to hire a full-time training director. However, they would be willing to hire Phil on a contract basis to carry out a few training projects. Rather than deplete his rapidly diminishing savings any further, Phil accepted the contract work. He did some of the work on company premises, but most of it back home in Houston.

Management was pleased with the quality of Phil's work. The company continued to grow and 13 months later, Phil was offered a full-time job as the company training director. His new position would give him more responsibility and more subordinates than his previous one.

A family conference was called, and it was decided that the family should relocate. Phil and his wife reasoned that it would be easier for her to find a computer programmer's job in Cleveland than it would be for him to find suitable employment in Houston. The couple also decided that when the family's economic survival depends on relocation, the children would have to adjust.

Phil said, "The family adjusted just fine. My wife found a great job as a systems programmer, and the two children found that there are decent kids in this world who live outside their neighborhood in Houston. We are pleased with the good fortune that came out of an unhappy set of circumstances."

Phil worked his way out of adversity because he was flexible. Although he did not initially plan to become a contract worker, he capitalized upon the opportunity when it presented itself. His flexibility paid off because he soon was offered full-time employment as a training director.

Comeback Scenario 103: Gino Roma, Part-Time Barber

Part-time self-employment can also help people who are not corporate employees. Gino Roma owned and operated a barbershop. Business declined as hair styling salons began to attract many of the people who formerly went to a barber for a haircut (instead of styling). "Not too many people anymore want to have their hair cut by a middle-aged man," said Gino. "They like to be styled by those young ladies." Revenue from the shop declined steadily to the point that Gino was working at close to the minimum wage. He closed his shop when his lease expired at the end of the year, and sold whatever equipment and supplies he could. For sentimental reasons, he kept his scissors, combs, and clippers.

Gino needed some means of contributing more to the support of his wife and two daughters. His wife's earnings as a check-out clerk in a supermarket were hardly sufficient to meet family expenses. Gino found a job as a laborer with the county highway department. Although the pay was low, the job offered a standard package of employee benefits. After the first week of work, Gino confronted the reality of his paltry take-home pay of $122. Yet he did not want to quit because of the potential of higher salary in the future and good job security and benefits.

Gino's straightforward solution to his financial dilemma was to operate a barbershop out of his home several nights a week and on Saturday. He used his credit card to purchase barber shop equipment suitable for his new enterprise, and located Gino's Barber Shop in his family room. Because of zoning laws, Gino was not able to advertise or place a barbershop sign in front of his house. Yet his customer base grew rapidly when neighborhood people realized they could get haircuts in the evening or did not have to spend a big chunk of Saturday waiting at a barbershop. Gino's survival plan worked well. His return to barbering helped him regain the rhythm of his life, and he was able to meet his family expenses.

Bouncing Back Characteristic 100: Create a New Venture with No Money

Bouncing back from career adversity by creating a new enterprise usually requires capital. Many of the people described in this chapter made substantial investments in their new business. Even Gino Roma needed about $1,500 to open a barbershop in his home. With a combination of business acumen and chutzpa, a new venture can be created with no money down. Such was the experience of a man who founded a marble and granite company.

Comeback Scenario 104: Garry Wilson, Marble Company Founder

Such was the experience of Garry Wilson of the Vintage Marble Company. Here is the letter he wrote describing his experiences:

> At 28 I was wrongfully fired from my $40,000 a year sales manager job at a marble and granite fabrication firm. I was unemployed and filing for bankruptcy when I read a magazine article about overcoming setbacks in business. With six hours left in the business day, I frantically called everyone I knew to tell them of the new marble and granite business I was starting.
> What a bluff—I didn't have a dime. But I did know the business and after two weeks of relentless hustling, I landed a $79,000 contract. So I negotiated a 40 percent deposit and quickly found a ship and bought the material needed. Vintage Marble Company was in business. Last year we grossed $420,000 and expect to do more than $750,000 this year. I avoided bankruptcy, paid off all my debts, and recently opened a new showroom in San Diego.[6]

Garry Wilson was bluffing less than he realized. The essence of an entrepreneurial venture is not a factory, mill, store, or office. Rather it is the spirit and imagination of the person who intends to make the product or provide the service. Furthermore, that same spirit and imagination can be utilized to fuel a career comeback.

Action Tips

Entrepreneurship, and other forms of self-employment, have considerable potential as career adversity fighters. As you think of entrepreneurship and self-employment as ways of improving your career, review these points and investigate these possibilities:

1. Evaluate whether you are entrepreneurial material.
2. Think of the various adversities entrepreneurship can overcome.
3. Go into competition with your former employer.
4. Convert your hobby into a business.
5. Search for a creative venture.
6. Purchase part of your company.
7. Try part-time self-employment.
8. Create a new venture with no money.

11
Holding Your Personal Life Together

Career adversity readily spills over into personal life, thus compounding the misery. Without careful attention to this rippling effect, the person facing a career crisis enters into a self-perpetuating cycle. Career adversity creates personal adversity which in turn makes it more difficult to bounce back from the problem that started the cycle.

Evidence of this rippling problem is found in the many case histories of people whose marriage crumbled under the weight of a prolonged career crisis. Several of these instances of career crisis followed by divorce—such as the entrepreneur with the earth satellite system—were described earlier. Preoccupation with a career disaster frequently makes it difficult for a person to pay proper attention to his or her domestic partner, thus creating resentment and anger on the other person's part.

To be a truly resilient manager or professional, it is necessary to hold one's personal life together during the crisis. Some people can intuitively handle the simultaneous demands of work and personal life when working in the midst of a crisis. Others need a more planned approach to keeping personal life under control while experiencing career turmoil. Here we describe some approaches to keep in mind in order to stabilize personal life while fighting a major career battle.

Bouncing Back Characteristic 101: Share Your Burden with Family and Friends

Faced with a career crisis it is easy to slip into the pattern of isolating oneself from family and friends. Isolation of this type creates two problems. First, it denies the person facing the crisis the emotional support so vitally needed in times of emotional turmoil. Second, the isolation creates strained feelings between the person in crisis and family and friends. Self-imposed isolation leads to others treating you as "touchy," thus creating further communication barriers.

The crisis of being fired creates a particular need for sharing your burden because being out of work can be such a lonely experience. Each day turns up its own joys and disappointments. A phone call to a friend to update him or her on your job search can be a useful way of dealing with your feelings. It's good to get somebody else (perhaps in addition to your spouse or partner) to share in the excitement of a good lead turned up and the despair of another rejection. An invaluable friend is someone who has successfully handled being fired.

A curious form of loneliness that occurs between jobs stems from the fact that many colleagues do not want you around. People with terminal illnesses often face the same plight. Managers who have felt the loneliness of being fired are often perplexed by their colleague's silence. One manager who was fired at one point in his life observes that one of the worst things is that no one wanted to associate with him anymore. He claims that friends and professional acquaintances become so uncomfortable around him that he ceased going out just to avoid the awkward confrontations.[1]

Comeback Scenario 105: Dan Bluestone, Middle Manager

A helpful aspect of sharing your burden with family and friends is to be open about your feelings and concerns. It may be necessary to hold a family conference to explain the situation. A former IBM middle manager who was demoted to a field sales position called together his wife and two children (teenagers), and told them:

> Something very annoying and hurtful has happened to me at the office. I am no longer a marketing manager. I've been given a small territory in which to knock on doors and sell typewriters. I don't like it, and I'm going to miss having my own office and assistant. It's a step backwards in my career. But I've accepted the situation. Big Blue has decided to put a lot of managers out in the field to increase

sales. IBM is still a great company, and I expect to soon be earning even more than I did in the past.

I may feel miserable, and my temper may be short for awhile, but I'll survive. My ego may be deflated, but I'm going to try to be a good husband and father. What is your reaction to my predicament?

Instead of anger, the man received approbation, hugs, and a promise of help from his entire family. The question posed by the man is an important part of sharing your emotional burden. By asking how others feel about your crisis, two-way communication is encouraged. People surrounding the person in crisis may sometimes resent all the attention he or she is getting, much like other family members who come to resent a physically sick or injured parent or child.

The feedback from family members is sometimes illuminating because it puts relationships in a new perspective. An attorney who had been disbarred described how the incident affected her marital relationship: "My misery and despair actually improved my relationship with Alec. He really opened up to me. Alec said that for the first time he really felt needed; that in the past I was always the stronger one. Now that I needed a shoulder to lean on, he could offer me support. Alec was genuinely sorry for what happened to me, but he enjoyed giving me emotional first aid. For the three months it took me to find new employment, he became the breadwinner, and it felt good to him.

"Nothing is worth having been disbarred, but at least it brought me closer to my husband. Alec revealed to me for the first time that he always wished he could help me, but that I was so strong and independent he didn't know how to help. He finally found an opening."

Communicating with your family about your burden can be overdone. Spare your mate. Instead, find an objective sounding board to listen to your feelings and career concerns. Such a person could be an outplacement counselor, a therapist, or a close friend. The main requirement is that he or she stay objective. Although you will want to share some of your feelings with your significant other, it is unfair to burden that person with the totality of your concerns. Incessant conversation about career concerns gets boring, and may inhibit romance. An effective counselor can help you maintain your primary intimate relationship as well as help you see your situation clearly.[2]

Bouncing Back Characteristic 102: Create Time for Dealing with Other Issues

A high school senior made a suicide attempt by taking an overdose of every pill she could find in the medicine cabinet. After being revived at the hospital, she was asked by a suicide counselor if she had ever spoken to her parents about her concerns. The young woman replied, "I tried and tried but nobody would listen to me. The family business was going bankrupt and my parents were going crazy over it. For two years all I ever heard was how bad things were in the store. Neither Mom nor Dad could listen to my problems. I would make some comment about needing new running shoes, and they would jump on me about not being understanding.

"It became so depressing living under those conditions. My good friends still care about what was happening inside of me, but my own parents acted as if they were the only people with problems."

A suicide attempt may be an immature reaction to not being listened to, but the young woman's story does illustrate an important point. Faced with the unremitting pressure of a career crisis, it is important for the individual to periodically set aside preoccupation with the crisis and deal with other family issues. Such advice, however, is not easy to follow. The stress generated by adversity typically interferes with concentration.

Don't Let Everything Else Slide.   One way of creating time for dealing with other issues is to say to yourself at the start of each day, "I know the big issue I'm facing today is still this horrible career problem. But that doesn't mean I'm going to let everything else in my life slide." The person would then budget a specific time slot for dealing with issues other than the career crisis. A specific recommendation would be to conduct a family dinner conversation that concentrates on any other issue but the career crisis.

Another way of creating a time slot for issues other than your career adversity would be to plan a social engagement that does not center on the crisis. A resilient manager might say to herself, "Tonight Roger is taking me out for dinner and dancing. I will talk about anything but the fact that if I don't come up with a new product for the company in the next three months, I will be an ex-product development manager. If he asks me how things are going in the office, I will tell him 'fine,' and then reverse the question."

A colleague of mine was on the verge of being denied tenure unless he could get two scholarly articles published in one year (certainly a back-to-the-wall situation). He gradually recognized that his preoccupation with this concern was monopolizing the conversation between himself and his girlfriend. One night when his girlfriend asked, "Any news about tenure?" the professor replied, "Nothing new since yesterday, Lisa. However, I don't want to talk about tenure tonight. I'm beginning to bore myself with the topic, and I must be boring you. Let's talk about the most significant thing that happened to you today."

A plausible reason a crisis may block out other issues is that people close to the person think that he or she is facing doom. Although you may feel you *are* facing doom, it is helpful to place the magnitude of your crisis in perspective for others. Ten years after graduating from college, a food administration major opened a restaurant that failed. In the process he had lost his savings and his share of a family inheritance. At a sparse dinner on the date of the liquidation sale of the restaurant's physical assets, he told his wife:

> I know my business has been wiped out, and I've lost a lot of money, and I have a big load to pay back. But my loss goes no further than that. I'm still an experienced, professional restaurant manager. I can no doubt find a good job in two months, and I could get a job managing a fast food restaurant by the weekend if I wanted to. We won't even have to relocate. Some of my dreams have been set aside, but my life is still intact.

In short, although career adversity can be overwhelming and preoccupying, concentrate on paying attention to significant others. Convey the impression that although you are facing problems, you will be able to get things under control. If you act too much in the disaster mode, your personal life will also suffer.

Bouncing Back Characteristic 103: Avoid Self-Defeating Behavior

Holding one's personal life together during a career crisis is made all the more difficult when the individual engages in self-defeating behavior. People close to the crisis sufferer may withdraw their emotional support as they watch him or her engage in self-defeating or self-destructive behavior. Furthermore, they may feel alienated from him or her and thus increase the isolation of the person in crisis. The self-defeating behaviors engaged in by some not so resilient people in response to crisis include the following:

- Procrastination over such matters as looking for a new job, dealing with irate creditors, attending to medical problems, paying bills, making household and automotive repairs, and taking care of routine household chores such as sewing and yardwork.
- Drinking earlier and earlier in the day, manifested in such behavior as returning from a job search at three in the afternoon and proclaiming, "I deserve a few drinks after the horrendous week I've faced."

- Increased cigarette consumption to the point that it results in visible symptoms such as smoker's cough and nicotine-stained fingers.

- Eating disorders including both over- and undereating to the point that it has a negative impact on the person's appearance.

- Drug abuse and the attendant use of household money and sale of assets in order to pay for the drugs.

- Repeated incidents of spouse abuse and child abuse, both verbal and physical.

- Throwing temper tantrums in response to minor disagreements with family members.

- Canceling of business and social appointments that are potentially beneficial in resolving the crisis, such as those with an outplacement counselor or a bank official.

- Staying up so late at night watching television, reading, or pacing the floor that the person sleeps late the next day, that he or she is late for work or the day's first job hunting appointment.

- Going into a defensive shell in order to avoid contact with people who can possibly be of help, such as family members, friends, and relatives. As the person becomes increasingly isolated from possible helpers, his or her capacity to resolve the crisis decreases.

How to Avoid Self-Defeating Behaviors. How can a person avoid self-defeating behavior when such behavior usually occurs without any intention to harm oneself or others? The best approach is to ask for constructive feedback from friends and family members. A person enmeshed in the emotional turmoil of a crisis might ask a spouse, "Can you help me by pointing to anything I've done lately that could be hurting my chances of overcoming the problem I'm facing?" If the question is asked in a tone that suggests the person really welcomes constructive feedback, the result could be illuminating. A friend of mine asked this question of his wife and was told, "I think I can help. You are drinking too much lately, and you attack too hard whenever we have a disagreement."

In the absence of feedback about possible self-defeating behavior, one can engage in self-analysis. One might ask himself or herself, "What am I doing lately that is damaging my personal life or making it difficult for me to overcome my career crisis?" Another approach would be to review, in checklist fashion, the symptoms of self-destructive behavior listed above and ask yourself about each one, "Am I doing this?"

Bouncing Back Characteristic 104: Keep Up Your Physical Appearance

Maintaining a favorable appearance is one part of holding your personal life together. Also, if you maintain or improve your physical appearance, you will feel self-confident and healthy enough to make a serious comeback attempt.

Physical appearance includes more than wardrobe and hair style. Equally important is to not look like you are in the midst of a crisis. White people are at a disadvantage in looking healthy when faced with a crisis because their skin can look ashen when they are distraught or depressed. The antidote is appropriate exposure to the outdoors along with regular exercise, which improves circulation enough to combat a pallor. White people, as well as people of color, can improve their appearance through exercise because of the healthy glow it provides beyond skin color.

Looking better and therefore feeling better can help a person deal effectively with a number of situations the crisis battler is likely to encounter in which a favorable appearance is an asset, including:

- Meeting with a top executive to make a last ditch effort to convince that person that your organizational unit is vital to the prosperity of the firm

- Applying for yet another job when you have already applied for 37 others

- Meeting with an irate creditor to convince him or her that although you are delinquent with your payments you know that business will pick up soon

- Attempting to convince a venture capitalist that your idea for a new business would be an excellent investment for him or her

- Cultivating new personal relationships that can help you maintain a decent life while you work your way out of adversity

Comeback Scenario 106: Bill Zanker, Self-Help Entrepreneur

The story of Bill Zanker, a millionaire who made his fortune in the adult education market, illustrates how a favorable appearance can help a person overcome career adversity. The adversity faced by playboy Zanker was being mediocre. To a power-driven, egotistical person, the fact of not being successful is a potent form of adversity. In the early 1980s, Zanker was a terminal graduate student in New York. An elegant evening meal meant ordering red wine with his hamburger. He describes the turning point in his life:

> When I first started the Learning Annex in 1980, the only businesswear I owned was a handful of Bar Mitzvah ties and a $99 polyester suit. It was perfect because everyone believed adult education was for hippies and secretaries who wanted to read Virginia Woolf. My agent thought I looked so cheap. She refused to represent me unless I bought a $1,000 Giorgio Armani suit.
>
> Zanker took the agent's advice seriously, and dredged up enough money to buy an Armani suit. He named the gray wool suit with a faint herringbone weave "Le Suit." For the next few months he wore Le Suit to every meeting, and the Learning Annex expanded rapidly. The following summer, Zanker made a public offering of stock for his company and raised $3.3 million. "It was like a bolt of self-confidence every time I put that suit on. I swear I walked and talked differently in it. Zanker explains the effect of such a nervy purchase: "Your life will never be the same. But you can't cheap out and buy the $800 suit. You have to break the $1,000."[3]
>
> We doubt that a $1,000 suit will change the lives of many people. Nevertheless, the valid message from Zanker's story is that if you are proud of your appearance, it will boost your self-confidence, thus helping you cope with a crisis.

Bouncing Back Characteristic 105: Strive for Emotional and Physical Intimacy

Preoccupation with adversity interferes with emotional and physical intimacy. The adversity sufferer becomes isolated and withdrawn rather than intimate as she or he worries about survival. Such behavior is self-defeating because achieving intimacy is necessary to deal effectively with the emotional turmoil associated with adversity. Having an intimate relationship helps ward off some of the feelings of isolation and abandonment associated with a career crisis. When middle managers lose their job, they feel it's a personal rejection.

Sharing the Burden.   Sharing one's burdens with family and friends is a starting point in achieving emotional intimacy. However, further actions may also be necessary. Intimacy results from emotional closeness, and this closeness can only be achieved through expressing feelings to a partner about many topics and issues. Expression of feelings is important because intimacy is rarely achieved by an exchange of factual information or simply sharing activities.

A challenge in achieving intimacy is that men and women often have a different perception of what constitutes intimacy. Women appear to be, on average, better connoisseurs of intimacy. Ted Huston, a psychologist who has studied 130 couples intensively, has observed these differences. He notes, "For the wives, intimacy means talking things over, especially talking about the relationship itself. The men, by and large, don't understand what the wives want from them. They say, 'I want to do things with her, and all she wants to do is talk.'"[4]

Communication Sessions. A practical tactic for achieving intimacy—during periods of adversity or at other times—would be to conduct regular communication sessions with one's partner. The sessions are likely to be the most effective if they take place during natural activities such as walking together, in a restaurant, or in bed. Scheduling a formal communication session can sometimes interfere with the intimacy it is intended to achieve. The problem is that the session may resemble a negotiation meeting about problems within the relationship.

During these communication sessions it is important to express feelings about the adversity as well as other aspects of life. Express both positive and negative feelings to prevent the sessions from becoming a forum for only gripes and discontents. The specific topics to communicate about usually arise naturally in response to the circumstances facing the partners. We asked several people to specify the topics they dealt with during close moments with their confidant. Here is a sampling of what they revealed:

- Hopes about each of our futures
- Whether or not one of us might have the AIDS virus and not be aware of it
- The fact that the other person sweats too much
- How peaceful the other person looked while sleeping
- How much they enjoy watching romantic movies together
- How close the two came to fitting each other's ideal mate
- The worst fears each person had about the future
- What made each person happy
- How good a job they felt each was doing as a parent

- How much each appreciated the relationship
- How much each worried about money
- The importance each attached to money
- The worst things each faced in past relationships
- How the other person felt about becoming one year older on his or her birthday
- The fears the other person had about getting older
- How happy each person was with his or her life so far

Emotional and Physical Intimacy Influence Each Other. Emotional and physical intimacy have a reciprocal relationship. Emotional intimacy leads to physical intimacy, and physical intimacy can sometimes facilitate emotional intimacy. Many couples are drawn closer to each intellectually and emotionally after making love. One of the best by-products of lovemaking for many people is the pillow talk that follows.

Physical intimacy helps coping with adversity in other ways in addition to facilitating emotional intimacy. The release of tension associated with a vigorous orgasm is helpful in managing any type of stress including that stemming from career crisis. Sex has to be frequent to be an instrumental part of stress management. Otherwise the frustration and disappointment associated with infrequent sex may create more problems than it solves.

Pleasing and vigorous sex helps cope with the stress associated with adversity in another important way: Good sex is good exercise, perhaps equivalent to a jog around the block, a one-mile bike ride, or nine holes of golf. And exercise is the natural way to reduce stress.

Bouncing Back Characteristic 106: Maintain a Sense of Humor

To both relieve tension and keep life in perspective during a career crisis, it is helpful to occasionally look at the humorous aspects of adversity. A good sense of humor helps keep personal life together because it makes the adversity sufferer more approachable and more human. Warm human relationships and intimacy are thus preserved during the period of hard times. Humor can take the form of witty comments about the adverse circumstances, poking fun at oneself, and good-news/

bad-news jokes. A starter kit of potentially humorous adversity comments follows:

Ancient joke about adversity in the retailing
business

> JAKE: How's business, Sam?
>
> SAM: Terrible, Jake. Things are getting worse every day.
>
> JAKE: How's that?
>
> SAM: On Monday I sold one suit. On Tuesday I didn't sell any suits. And business was even worse on Wednesday.
>
> JAKE: You make no sense, Sam. How could business be worse on Wednesday than Tuesday, if you didn't sell even one suit on Tuesday?
>
> SAM: The man who bought the suit on Monday returned it on Wednesday.

Good-News/Bad-News Quips

The good news is that I will finally be able to spend more time with the family and fixing up things around the house. The bad news is that I've been fired.

The good news is that I've finally found a solution to the problem of our children being too dependent on us. The bad news is that they are going to have to find a way to finance their own college. My business is facing bankruptcy.

Miscellaneous Quips

When I agreed to help the community study the problems of the homeless, I didn't know that I would be joining their ranks.

I've been demoted so far down into the organization that the gang at the office gave me a black lunch box to take to work.

I now know the true meaning of the term "consultant." That's an unemployed person with a new set of business cards.

Asked why he gave a five-dollar bill to a beggar, the advertising account executive said to his girlfriend, "I empathize with the guy. If I don't land a big account this month, I'll be joining him on the street corner. And then I'll want people to give me a five-dollar handout."

Action Tips

Career adversity poses a threat to your personal life. To keep your personal life together while facing adversity, remember to:

1. Share your burden with family and friends (but don't overdo it).

2. Create time for dealing with issues other than your career adversity.

3. Avoid self-defeating behavior (such as alcohol abuse and missing important appointments).

4. Keep up your physical appearance.

5. Strive for emotional and physical intimacy.

6. Maintain a sense of humor.

12

Preparing in Advance for a Crisis

Ambitious people typically face at least one career crisis because they place themselves at risk through such means as holding an executive position, owning and operating a business, or stepping on the toes of an insecure executive. Furthermore, many successful people face more than one crisis in their career. It is therefore valuable for most people to assume that someday they will face a serious career reversal, and to prepare in advance to soften its blow. It is even conceivable that astute planning will help you prevent a major career crisis.

Van Gordon Sauter, a writer and former president of CBS News, commented during a late stage in his career that it is almost inevitable that at some point a person will turn on you. Sauter's suggestion for dealing with the inevitable is to adopt the strategy of Clyde Beatty, the legendary circus animal trainer.[1]

> When Beatty was attacked, he was able to cope because he had always known that someday he would temporarily lose control of the lion cage, that some cat would come at him and get him. And he always knew how he was going to get out of the cage. The key thing was that even in the greatest crisis he could never let the other cats know that he was in trouble. If they knew he was vulnerable, he was gone. It's much the same in our lives.

You can decrease your vulnerability to the career crisis created by a vindictive corporate feline, as well as other factors, by incorporating the tactics described below into your career planning. By so doing you should be able to soften the blow of your next—and hopefully, only—career crisis.

Bouncing Back Characteristic 107: Develop a Crisis Mentality

Crisis management expert, and former American Motors CEO, Gerald Meyers agrees with one of the key premises of this book—crises in business are so frequent they are almost inevitable. Because of their inevitability, managers need to learn crisis management techniques. Many of Meyers' strategies deal with managing the organization's crisis. One of his suggestions, however, deals with managing an individual's own crisis. Meyers recommends that managers develop a crisis mentality, because job security is a fictitious state in our present business environment.

> Once you can accept that crisis is not beyond the realm of possibility, you can deal with it positively [says Meyers]. We're taught to think success, which is good—as far as it goes. But it's not complete. You must also develop an attitude that takes into account the unexpected disaster. It's not just the CEO who must cope with it, but all company executives.[2]
>
> Meyers believes that by successfully managing crises, companies sharpen their competitive edge. Similarly, individuals can become more competitive by handling crises and preparing in advance to make the crisis less devastating.

Develop a Career Insurance Protection Plan.   Most people pay substantial premiums to insure their automobiles, homes, health, and life, but few think of insuring their careers. Leading employment agency executive and author, Robert Half has formulated suggestions to provide the individual with an insurance protection plan. In Half's plan, "There is no premium to pay and the dividends can be enormous." Specifically, he suggests there are key steps you can take now that will help you cope should the axe fall. The same suggestions can be used to help win a promotion or land a better job. Half suggests the following policies to insure you against the ravages of being fired or laid off:[3]

Keeping an ongoing file of all your accomplishments. Make note of every concrete accomplishment, even if it seems minuscule at the time. The most effective tactic for holding onto your job when others are being dismissed is to be able to document the contributions you have made to the organization. Cite verifiable, tangible accomplishments such as increased sales or decreased costs. Documentation of this type is much more impressive than statements of other people's opinions about your accomplishments.

Be prepared for any contingency by maintaining a constantly updated resume. Revise your resume regularly, making sure to include your major accomplishments and key occupational skills. The latter would include selling ability, communication skills, computer skills, negotiating ability, conflict-resolution skills, problem-solving skills, and data analysis skills. Half cautions that an inferior or outdated resume can be a job candidate's worst enemy, and we concur.

Sharpen your communication skills. Studies conducted by an independent research firm provide additional support for the link between career success and the ability to communicate effectively with superiors, subordinates, and peers. Written communication skills are also important. Impoverished communication skills decrease one's chances of landing a new position should the need arise.

Keep records of the people you meet in business, as well as socially, who could conceivably be sources of job leads or who might even be in a position to hire you themselves. As a veteran executive stated, "Despite your education and experience, you're only as good as your Rolodex in today's business environment."[4] Your network of contacts may take years to establish but it can prove invaluable. Keep files with names, addresses, telephone numbers, and other pertinent data. Many people today store this information in a computer as a substitute for a card-based filing system. If it seems appropriate, keep in touch with people in your network by sending a holiday greeting card or a newspaper or magazine clipping of potential interest to the individual.

Strive toward becoming indispensable. Employees who try harder, who volunteer for additional responsibility, who demonstrate outstanding knowledge of company operations, and who have a good track record of problem solving are among the last to be laid off—even during dire business conditions.

Persist in your professional education. Keep abreast of information in your field by reading relevant trade publications, newspapers, books, and newsletters. The more relevant work-related information you have, the greater the chances of keeping your current job or finding a new one if necessary.

Work at being pleasant and courteous. Employees at all levels who are personable, friendly, and cooperative are often the first to be hired and the last to be fired. Self-development of interpersonal skills is therefore yet another form of career insurance.

"The bottom line," advises Half, "is that people who ignore the simple steps necessary to 'insure' their careers do so at their own risk."[5]

Bouncing Back Characteristic 108: Formulate a Contingency Plan

Many people have problems coping with adversity, both on and off the job, because they fail to develop alternative plans in case the original plan goes astray. Such contingency planning is a normal part of business, but many people fail to develop contingency plans for themselves. The contingency plan can be applied to one's area of responsibility or to one's career.

Comeback Scenario 107: Casper Winters, Marketing Executive

A marketing executive in the machine tool industry, Winters helped his firm survive foreign competition that threatened to put him out of business. He accomplished this feat by establishing a contingency plan of what the company would do in case the demand for their major product took a nosedive. His idea was for his firm to use its manufacturing capability to help other companies manage an overload in demand for their products.

Winter's company soon encountered a crisis. Its main product became noncompetitive when a Japanese company developed a duplicate version that sold for one-third the price of the product offered by Winter's company. In response to this problem, Winter's company followed up on inquiries they had already made about doing subcontract manufacturing for other companies. By helping these other companies with their overload, the domestic machinery maker was able to avoid substantial layoffs. Within three years, the company developed an industrial robot for making quality control inspections. The new product provided them an adequate level of business.

Winters thus staved off adversity for his company, and his career, by quickly formulating a contingency plan to avert disaster. Give serious thought to this issue: "What would you do if you lost your major customer, account, line of business, or source of funding?"

Develop a Back-Up Career.   Personal contingency planning to prevent or soften the blow of a crisis usually involves developing a back-up career. As described previously, if you lose your job because of poor business conditions, finding a new job may be difficult. Other companies you might want to work for may also be faced with hard times. The job market consequently becomes limited or highly competitive. A side business, a hobby, or an unusual skill can be converted into a full-time or part-time job.

Contingency plans can also be drawn for a career switch in ways other than becoming an entrepreneur. You can take the skills or contacts you have developed in one career and apply them to a second. Many managers and professionals who have lost their corporate jobs have switched to selling real estate or investments.

Comeback Scenario 108: Todd Chans, Bank Officer

Chans, a bank officer with an MBA who had lost his job in a merger, describes why his career switch into real estate, at age 42, made sense:

> You have to realize that most people who enter real estate sales have very limited business backgrounds. They gave lots of enthusiasm but very few contacts and very limited knowledge of mortgages. Also, they sometimes don't conduct themselves in a highly professional manner. My business experience and professionalism gave me the edge over many other realtors. In a short period of time, I became one of the highest producers in our office.

Similarly, many managers and professionals have made a career switch into selling securities and other investments. The network of contacts they have developed over the years, and their lengthy background in business gives them an edge over newcomers to the business world.

Comeback Scenario 109: Ed Birnbaum, Human Resources Director

Birnbaum, a 56-year-old director of human resources, lost his position when his company pressured him into early retirement. As early retirement day approached, the man reflected upon the hundreds of people he had known and helped in his 31 years with the same company. He explains why he joined a securities firm as a financial consultant (securities sales representative):

I needed more income than I would be obtaining from my early retirement pension, and I also wanted to fill my time with challenging activities. I had heard of many mid-career professionals entering the stock brokerage business because of their emotional maturity and work experience. Although I was almost in the retiree age range, I thought I could serve a particular niche in the market.

My proposal to the firm was that I would specialize in helping clients with retirement planning. As a personnel director, I had dealt extensively with company retirement plans. Of course, I also had some personal experience along those lines. The securities firm agreed with my thinking, and we were both right. I was able to develop a stable clientele, specializing in helping mid- and late-career people plan for their retirement. I was both earning a good supplementary income and having fun. Besides that I think I was actually helping people.

Ed Birnbaum overcame adversity because he formulated a sensible plan for making a career shift. He transferred his experience and expertise as a counselor in human resources to a financial counselor specializing in retirement planning.

Bouncing Back Characteristic 109: Build Up Financial Reserves

Career setbacks bring about psychological problems such as a loss of self-esteem, blows to the ego, and even depression. Setbacks such as being fired, demoted, or losing a major customer also create financial problems. Beset with financial problems, many people become tense and depressed. Building up financial reserves is therefore an important strategy for both preventing a crisis or softening the blow of one that does occur.

In some instances the organization provides financial reserves for top executives through golden parachutes. The executive is guaranteed a substantial sum of money paid out over several years should he or she suffer a job loss because of a takeover by another firm. For some executives the golden parachute can amount to several million dollars in cash. A select few other executives work under an employment contract whereby the person is paid full wages for a specified period of time, even if he or she is fired or squeezed out in some other way.

Golden parachutes and lucrative employment contracts are particularly helpful because they give the fired manager time to find new employment or establish a new business. Because the dismissed manager is receiving a full salary, he or she can take the time to make a sensible employment decision.

Substantial financial reserves also give the individual more flexibility in responding to an adverse employment situation. Such was the case with a communications (public relations) specialist.

Comeback Scenario 110: Andrea Young, Communications Specialist

Young used her financial reserves, combined with a business on the side, to help her cope with job adversity. "My job within the company started turning sour when a new vice president was appointed," said Andrea. "When his predecessor was in power, everything was going okay. I knew what my job was, and I was getting it done."

> LaChance, the new VP, and I never had the right chemistry. He would find a flaw in any project I completed. The main part of my job was to get favorable media placements for our company. I thought I was doing a professional job, but I could never please LaChance. One incident will always stick in my mind. I worked my hardest to get the firm some publicity on a new product. We did get several media placements, and I was happy with the outcome.
>
> LaChance, however, was not happy. He told me I wasn't getting out the proper message about the company, He thought the world was eager to know all about his philosophy of running a business. He also thought that he was newsworthy, which he certainly wasn't.
>
> After that incident, bit by bit, LaChance tried to make life miserable for me. My assignments became less and less professionally challenging. I decided to quit, rather than suffer in a job in which my best talents were being underutilized. Finding a new job at a suitable level proved to be very difficult. The few good leads I turned up were below my level at the time.
>
> My solution was to start my own one-person communications consulting firm. But I knew that opening a business would require a substantial investment because it would probably take me a long time to attract enough clients to make a living. My decision was to give self-employment a try because I was no longer entirely dependent on my corporate salary. I had started a small, part-time business selling African art to individuals in the community. Because I operated the business out of my home, my only expenses were phone calls and an occasional trip to my source of supply in New York City. I had been netting about $400 per month for several years, and I had put most of the profits in bank certificates of deposits and municipal bonds.
>
> To start my own public relations business, I relied on my savings, and still kept my small African art business going. In this way I was

able to meet expenses until I attracted enough public relations clients. A serendipitous circumstance was that my art sales led to a couple of clients, and a few of my public relations clients bought some African art to decorate executive offices.

To prepare for the financial demands of a career crisis, establish a line of credit long before you face a crisis. Get as much credit lined up as possible in which you are given checks to activate a loan whenever needed. Although the interest on line of credit accounts may be higher than for other types of loans, the additional expense pays for itself in peace of mind. Imagine trying to negotiate a loan *after* you are no longer employed? To prevent your line of credit from being cancelled, activate it periodically by making a small loan and paying it back quickly.

Bouncing Back Characteristic 110: Be Alert to Early Warning Signals

Organizational crisis specialist Steven Fink writes that what we typically think of as a crisis—that turbulent cacophony of events tumbling out of control—is really the second crisis stage. Usually there is a previous stage, which he labels the *warning* or *prodromal* phase. Management can often do something about the precrisis sequence:

> You and your managers should understand that anytime you are *not* in a crisis, you are instead in a precrisis or prodromal mode. In sound crisis management planning, you must train yourself and your managers to examine *every* out-of-the ordinary situation for what it is—a warning, a prodrome, a precrisis. It is helpful at this stage to pose the question, "What is the worst thing that could happen?"[6]

What Fink recommends for managing an organizational crisis also applies to the individual. Be alert to the prodromal phase of a crisis. Look for straws in the wind before the last straw catapults you into a crisis. Here are some events and circumstances that could be early warning signals of a career crisis:

- You stop receiving intraoffice mail other than routine correspondence.
- You are rarely asked your opinion on important organizational issues.
- Your major customer has dropped its standing order, and now places orders less frequently.

- Several of your customers begin to take longer to pay their accounts receivable with your company.

- Your business partner becomes noncommunicative and evasive.

- You are not brought into discussions about a pending corporate takeover when you should be, according to your level of responsibility.

- Your performance evaluations are much lower and are characterized by much nitpicking by your boss.

- You begin making loan payments, whether business or personal, with borrowed money.

- You begin to receive many calls from creditors demanding payments on bills outstanding.

To prevent a crisis, or to soften its blow, act these precrisis signals before they fulminate into a crisis. Such actions are analogous to cutting one's losses in the stock market by selling a stock that is tumbling before it tumbles even further. By pitching out, you prevent further erosion of your assets and further mental anguish.

Combat a Problem Early.   Many of the signals presented above can serve as a good reason for confronting a problem before it becomes a crisis. For example, if your performance evaluations are taking a nosedive, discuss with the boss what the real problem might be. The evaluations could signal that you and your boss disagree on what you should be accomplishing or that the two of you have entered into a personality conflict. Another example is that by confronting the fact that your major customers have delayed payments, you may discover that the quality of your product or service has become unacceptable.

Comeback Scenario 111: Jack Morrison, Factory Superintendent

Morrison, a former factory superintendent working in Toronto, knew when to quit in order to prevent the further erosion of his career. Jack made the final decision to purchase a $3-million computerized inventory control system, based on recommendations and surveys from his supervisors. The system was installed a year later than anticipated due to a series of mishaps.

After the system was installed, many bugs surfaced which had to be worked out. The debugging process took more than six months, pushing the starting date 18 months beyond schedule. Four months were needed after the system was running to properly train the operators.

Once the system was operational, it was supposed to reduce human resources by 50 percent and save substantial time and money. The system was also designed to support more than one product simultaneously, thus reducing the amount of warehouse space and concomitant expense.

The supervisors operating the system analyzed the situation and determined that only seven out of the 60 warehouse jobs could be eliminated. It was also discovered that the system had a number of hidden costs. Among them were operator training, lost time when the system was down for repairs, and the waste that resulted from the confusion when inventories were being handled for more than one department.

Five years later top management made the decision to remove the system and sell it for scrap. The system was declared obsolete, and implementing the project was regarded as a serious error in judgment. Although Jack was not demoted or asked to resign, he was blamed for the faulty inventory control system. Jack knew his growth potential in the company was now limited. Rather than stay on an indefinite plateau, Jack quietly and methodically conducted a job campaign. He found a job with a computer manufacturer as an assistant director of manufacturing. Three years later, he was promoted to director.

Jack circumvented substantial career adversity by finding a new position. Although he was not fired or asked to resign, he had lost substantial political clout in his firm. When this happens, it is time to move on.

Bouncing Back Characteristic 111: Maintain a Program of Exercise and Relaxation

Person after person we spoke to about bouncing back from adversity said the process required mental and physical toughness. The stress generated by adversity grinds you down. Unless you have a good reservoir of mental and physical energy you may not make it through the crisis without permanently downscaling your lifestyle or damaging your mental and physical health. A life-sustaining strategy for preparing for a career crisis is therefore to put yourself in good mental and physical shape. An unswerving regimen of exercise and relaxation will be needed. Two human resource managers make this succinct observation:

> Resilient managers find ways to unwind, to back away and gain some distance from work problems. Exercise and recreation help to renew body and soul, and to build the capacity to withstand the inevitable pressures of high risk/high reward jobs.[6]

Bouncing Back Characteristic 112:
Become a Free Agent
Manager

"They did it to me, so I'll do it to them," said the jaundiced sales manager as he wooed away three big accounts from his former employer. In today's turbulent corporate environment, it may be necessary to place your own interests above those of the organization. If every manager and professional is entirely self-interested, self-centered, and self-aggrandizing their employers may suffer, thus becoming less competitive. As a consequence, every employee and stockholder will suffer. Nevertheless, if you are ready to reject before being rejected, or to jump ship before being shoved overboard, you will be able to soften the blow of a forthcoming crisis.

Business professor Paul Hirsch labels this being prepared approach "becoming a free agent manager." Free agent managers and professionals have developed skills far different from those taught in traditional MBA and executive development programs (except for those programs offering a seminar in organizational power and politics). First, free agent managers are loyal primarily to themselves because sacrificing personal goals for the organization will no longer be rewarded or appreciated by the organization. After a merger, even the most loyal organization person might be put on the hit list.

Second, free agent managers and professionals protect themselves and learn to survive in their own environment. Previously guaranteed perks such as pension plans and fringe benefits can no longer be perceived as automatic. As a result managers must develop their own protection plans. Third, the recommended new breed of managers are still committed to their careers, but they see the company as a temporary arena in which to apply their skills and knowledge. This attitude is imperative because the organization will not hesitate to fire managers in order to reach its financial objectives—particularly a good return to shareholders.

Fourth, free agent managers and professionals regard temporary setbacks, such as being fired, as challenges. They realize that downsizing decisions are made by people who do not know them personally and who have very little concern for human welfare. "Remote-control management," says Hirsch, "is inevitable as mergers and acquisitions place a greater emphasis on efficiency (as measured by headcount) than on effectiveness."[7]

Finally, free agent managers strive to be in control of their own destiny. Proactive rather than reactive strategies and tactics are required to increase their visibility in the organization and in their industry.

Pack Your Own Parachute. If you want to "pack your own parachute" and thus become a free agent manager or professional, Hirsch urges you to take the following steps:

1. *Maintain your mobility.* Because jobs are only temporary, assume that you will move on your own terms should the need arise.

2. *Avoid long-term or group assignments where your accomplishments cannot be clearly defined.* Minimize the number of task force assignments you accept, opt for individual problem solving over group decision making, and avoid attempting to solve the unsolvable.

3. *Become a generalist rather than a specialist.* You will usually need to build your reputation by being an expert about something, but after your career is solidly launched, branch out into more general assignments. Overspecialization can hinder movement from one corporation to another. Remember, however, that a delicate balance must be achieved. Strive to become a generalist who also has a well-defined bag of tricks in his or her repertoire. For example, headhunters usually pursue an executive with a track record of accomplishing a specific task such as cost cutting, boosting sales, or mobilizing distributors.

4. *Return calls from headhunters thus maintaining your marketability.* Not returning calls is a tip-off that you are not willing to test the waters.

5. *Cultivate networks that enhance your visibility outside your organization.* Participation in professional associations (such as the National Association of Accountants or the Purchasing Managers Association), community activities, and so on, makes you visible as a competent manager or professional.

By following these guidelines you are better equipped to deal with the ravages of mergers and acquisitions, personality conflicts with top executives, and business failures.

Bouncing Back Characteristic 113: Ask for a Bronze Parachute

Golden parachutes are generous compensation packages that give senior executives a soft landing should they be squeezed out in a takeover.

Some of these parachutes ease the dismissed executive's pain with up to $3 million in cash and stocks. A new trend has emerged of giving upper-level managers "bronze parachutes." These are less generous severance plans than golden parachutes, but more comprehensive than the severance plans designed for lower-level employees. A bronze parachute, for example, might include a lump sum cash payout of $250,000.

Bronze parachutes are distinctive in the amounts of money involved, and the way in which they can be triggered. Most golden parachutes are triggered by a takeover and subsequent termination of the executive. Bronze parachutes usually accompany termination. However, they can also be triggered if the manager voluntarily leaves the company for valid reasons. Included here are company relocation, a forced demotion, or a change in compensation.[8]

Having a bronze parachute on reserve will thus help you prepare for a potential crisis. Because these arrangements are not a standard item, you will have to negotiate tactfully for a bronze parachute. Make sure, however, that you are considered a very valuable manager before demanding one. If you do not enjoy a most favored status, you might be pushed out of the corporate plane without any parachute.

Bouncing Back Characteristic 114: Develop a Flexible Definition of Success

Some career crises are traumatic by objective standards. They may deprive you temporarily from meeting your financial obligations, create battles with creditors, leave you unable to dine in restaurants or take vacations away from home, and generate extensive legal fees. Yet many other career crises reside in the head of the crisis sufferer. As a 10-year-old girl said to her tearful father who was describing his recent demotion, "So what Daddy. You're still going to be my father aren't you?" The young lady hit it on the head—a demotion is only a crisis if status is agonizingly important to the demoted person. Her demoted father still had a daughter, his wife, his possessions, his education, his knowledge, and wisdom, and a decent job. All he lost was some prestige.

Many career crises thus only exist because people suddenly become unsuccessful according to an external definition of success. if a manager believes that the cut-off point for career failure is $149,999 per year, that person will be unsuccessful unless he or she earns $150,000 per year. People who readily rebound from career adversity, focus on the process of what they do, not the results they achieve.[9] They love their work for its own sake, and do not think so much about the money, prestige, and recognition it brings.

Enthusiasm Helps.   Successful career professionals have tremendous enthusiasm. Speak to them about their work and they sound like basketball coaches describing their winning team. If you are more enthusiastic about the nature of your work than the success trappings it brings, you won't be so crushed when somebody decides that your results are not so hot. "If you don't like my ideas, I'll move on to another sandbox," a sales promotion manager told her boss. Being fired may have created vexing short-term inconveniences, but the manager's list of tangible accomplishments and love for promotional gimmicks will enable her to practice her craft in another setting. Her boss's decision to fire her was just someone else's subjective judgment about what constitutes good ideas for sales promotion.

Look Inward Rather than Outward.   Resilient managers and professionals prepare for and prevent many crises by looking inward rather than outward. With self-confidence and pride they know that their work is meritorious in its own right, whether or not they can please every powerful person who judges their performance. Resiliency is an inner quality that brings peace of mind in the midst of environmental turbulence. The inner quality of resilience combined with sensible planning and the right tactics will help you bounce back from adversity. Good luck, and let me know what happens.

References

Preface

1. David Broder, "Biden Will Be Better Candidate Down the Road," syndicated column, January 6, 1988.

Chapter 1

1. Warren Bennis and Burt Nanus, "The Leadership Tightrope," *Success*, March 1985, p. 62.

2. Salvatore Didato, "Commitment, Control, Courage Are Traits of the Survivors Among Us," Gannett News Service syndicated column, March 3, 1987.

3. The Stam case history is quoted and paraphrased from Oliver L. Niehouse, "Stress and the Hardy Executive," *Industry Week,* November 12, 1984, pp. 96–97; the characteristics are also from Niehouse, "Stress and the Hardy Executive," p. 97.

4. Case history quoted and paraphrased from Michael M. Lombardo and Robert W. Eichniger, "Rescuing Derailed Executives," *Issues & Observations* (Center for Creative Leadership), Fall 1988, pp. 2–5.

5. The information about Yang is from Reva Tooley, "Handling Setbacks," *Working Woman*, February 1988, p. 72.

6. Timothy Dougherty, "Working Beyond Disabilities," Rochester *Democrat and Chronicle,* July 6, 1987, pp. 1D–2D.

7. Abraham Zaleznik and Manfred F. R. Ket de Vries, *Power and the Corporate Mind* (Chicago: Contemporary Books, 1985), p. 213.

8. A. David Silver, "Profit from Disaster: The ABCs of Survival," *Success!*, November 1988, p. 67.

9. Victor Kiam, "Reject Rejection," *Success!*, December 1986, p. 12.

10. *Ibid.*, excerpted and paraphrased.

11. Quoted in "Be Nice to the Dullard; He Might Become Boss," Associated Press story, July 13, 1985.

Chapter 2

1. Robert Bell, *Surviving the 10 Ordeals of the Takeover* (New York: AMACOM, 1988), pp. 123–137. Several of the items in the list contained in this section of the chapter are from Bell.

2. "Corporate Acquisitions: The Day After," *Personal Report for the Executive,* December 15, 1988, p. 4.

3. Bell, *Surviving 10 Ordeals*, pp. 135–36.

4. Toni Apgar, *Mastering Office Politics* (New York: National Institute of Business Management, 1988), p. 66.

5. William LeMoult, "Mergers and Management Values," *Personnel Administrator*, July 1989, p. 42.

6. Several of the suggestions below are based on "Postmerger Survival," *Executive Strategies*, August 22, 1989, p. 4.

7. "Unbearable New Boss," *Executive Strategies*, October 3, 1989, p. 2.

8. "Keep the Boss Informed in Lean and Mean Times," *Personal Report for the Executive*, March 15, 1989, pp. 2–3.

9. "There's Life After Termination," *Personal Report for the Executive*, April 15, 1989, p. 7.

Chapter 3

1. Carole Hyatt and Linda Gottlieb, *When Smart People Fail: Rebuilding Yourself for Success* (New York: Penguin Books, 1988), p. 21.

2. "Helping Employees Through Personal Crises," *Personal Report for the Executive*, September 1, 1986, p. 8.

3. Steve Fishman, "Facing Up to Failure," *Success!*, November 1984, p. 53.

4. Ibid., p. 52.

5. Hyatt and Gottlieb, *When Smart People Fail*, p. 155.

6. Julius Segal, *Winning Life's Toughest Battles: Roots of Human Resilience* (New York: Ivy Books/Ballantine, 1986), p. 64.

7. Hyatt and Gottlieb, *When Smart People Fail*, p. 177.

8. Peggy Moran, "Amazing Things," *Upstate* (Rochester, N.Y. *Democrat and Chronicle*), January 18, 1987, p. 3.

9. Reva Tooley, "Handling Setbacks," *Working Woman*, February 1988, p. 74.

Chapter 4

1. Jonathan D. Quick, Debra L. Nelson, and James Campbell Quick, "Successful Executives: How Independent?" *Academy of Management Executive*, May 1987, p. 139.

2. Julius Segal, *Winning Life's Toughest Battles* (New York: Ballantine/Ivy Books, 1986), p. 20.

3. These suggestions are adapted from Carole Hyatt and Linda Gottlieb, *When Smart People Fail: Rebuilding Yourself for Success* (New York: Penguin Books, 1988), pp. 185–187.

4. *Ibid.*, p. 186.

5. The facts here are as reported in Michael Oneal, "Harley-Davidson: Ready to Hit the Road Again," *Business Week*, July 21, 1986, p. 70; Vaughn L. Beals, "Operation Recovery," *Success*, January/February 1989, p. 16.

6. Dan Hurley, "Getting Help from Helping," *Psychology Today*, January 1988, p. 64.

7. *Ibid.*

8. Reva Tooley, "Handling Setbacks," *Working Woman,* February 1988, p. 72.

9. David Robino and Kenneth DeMeuse, "Corporate Mergers and Acquisitions: Their Impact on HRM," *Personnel Administrator,* November 1985, p. 33.

Chapter 5

1. These results are described in Tara Bradley-Steck, "Looking at the Bright Side Has Rewards," Associated Press story, June 21, 1987.

2. "Beyond Positive Thinking: New Facts About Ancient Wisdom," *Success,* December 1988, p. 32.

3. Alice Lake, "Can't Cope? Try Hope," *Woman's Day,* February 11, 1986, p. 42; all but suggestions 6 and 7 are from this article. The examples, however, are from the present author.

4. Martha T. Moore, "DeLorean Plans New Venture into Car Making," Gannett News Service syndicated story, June 6, 1987; "DeLorean Still Wheeling Along," Rochester *Democrat and Chronicle,* December 12, 1989, p. 1C.

5. Kurt Anderson, "A Spunky Tycoon Turned Superstar," *Time,* April 1, 1985, p. 32.

6. *Ibid.,* p. 33.

7. The Neuharth story, including the quote, is from Peter Prichard, *"USA Today* Wasn't First Newspaper Al Neuharth Started," Gannett News Service syndicated story, September 16, 1987; Al Neuharth, *Confessions of an S.O.B* . (New York: Doubleday, 1989), pp. 26–33.

8. Barry M. Staw and Jerry Ross, "Commitment in an Experimenting Society: A Study of the Attribution of Leadership From Administrative Scenarios," *Journal of Applied Psychology,* June 1980, pp. 249–260.

9. "Beyond Positive Thinking," p. 34.

10. *Ibid.*

Chapter 6

1. Anecdote and quote from "Turn a Disadvantage Into an Advantage," *Sparks from the Anvil,* undated, pp. 1–3.

2. Leah Rosch, "Turning a Career Crisis into a Chance for Growth," *Working Woman,* September 1988, p. 118.

3. William Friend, "Getting Set for a Setback," *Association Management,* March 1984, p. 73.

4. John Ramee, "Managing in a Crisis," *Management Solutions,* February 1987, pp. 28–29.

5. Julius Segal, *Winning Life's Toughest Battles* (New York: Ivy Books/ Ballantine, 1986), pp. 34–39.

Chapter 7

1. Carole Hyatt and Linda Gottlieb, *When Smart People Fail: Rebuilding Yourself for Success* (New York: Penguin, 1988), p. 35.

2. David Broder, "Biden Will Be Better Candidate Down the Road," syndicated column, January 6, 1988.

3. "Great Comebacks: First Annual Awards," *Success!*, July/August 1986, p. 35.

4. "Rescuing Flops—Or How to Buy Cat Litter and Sell Sawdust," *Business Week*, December 3, 1984, p. 128.

5. Susan Okula, "Paralysis of Legs Gives Insight into Client Needs," Associated Press syndicated story, November 23, 1986.

6. Myron Peretz Glazer and Penina Migdal Glazer, "Whistle-blowing," *Psychology Today*, August 1986, p. 43.

7. Don Lee Bohl (ed.), *Tying the Corporate Knot*, American Management Association Research Report (New York: AMACOM, 1989), p. 16.

Chapter 8

1. As reported in Stewart Toy, "Will Samurai Marketing Work for Suzuki?" *Business Week*. June 27, 1988, pp. 33–34.

2. "They Turned Disaster into Victory," *Success*, July/August 1987, p. 36.

3. Mei-Mei Chan, "Louis L'Amour: Fastest Pen in the West," *USA Weekend*, May 30–June 1, 1986, p. 4.

4. Reprinted with permission from "Gold in the Gutter," *Success!*, July/August 1988, p. 38.

5. "A Bird in the Hand," *Success!*, July/August 1986, p. 34.

6. John Hartsock, "Trouble in 'Oasis,'" Rochester *Democrat and Chronicle*, September 1, 1985, and updated with interview conducted in January 1989.

7. As reported in "A Setback Didn't Fence Him in," *Nation's Business*, April 1984, pp. 59–60.

Chapter 9

1. "When Power Investors Call the Shots," *Business Week*, June 20, 1988, p. 127.

2. Based on "The Biography of Walter E. Dundy," in Hugo Rizzoli, *Clinical Neurosurgery* (Baltimore: Williams & Wilkins, 1985).

3. Adapted from Priscilla Petty, "His Road to the Vice Presidency Contained Several Career Detours," Gannett News Service syndicated story, January 11, 1983.

4. Joseph A. Morabito, "Managing Post-Merger Group Moves," *Personnel Journal*, May 1989, p. 76.

Chapter 10

1. David L. Birch, "Thriving on Adversity," *Inc.*, March 1988, pp. 80–81.

2. Information from the Dun & Bradstreet Corporation, as cited in Ramon J. Aldag and Timothy M. Stearns, *Management, 2nd ed.* (Cincinnati: South-Western Publishing Co., 1991), pp. 744–745.

3. As reported in Bruo Utal, "Behind the Fall of Steve Jobs," *Fortune*, August 15, 1985, pp. 20–24; Deborah C. Wise, "The Palace Revolt at Apple Computer," *Business Week*, June 17, 1985, p. 38; Katherine M. Hafner and Ri-

chard Brandt, "Steve Jobs: Can He Do It Again?" *Business Week,* October 24, 1988, p. 74.

4. "Stretching the Imagination," *Success!,* August 1986, p. 41.

5. "Fortunes Revived by a 'New Toy,'" *Nation's Business,* May 1984, pp. 69–70.

6. Letter adapted from "Bulletin Board," *Success!,* April 1988, p. 41.

Chapter 11

1. Elizabeth K. Kellar, "What Every Manager Should Know About Being Fired," *Public Management,* February 1979, p. 2.

2. Carole Hyatt and Linda Gottlieb, *When Smart People Fail* (New York: Penguin Books, 1988), p. 83.

3. "The Secret of the $1,000 Suit," *Success,* September 1987, p. 66.

4. Quoted in Daniel Goleman, "Intimate Differences," *The New York Times* syndicated story, April 19, 1986.

Chapter 12

1. Reva Tooley, "Handling Setbacks," *Working Woman,* February 1988, pp. 72–73.

2. Quoted in "Crisis Management to the Rescue," *Personal Report for the Executive,* October 15, 1985, p. 7.

3. "Career 'Insurance' Protects DP Professionals from Setbacks, Encourages Growth," *Data Management,* June 1986, p. 33.

4. Quoted in "Career 'Insurance' Protects DP Professionals," p. 33.

5. Quoted in "Career 'Insurance' Protects DP Professionals."

6. Steven Fink, *Crisis Management: Planning for the Inevitable* (New York: AMACOM, 1986), p. 21.

7. Donald Zauderer and Joseph Fox, "Resiliency in the Face of Stress," *Management Solutions,* November 1987, p. 35.

8. Paul Hirsch, *Pack Your Own Parachute* (Reading, Mass.: Addison-Wesley Publishing Company, 1987). The summary and analysis of Hirsch's work cited here is based on a book review by John W. Slocum, appearing in *Academy of Management EXECUTIVE,* February 1988, pp. 75–76.

9. *Executive Insights,* AMA Council Report (Saranac Lake, N.Y.: AMA Publication Services, 1989), p. 18.

Index

About the Author

Andrew J. DuBrin, a licensed psychologist, has authored 34 management texts, trade books, and general interest books, including the best-selling *Winning Office Politics: DuBrin's Guide for the '90s*. He is a professor at the Rochester Institute of Technology where he teaches organizational behavior and career management. Dr. DuBrin conducts seminars and workshops on career management and has served as a consultant to numerous individuals and professional organizations.